1984

A Practical Guide
to the UNIX™ System

The Benjamin/Cummings Series in Computing and Information Sciences

G. Booch
Software Engineering with Ada (1983)

H. L. Capron, B. K. Williams
Computers and Data Processing, Second Edition (1984)

D. M. Etter
Structured FORTRAN 77 for Engineers and Scientists (1983)

D. M. Etter
Problem Solving with Structured FORTRAN 77 (1984)

P. Linz
Programming Concepts and Problem Solving: An Introduction to Computer Science Using Pascal (1983)

W. Savitch
Pascal Programming: An Introduction to the Art and Science of Programming (1984)

R. Sebesta
Structured Assembly Language Programming for the VAX II (1984)

R. Sebesta
Structured Assembly Language Programming for the PDP-11 (1984)

M. Sobell
A Practical Guide to the UNIX System (1984)

M. Sobell
A Practical Guide to XENIX (1984)

M. Sobell
A Practical Guide to UNIX System V (1985)

A Practical Guide
to the UNIX™ System

Mark G. Sobell

The Benjamin/Cummings Publishing Company, Inc.
Menlo Park, California • Reading, Massachusetts
London • Amsterdam • Don Mills, Ontario • Sydney

Sponsoring Editor: Alan Apt

Book and Cover Design: Marilyn Langfeld

Cover Illustration: Tom Cervenak

Text Illustration: David Fields

Library of Congress Cataloging in Publication Data

Sobell, Mark G.
  A practical guide to the UNIX system.

  Includes index.
  1. UNIX (Computer operating system) I. Title.
II. Title: Practical guide to the U.N.I.X. system.
QA76.6.S61673   1984   001.64'2   83-21069
ISBN 0-8053-8910-5

 bcdefghij-HA-8987654

The Benjamin/Cummings Publishing Company
2727 Sand Hill Road
Menlo Park, CA 94025

for Laura

PREFACE

A Practical Guide to the Unix System is an alternative to current UNIX system books that either overwhelm the reader with unnecessary detail or give only a superficial introduction to the system. This book is for people with some computer experience but little or no experience with the UNIX system.

A Practical Guide to the Unix System shows you how to use your UNIX system right from your terminal. The first nine chapters of the book (Part I) are step-by-step tutorials covering the most important aspects of the UNIX operating system:

Word Processing.   Chapters 6 and 7 show you how to use the built-in word processing capabilities of your UNIX system to produce professional documents, including manuscripts, letters, and reports.

Organizing Information.   In Chapters 2, 3, and 4 you will learn how to create, delete, copy, and move information on your system. You will also learn how to use the UNIX system files to organize all the information stored on your computer.

Electronic Mail and Telecommunications.   Chapter 3 and Part II include information on how to use the UNIX system utility programs to communicate with users on your system and other systems.

Using the Shell.   In Chapter 5, you will learn how to send output from a program to the printer, to your terminal, or to a file—just by changing a command. You will also learn how to combine UNIX utility programs to solve problems right from the command line.

Bourne Shell and C Shell Programming.   Once you have mastered the basics of the UNIX system, the creative aspects of the system are open to you. Chapters 8 and 9 show you how to use the Shell to write your own programs composed of UNIX system commands. This is the only book currently available that explains how both the Bourne and C Shells can be used to write custom programs for *your* applications.

XENIX.   XENIX is an implementation of UNIX. Appendix D presents an overview of XENIX, discusses its advantages and disadvantages, and explains how to use this book with XENIX.

Using the UNIX Utility Programs.   Part II offers a comprehensive, detailed reference to the major UNIX utility programs, with numerous examples. If you are already familiar with the UNIX system, this part of the book will be a valuable easy-to-use reference. If you are not an experienced user, you will find Part II useful once you have mastered the tutorials in Part I.

This book would not have been possible without the help and support of everyone at Relational Database Systems, Inc., the developers of **informix**. Special thanks to Laura King, Roger Sippl, and Roy Harrington (all of RDS) for introducing me to the UNIX system. My mother, Dr. Helen Sobell, provided invaluable comments on the manuscript at several junctures. Raphael Finkel of the University of Wisconsin and Randolph Bentson of Colorado State University each reviewed the manuscript several times, making many significant improvements. Dr. Harry Garland and Dr. Roger Melen (president and vice president of Cromemco) both provided much-needed support during the early manuscript stages. Robert Veroff of the University of New Mexico, Udo Pooch of Texas A & M, Judy Ross, and Bob Greenberg also reviewed the manuscript and made useful suggestions.

Many people improved the accuracy and continuity of the original manuscript; the author accepts responsibility for any remaining errors.

MARK G. SOBELL

BRIEF CONTENTS

DETAILED CONTENTS

Part I
THE UNIX OPERATING SYSTEM

1

INTRODUCTION TO THE UNIX OPERATING SYSTEM

UNIX is the name of a computer operating system and its family of related utility programs. Over the past few years, the UNIX operating system has gained unprecedented popularity. This chapter discusses operating systems and presents a brief history of the UNIX system that explains why it is becoming so popular.

The UNIX operating system was developed at Bell Laboratories in Murray Hill, New Jersey—one of the largest research facilities in the world. Since the original design and implementation of the UNIX operating system by Ken Thompson in 1969, many people have contributed to it.

THE HISTORY OF THE UNIX OPERATING SYSTEM

When the UNIX operating system was developed, many computers still ran single jobs in a *batch* mode. Programmers fed these computers input in the form of punch (IBM) cards and didn't see the program again until the printer produced the output. Because these systems served only one user at a time, they did not take full advantage of the power and speed of the computers. Further, this work environment isolated programmers from each other. It did not make it easy to share data and programs, and did not promote cooperation among people working on the same project.

The UNIX time-sharing system provided two major improvements over single-user, batch systems. It allowed more than one person to use the computer at the same time (the UNIX operating system is a *multiuser* operating system), and it allowed a person to communicate directly with the computer via a terminal (it is *interactive*).

The UNIX system was not the first interactive, multiuser operating system. An operating system named Multics was in use briefly at Bell Labs before the UNIX operating system was created. The Cambridge Multiple Access System had been developed in Europe, and the Compatible Time Sharing System (CTSS) had also been used for several years. The designers of the UNIX operating system took advantage of the work that had gone into these and other operating systems by combining the most desirable aspects of each of them.

The UNIX system was developed by researchers who needed a set of modern computing tools to help them with their projects. It allowed a group of people working together on a project to share selected data and programs, while keeping other information private.

Universities and colleges have played a major role in furthering the popularity of the UNIX operating system through the "four year effect." When the UNIX operating system became widely available in 1975, Bell Labs offered it to educational institutions at minimal cost. The schools, in turn, used it in their computer science programs, insuring that all computer science students became familiar with it. Because the UNIX system is such

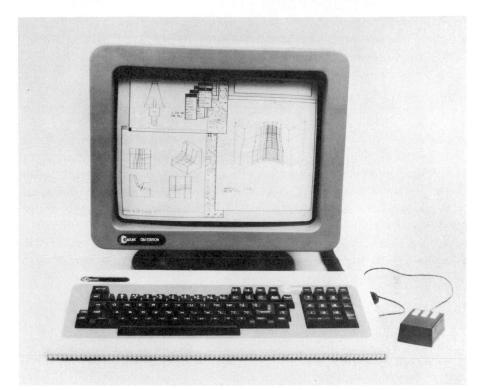

A graphics workstation that simultaneously displays different *windows* containing graphics or text. The *mouse* on the right is used to move a pointer on the screen to execute commands and to open, close, and change the size of the windows. This workstation is based on the UNIX operating system. (Photograph courtesy of Cadlinc, Inc.)

an advanced development system, the students became acclimated to an optimum programming environment. As these students graduated and went into industry, they expected to work in a similarly advanced environment. As more of these students worked their way up in the commercial world, the UNIX operating system found its way into industry.

In addition to introducing its students to the UNIX operating system, the Computer Science Department of the University of California at Berkeley made significant additions and changes to it. They made so many popular changes that one version of the UNIX operating system is now called the Berkeley UNIX system. Some of the features developed at Berkeley appear in releases from Bell Labs, and many are being adopted by software companies that specialize in adapting the UNIX system to different computers. It is this heritage—development in a research environment and enhancement in a university setting—that has made the UNIX operating system such a powerful software-development tool.

THE UNIX SYSTEM ON MICROCOMPUTERS

In the mid-1970s minicomputers began challenging the large mainframe computers. Minicomputer manufacturers demonstrated that in many applications their products could perform the same functions as mainframe machines for much less money. Today microcomputers are challenging the minis in much the same way. Powerful 16-bit processor chips, plentiful, inexpensive memory, and lower-priced hard-disk storage have allowed manufacturers to install multiuser operating systems on microcomputers. The cost and performance of these systems are rivaling those of the minis.

WHY IS THE UNIX SYSTEM POPULAR WITH MANUFACTURERS?

Advances in hardware technology are creating the need for an operating system that can take advantage of available hardware power. CP/M™, the standard for 8-bit microcomputers, does not fill the need. Among other reasons, CP/M and its multiuser derivative MP/M™ lack file structures that can reasonably support the large number of files normally stored on a hard-disk system.

With the cost of hardware dropping, hardware manufacturers cannot afford to develop and support proprietary operating systems. In a similar manner, application-software manufacturers cannot afford to convert their products to run under many different proprietary operating systems. Software manufacturers have to keep the price of their product down—in line with the price of the hardware.

Hardware manufacturers need a generic operating system that they can easily adapt to their machines. They want to provide a hospitable environment for third party software. Software manufacturers need a generic operating system as a common environment for their products.

The UNIX operating system satisfies both needs. Because it was initially designed for minicomputers, the UNIX operating system file structure takes full advantage of large, fast hard disks. Equally important, the UNIX operating system was intended to be a multiuser operating system, not mod-

An office workstation that combines voice, text, and graphics capabilities. A *mouse* is shown at the right of the picture, and the integral telephone is on the left. This workstation is based on the UNIX operating system. (Photograph courtesy of Sydis, Inc.)

ified to serve several users as an afterthought. Finally, because the UNIX system was originally designed as a development system, it provides an ideal working environment for a software company.

The advent of a standard operating system legitimized the birth of the software industry. Now software manufacturers can afford to make one version of one product available on many different machines. No longer does one speak of ". . . the company that makes the MRP package for the IBM machine," but rather ". . . the company that makes the MRP package for the UNIX operating system." The hardware manufacturer who offers a UNIX-based system can count on third-party software being available to run on the new machine.

IS THE UNIX SYSTEM BEING ACCEPTED?

The UNIX operating system is gaining widespread commercial acceptance. UNIX system user groups are springing up, UNIX system magazines are starting to appear, and articles on the UNIX operating system are becoming more plentiful. The UNIX operating system is available on many machines, from smaller microcomputers and minicomputers to the largest mainframes. Even non-UNIX operating systems, such as MS-DOS™, are beginning to adopt some of the traits of the UNIX system. In addition, many companies are manufacturing operating systems, such as CROMIX,® that are very similar to the UNIX system.

HOW CAN THE UNIX OPERATING SYSTEM RUN ON SO MANY MACHINES?

An operating system that can run on many different machines is said to be portable. About 95% of the UNIX operating system is written in the C programming language. And C can be portable because it is written in a higher-level, machine independent language. (The C compiler is actually written in itself, C.)

The C Programming Language

Ken Thompson originally wrote the UNIX operating system in PDP-7 assembly language. Assembly language is a machine-dependent language—programs written in assembly language work on only one machine, or, at best, one family of machines. Therefore, the original UNIX operating system could not easily be transported to run on other machines.

In order to make the UNIX system portable, Thompson developed the B programming language, a machine-independent language. Dennis Ritchie developed the C programming language by modifying B, and with Thompson, rewrote the UNIX system in C. After this rewrite, it could easily be transported to run on other machines.

That was the start of C. You can see in its roots some of the reasons it is such a powerful tool. C can be used to write machine-independent programs. A program that is designed to be portable, and is written in C, can be easily moved to any computer that has a C compiler. As C and the UNIX operating system become more popular, more machines have C compilers.

C is a modern systems language. You can write a compiler or an operating system in C. It is highly structured, but it is not necessarily a high-level

This terminal screen shows a relational database management system (DBMS) displaying information about a customer and the customer's order. This DBMS was written in C for the UNIX system, enabling it to run on many different machines. A DBMS is a necessary component of a wide range of application programs. (**informix** screen courtesy of Relational Database Systems, Inc.)

language. C allows a programmer to manipulate bits and bytes, as is necessary when writing an operating system. But it also has high-level constructs that allow efficient, modular programming.

C is becoming popular for the same reasons the UNIX operating system is successful. It is portable, standard, and powerful. It has high-level features for flexibility and can still be used for systems programming. These features make it both useful and usable.

WHAT IS AN OPERATING SYSTEM?

An operating system is a control program for a computer. It allocates computer resources and schedules tasks. Computer resources include all the hardware: the central processing unit, system memory, disk and tape storage, printers, terminals, modems, and anything else that is connected to or inside the computer.

An operating system performs many varied functions almost simultaneously. It keeps track of filenames and where each file is located on the disk, and monitors every keystroke on each of the terminals. Memory must be allocated so that only one task uses a given area of memory at a time. Other operating system functions include fulfilling requests made by users, running accounting programs that keep track of the use of resources, and executing backup and other maintenance utilities. An operating system schedules tasks so that the central processor is only working on one task at a given moment, although the computer may appear to be running many programs at the same time.

OVERVIEW OF UNIX SYSTEM FEATURES

The UNIX operating system has many unique features. Like other operating systems, the UNIX system is a control program for computers. But it is also a well-thought-out family of utility programs (see Figure 1-1) and a set of tools that allows the user to connect and use these utilities to build systems and applications. This section discusses both the common and unique features of the UNIX operating system.

Utilities

The UNIX system includes a family of several hundred utility programs. These utilities perform functions that are universally required by users. An example is **sort**. The **sort** utility puts lists (or groups of lists) in order. It can put lists in alphabetical or numerical order, order by part number, author, last name, city, zip code, telephone number, age, size, cost, and so forth. The **sort** utility is an important programming tool and is part of the standard UNIX system. Other utilities allow you to display, print, copy, search, and delete files. There are also text editing, formatting, and typesetting utilities. The **man** (for manual) utility provides online documentation of the UNIX system itself. Because the UNIX system provides these frequently used utilities, you don't have to write them. You can incorporate them in your work, allowing you to spend more of your time working on the unique aspects of your project, and less time on the aspects that are common to many other projects.

Figure 1-1: The UNIX System

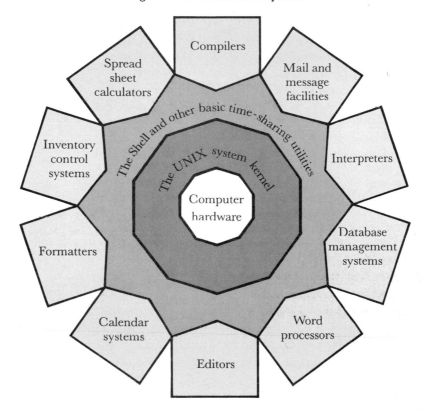

The UNIX System Can Support Many Users

The UNIX operating system is a multiuser operating system. Depending on the machine being used, a UNIX system can support from one to over one hundred users, each concurrently running a different set of programs. The cost of a computer that can be used by many people at the same time is less per user than that of a computer that can only be used by a single person at a time. This is true because one person cannot generally use all of the resources a computer has to offer. No one can keep the printer going 24 hours a day, keep all the system memory in use, keep the disk busy reading and writing, keep the tape drives spinning, and keep the terminals busy. A multiuser operating system allows many people to use the system resources almost simultaneously. Thus, resource utilization can approach 100% and the cost per user can approach zero. These are the theoretical goals of a multiuser system.

The UNIX System Can Support Many Tasks

The UNIX operating system allows you to run more than one job at a time. You can run several jobs in the background while giving all your attention to the job being displayed on your terminal. This *multitasking* capability allows you to be more productive.

The Shell

The Shell is the utility that processes your requests. When you enter a command at a terminal, the Shell interprets the command and calls the program you want. There are two popular shells in use today, the Bourne Shell (standard UNIX system) and the C Shell (Berkeley UNIX system). More shells are available, including menu shells that provide easy-to-use interfaces for computer-naive users. Because separate users can use different shells at the same time on one system, a system can appear different to different users. The choice of shells demonstrates one of the powers of the UNIX operating system: the ability to provide a customized user interface.

The Shell is also a high-level programming language. You can use this language to combine standard utility programs to build entire applications in minutes instead of weeks. Using the tools described in this book, you can even construct many useful applications right on the command line. A Shell program can, for example, allow an inexperienced user to easily perform a complex task. The Shell is one of the UNIX system tools that makes your job easier.

File Structure

A *file* is a set of data, such as a memo, report, or group of sales figures, that is stored under a name, frequently on a disk. The UNIX system file structure is designed to assist you in keeping track of large numbers of files. It uses a hierarchical or treelike data structure that allows each user to have one primary directory with as many subdirectories as required.

Directories are useful for collecting files pertaining to a particular project. In addition, the UNIX system allows users to share files by means of *links,* which can make files appear in more than one user's directory.

Security—Private and Shared Files

Like most multiuser operating systems, the UNIX system allows you to protect your data from access by other users. The UNIX system also allows

The heart of a computer system: the Central Processing Unit (CPU).
This CPU contains two microprocessor chips, an MC68000 (the large
rectangular grey object) and a Z80A (just above the MC68000).
(Photograph courtesy of Cromemco, Inc.)

you to share selected data and programs with certain users by means of a
simple but effective protection scheme.

Filename Generation

Using special characters that the Shell command processor recognizes, you
can construct patterns. These patterns can generate filenames that can be
used to refer to one or more files whose names share a common character-
istic. Commands can include a pattern when you do not know the exact
filename you want to reference, or when it is too tedious to specify it. A single
pattern can also be used to reference many filenames.

Device-Independent Input and Output

Devices (such as a printer or terminal) and disk files all appear as files to
UNIX programs. When you give the UNIX operating system a command,
you can instruct it to send the output to any one of several devices or files.
This diversion is called output *redirection.*

In a similar manner, a programs's input that normally comes from a
terminal can be redirected so that it comes from a disk file instead. Under the

UNIX operating system, input and output are *device-independent*; they can be redirected to or from any appropriate device.

As an example, the **cat** utility normally displays the contents of a file on the terminal screen. When you enter a **cat** command, you can cause its output to go to a disk file, or the printer, instead of the terminal.

Interprocess Communication

The UNIX system allows you to establish both pipes and filters on the command line. A *pipe* redirects the output of a program so that it becomes input to another program. A *filter* is a program designed to process a stream of input data and yield a stream of output data. Filters are often used between two pipes. A filter processes another program's output, altering it in some manner. The filter's output then becomes input to another program. Pipes and filters are frequently used to join utilities to perform a specific task.

WHAT ARE THE LIMITATIONS OF THE UNIX SYSTEM?

The most commonly heard complaints about the UNIX operating system are that it has an unfriendly, terse, treacherous, unforgiving, and non-mnemonic user interface. These complaints are well founded, but many of the problems have been rectified by newer versions of the operating system and some application programs. Those problems that haven't been addressed directly can usually be solved by writing simple Shell programs.

The UNIX system is called unfriendly and terse because it seems to follow the philosophy that "no news is good news." The **ed** editor does not prompt you for input or commands, the **cp** (copy) utility does not confirm that it has copied a file successfully, and the **who** utility does not display a banner before its list of users.

This terseness is useful because it facilitates *redirection,* allowing the output from one program to be fed into another program as its input. Thus, you can find out how many people are using the system by feeding the output of **who** into a utility that counts the number of lines in a file. If **who** displayed a banner before it displayed the list of users, you could not make this connection. If you want **who** to display a banner, you can write a two-line program using the Shell so that *your* copy of **who** displays a banner.

In a similar manner, although it would be nice if **ed** prompted you when you were using it as an interactive editor, it would not be as useful when you

A memory board. The chips on this board can hold 524,288 bytes (characters) of information. Each byte is composed of 8 bits; the total capacity of the board is 4,194,304 pieces of information. (Photograph courtesy of Cromemco, Inc.)

wanted to feed it input from another program and have it automatically edit a group of files.

The UNIX system was designed for slow hard-copy terminals. The less a program printed out, the sooner it was done. With high-speed terminals, this is no longer true. Editors that display more information (e.g., **vi**) are being developed to run on the UNIX system with these newer, high-speed terminals.

The Shell user interface can be treacherous, however. A typing mistake on a command line can easily destroy important files, and it is possible to inadvertently log off the system. You must use caution when working with a powerful operating system. If you want a foolproof system, you can use the tools the UNIX system provides to modify the Shell. Some manufacturers are producing menu-driven user interfaces that make it very difficult to make mistakes with such far-reaching consequences. The C Shell has optional built-in safeguards against many of these problems.

Due to its simplicity, the UNIX operating system has some limitations. The original UNIX operating system was not able to lock files, an important feature in a multiuser operating system. Mechanisms to synchronize separate jobs were poorly implemented. The objection that is perhaps the most serious and hard to overcome is that the UNIX operating system does not have a guaranteed hardware-interrupt response time. This prevents a standard UNIX system from being used in some real-time applications.

SUMMARY

Although the UNIX operating system has some shortcomings, most of them can be rectified using the tools that the UNIX system itself provides. The unique approach that the UNIX operating system takes to the problems of standardization and portability, combined with its strong foothold in the professional community, its power as a development tool, and chameleon-like user interface, is causing it to emerge as the standard choice of users, hardware manufacturers, and software manufacturers.

2

GETTING STARTED

This chapter explains how to log on to, and use, the UNIX system. It discusses several important names and keyboard keys that are specific to you, your terminal, and your installation. Following a description of conventions used in this book, you are led through a brief session with your UNIX system. Once you have learned how to log on and off, the chapter explains how to correct typing mistakes and terminate program execution. Finally, you are introduced to some important utilities that manipulate files. With them you can edit files, obtain lists of filenames, display the contents of files, and delete files.

BEFORE YOU START

One of the best ways to learn is by doing. Chapters 2 through 9 are designed to be read and used while you are sitting in front of a terminal. You can learn about the UNIX system by running the examples in this book and by making up your own. Feel free to experiment with different commands and utilities. The worst thing that you can do is erase one of the files that you have created. Because these are only practice files, you can easily create another.

Before you log on to a UNIX system for the first time, take a couple of minutes to find out the answers to the following questions. Ask the system administrator, or someone else who is familiar with your installation. Make note of the answers; they will be useful as you proceed.

What Is My Login Name? This is the name that you use to identify yourself to the UNIX system. It is also the name that other users use to send you electronic mail and messages.

What Is My Password? On systems with several users, passwords prevent others from gaining access to your files. To start with, the system administrator assigns you a password. You can change your password at any time.

Which Key Ends a Line? Different terminals use different keys to move the cursor to the beginning of the next line. Find out which key your terminal uses.

This book always refers to the key that ends a line as the (RETURN) key. Your terminal may have a (RET), (NEWLINE), (ENTER), or other key. Each time this book asks you to "press the (RETURN) key" or "press (RETURN)," press the equivalent key on your terminal.

Which Key Deletes a Character? (CONTROL-H) (press **H** while holding the (CONTROL), (CNTRL), or (CTRL) key down) will often back up over and delete the characters you just entered, one at a time. There is usually another key, frequently #, that can also be used to delete characters. This key is called the *delete character* key. Find out which key you can use. If you like, you can change the key to one that is more convenient. Refer to page 364 for examples of how to make this change.

Which Key Deletes a Line? The standard key that deletes the entire line you are entering is @. This key is called the *delete line* or *line kill* key (or character). Find out which key you can use. This key can also be changed. Refer to page 363 for examples of how to make this change.

Which Key Interrupts Execution? There is one key that interrupts almost any program you are running. On most systems it is labeled (RUBOUT), (DEL), or (DELETE). You may have to hold the (SHIFT) key down while you press this key to make it work. Find out which key you can use.

What Is the Termcap Name for My Terminal? You'll need to know this name if you use the visual editor (vi), described in Chapter 6. Some other application programs that run on UNIX systems also need this information.

Which Shell Will I Be Using? You will probably be using either the Bourne Shell or the C Shell. They are very similar in many respects. The examples in this book show the Bourne Shell, but are generally applicable to both shells. Differences between the shells are described in Chapter 9.

Conventions

This book uses conventions to make its explanations shorter and clearer. These conventions are described in the following paragraphs.

Keys and Characters. (SMALL CAPS) are used in this book to indicate three different items.

- Important terminal keys, such as the (SPACE) bar and the (RETURN), (ESCAPE), and (TAB) keys
- The characters that keys generate, such as the (SPACE)s generated by the (SPACE) bar
- Terminal keys that you press in conjunction with the (CONTROL) key, such as (CONTROL-D) (Even though **D** is shown as an uppercase letter, you do not have to press the (SHIFT) key; enter (CONTROL-D) by holding the (CONTROL) key down and pressing **D**.)

Utility Names. Names of utilities and common programs are printed in **this typeface**. Thus you will see references to the **sort** utility and the **vi** editor.

Commands. All commands that can be entered at the terminal are printed in a **bold** typeface. This book refers to the **ls** utility, or just **ls**, but instructs you to enter **ls −a** on the terminal.

Prompts and RETURNs. All examples include the Shell prompt (the signal that the UNIX system is waiting for a command) as a dollar sign (**$**). Your prompt may differ—another common prompt is a percent sign (**%**). The prompt is printed in a regular typeface because you do not enter it. It is important not to enter the prompt on the terminal when you are experimenting with examples from this book.

All examples *omit* the (RETURN) keystroke that you must use to terminate them. This aspect of giving a command is discussed in detail in the next section. An example of a command line is

```
$ vi newfile
```

If you were using the previous example as a model for calling the **vi** utility, you would enter **vi newfile** and then press the (RETURN) key. This method of giving examples makes the example in the book and what appears on your terminal screen the same.

Filenames. All filenames appear in lowercase letters in a **bold** typeface. Examples of files that appear in the text are: **memo5**, **letter.1283**, and **reports**. Filenames can include uppercase letters, but the examples in this book avoid such filenames for clarity.

Screens and Examples. In the screens and examples throughout this book, the items that the user enters are printed in **bold-faced** type. In the first line of Screen 2-1, the word **login:** is printed in a regular typeface because it was displayed by the UNIX system. The word **jenny** is shown in boldface to indicate that the user entered it.

USING THE UNIX SYSTEM

Now that you are acquainted with some of the special characters on the keyboard and the conventions used in this book, it will be easier to start using your UNIX system. This section leads you through a brief session, explaining how to log on, change your password, and log off.

Logging On

Since the UNIX operating system can be used by many people at the same time, it must be able to differentiate between you and other users. You must identify yourself before the UNIX system will process your requests.

Screen 2-1

```
login: jenny
password:

Welcome to UNIX!

$
```

Screen 2-1 shows how a typical login procedure appears on the terminal screen. Your login procedure may look different. If your terminal does not have the word login: on it, check to see that the terminal is turned on, then press the (RETURN) key a few times. If login: still does not appear, try pressing (CONTROL-Q). You can also try pressing the (BREAK) key and then the (RETURN) key again. If these procedures don't work, check with the system administrator. (If LOGIN: appears in uppercase letters, proceed. This situation is covered shortly.)

You must terminate every message or command to a UNIX system by depressing the (RETURN) key. (RETURN) signals that you have completed giving an instruction and that the operating system should commence execution of the command or respond to the message. UNIX programs do not generally respond if a communication is not terminated with a (RETURN) keystroke.

The first line of Screen 2-1 shows the UNIX system login: prompt followed by the user's response. The user entered **jenny**, her login name, followed by a (RETURN). Try logging on, making sure that you enter your login name exactly as it was given to you. The routine that verifies the login name and password is *case-sensitive* —it differentiates between uppercase and lowercase letters.

The second line of Screen 2-1 shows the password: prompt. If your installation does not require a password, you will not see this prompt. In the example, the user *did* respond to the prompt with a password followed by a (RETURN). For security, the UNIX operating system never displays a password. Enter your password in response to the password: prompt.

You will see a message and a prompt when you successfully log on. The message, called the *message of the day,* is generally something like Welcome to UNIX! and, if you are using the Bourne Shell, the prompt is usually a dollar sign ($). The C Shell generally prompts you with a percent sign (%) or a number followed by a percent sign. These prompts indicate that the system is waiting for you to give it a command.

If the login prompt appears in all uppercase letters (LOGIN:), everything you enter will also appear in uppercase letters. The UNIX system thinks you have a terminal that can only display uppercase characters. It sends uppercase characters to the terminal and translates everything you enter into lowercase for its internal use. If you are having this problem and your terminal is capable of displaying both uppercase and lowercase characters, give the following command *after you log on.*

```
$ STTY -LCASE
$
```

If you enter an invalid login name or password, the **login** utility displays the following message, after you finish entering both your login name *and* password.

```
Login incorrect
```

This message indicates that you have entered either the login name *or* password incorrectly, or that they are not valid. The message does not differentiate between an unacceptable login name and an unacceptable password. This policy discourages unauthorized people from guessing at names and passwords in order to gain access to the system.

Once you log on, you are communicating with the command interpreter known as the Shell utility. The Shell plays an important part in all your communication with the UNIX operating system. When you enter a command at the terminal (in response to the Shell prompt), the Shell interprets the command and initiates the appropriate action. This action may be executing your program, calling a standard program such as a compiler or one of the UNIX utility programs, or giving you an error message telling you that you have entered a command incorrectly.

Changing Your Password

Screen 2-2

```
$ passwd
Changing password for jenny
Old password:
Type new password:
Retype password:
$
```

When you first log on to a UNIX system, you may not have a password, or you may have a password that was assigned by the system administrator. In either case, it is a good idea to give yourself a new password. An optimal password contains a combination of numbers and uppercase and lowercase letters and is seven or eight characters long. Don't use names or other familiar words that can be easily guessed.

Screen 2-2 shows the process of changing a password using the **passwd** utility. For security reasons, none of the passwords that the user enters are ever displayed by this or any other utility.

Give the command **passwd** (followed by a (RETURN)) in response to the Shell prompt. This command causes the Shell to execute the **passwd** utility. The first item **passwd** asks you for is your *old* password. **passwd** verifies this password to insure that an unauthorized user is not trying to alter your password. Next, **passwd** requests the new password. Your password should contain six to eight printable characters in an easy-to-remember sequence. Next, in order to verify that you did not make a mistake typing it, **passwd** asks you to retype the new password. If the new password is the same both times that you enter it, your password is changed. If the passwords differ, it means that you made an error in one of them; **passwd** displays the following message.

Mismatch—password unchanged.

The Shell displays its prompt following this message. You must execute **passwd** again to change your password.

If your password contains too few characters, **passwd** encourages you to choose a longer password by displaying the following message.

Please use a longer password:

At this point, you can enter a longer password (try eight characters) or, if you really want to use a short password, retype the same password. If you enter the short password a few times, **passwd** gives up and lets you have the password of your choice.

You have now changed the way you will log on. You must always enter your password *exactly* the way you created it. If you created the password using a combination of uppercase and lowercase letters, you must use this same combination each time. If you forget your password, the system administrator can help straighten things out. Although no one can determine what your password is, the administrator can change it and tell you your new password.

Logging Off

Once you have changed your password, log off and try logging back on using your new password. You can log off by pressing (CONTROL-D) in response to the Shell prompt. If this doesn't work, try giving the command **logout**.

CORRECTING MISTAKES

This section explains how to correct typing and other errors you may make while you are logged on. (The techniques covered here do not generally work to correct errors made while you are entering your name and password.) Log on to your system and then try making and correcting mistakes as you read this section. Log off when you want to stop using the system.

Because the Shell and most other utilities do not interpret the command line (or other text) until after the (RETURN) key is pressed, you can correct typing mistakes before you press (RETURN). There are two ways to correct typing mistakes. You can delete one character at a time or you can back up to the beginning of the command line in one step. After you press the (RETURN) key, it is too late to correct a mistake; you can either wait for the command to run to completion or stop execution of the command. Refer to the subsequent section on "Stopping Program Execution."

Deleting Characters

While entering characters from the keyboard, you can backspace up to and over a mistake by pressing the delete character key (#), one time for each character you want to delete. (Use the delete character key you inquired about at the start of this chapter in place of # throughout this book.) As the cursor moves to the left, the characters it moves over are discounted, even if they still appear on the screen. A Teletype™ or other hard-copy terminal displays a # each time you press the delete character key; this type of terminal cannot backspace. The delete character key backs up over as many characters as you wish. It will not, however, back up past the beginning of the line.

Deleting an Entire Line

You can delete the entire line you are entering, anytime before you press (RETURN), by pressing the delete line key (@). (Use the delete line key you inquired about at the start of this chapter in place of @ throughout this book.)

When you press the @ key, the cursor moves down to the next line and all the way to the left. The Shell does not give you another prompt, but it is as though the cursor is sitting just following a Shell prompt. The operating system does not remove the line with the mistake on it, but ignores it. Enter the command (or other text) again, from the start.

Stopping Program Execution

Sometimes you may want to stop a running program. One of the UNIX programs may be performing a task that takes a long time, such as displaying the contents of a file that is several hundred pages, or copying a file that is not the file you meant to copy.

To stop program execution, press the interrupt execution key (DEL). (Use the interrupt execution key you inquired about at the start of this chapter in place of DEL throughout this book.) When you press this key, the UNIX operating system sends a terminal interrupt signal to all of your programs, including the Shell. Exactly what effect this signal has depends upon the program. Some programs stop execution immediately. Other programs take other appropriate actions. The Shell displays a prompt and waits for another command.

CREATING AND EDITING A FILE USING ed

As stated in Chapter 1, the UNIX system includes several hundred utility programs. The next sections describe four utilities that you can use to create and manipulate files. The screens and command lines in these (and other) sections are examples that you can experiment with while you are logged on to your system. This section shows you how to create a file with the **ed** utility, a text editor.

A *text file* is a collection of information that you can refer to by a *filename*. It is stored on a disk. Text files typically contain memos, reports, messages, program source code, lists, etc. An *editor* is a utility program that allows you to create a new text file or change a text file that already exists. There are many editors in use on UNIX systems. This chapter discusses **ed**. Chapter 6 discusses the **vi** editor. Although **vi** is more complex than **ed**, you may want to use **vi** if your system has it. **vi** makes editing easier by displaying a full screen of text at a time and allowing you to see what you're working on. Because **vi** displays a full screen of the text you are editing, it is called a *screen editor*. Because **ed** displays only one line of text at a time, it is called a *line editor*.

This discussion of **ed**, the simplest UNIX system line editor, covers only a few of its commands. Although using the full set of commands makes editing a text file easier, the subset of **ed** commands discussed here allows you, in principle, to accomplish anything you could accomplish using the entire set of **ed** commands.

Line Numbers

A *line* is a sequence of characters that begins just after the end of the previous line and ends with a (NEWLINE) character (ASCII value of 10 decimal). A line is independent of sentences and their punctuation. When you press the (RETURN) key, the system recognizes it as a (NEWLINE). The system displays a (NEWLINE) by sending the terminal the appropriate characters to end a line.

As you add and remove text, **ed** keeps track of the line you're working on by means of an invisible *line number.* The first line of text is line number one; the second, line number two; and the third, number three. Each line in the file is numbered in this manner. The numbers are not associated with any particular line, but rather with a line's position within the file. If, for example, you remove line three, line four becomes line three, line five becomes line four, and so on. If you add a line in between other lines, **ed** adjusts the line numbers accordingly.

Even though line numbers are not visible, you can reference any line (or group of lines) of text by line number when giving an **ed** command such as Display or Delete. Because you may need to reference a group of lines that ends with the last line in a file, you can refer to the last line with a dollar sign.

The Current Line. One particular line is almost always the *current* line. When you first call the editor, the file's last line is the current line. (If you are editing a new file, there is no current line.) After any command, the current line is dependent on the last line that you have accessed, entered, or deleted. If you have just displayed or entered a line, then that line is the current line. If a line has just been deleted, the line following the deleted line is the current line. Just as you can use a dollar sign to refer to the last line in a file, you can use a period to refer to the current line.

Addresses. Anywhere **ed** requires an address, you can use a line number to specify a line. You can specify a group of lines by using an address composed of the first and last line numbers, separated by a comma. For example, **4 ,7** represents lines four through seven, **17,$** represents lines 17 through the last line of the file, and **1,**. represents the beginning of the file through the current line.

Calling ed

Call **ed** by entering **ed** followed by a (SPACE) and the name of the file you want to edit. Refer to the first line of Screen 2-3, where the user is editing a file named **demo**. **ed** displays a question mark and the name of the file to indicate that this is a new file. If you are editing a file that already exists, **ed** displays the number of characters in the file in place of this line.

Screen 2-3

```
$ ed demo
?demo
a
This is the first line of text.
All of this text will become the file named demo.
This line has a mastake on it.
This is the last line.
```

Unlike the Shell, **ed** has no prompt. At this point, **ed** is in the *Command Mode* and responds to any of the **ed** commands. Because **ed** is case-sensitive, you must enter the commands as shown (i.e., do not enter an uppercase **A** when an **a** is called for). You will be using **ed** until you exit from the editor and have the Shell prompt back. While you use the editor, only editor commands are valid. Without the use of a special command (!) you cannot run other UNIX programs, such as **passwd**, while you are running the editor. In the same manner, once you exit from the editor and return to the Shell, you will no longer be able to use editor commands. This section covers the Append, Delete, Display, Substitute, Write, and Quit **ed** commands.

Entering Text

Once **ed** is in the Command Mode, enter the letter **a** (for append) followed by a (RETURN). This puts **ed** in the Append Mode. While in this mode, **ed** considers *anything* that you enter on the keyboard to be text and places it in the file you are creating. To get back to the Command Mode, enter a period on a line by itself, followed by a (RETURN). If you notice a mistake on the line that you are entering, you can use the delete character or delete line keys to correct the error. In Screen 2-3, the user entered four lines of text and then returned to the Command Mode.

Displaying Text

When **ed** is back in the Command Mode, you can use other **ed** commands. The Display command is **p** (for print). When used without an address, the **p** command displays the current line. You can precede **p** with an address consisting of a line number or a range of line numbers. The first command of Screen 2-4 displays the entire file because the user addressed the first through the last lines (**1,$**). Next, the screen shows the command **3p** displaying the third line of text.

Screen 2-4

```
1,$p
This is the first line of text.
All of this text will become the file named demo.
This line has a mastake on it.
This is the last line.
3p
This line has a mastake on it.
```

Deleting Text

Just as you can display text, you can delete it. Line numbers work with the Delete command, **d** (for delete), in a manner analogous to the way they work with the **p** command. The first command in Screen 2-5 deletes line three.

Screen 2-5

```
3d
2a
This line used to have a mistake on it.
.
3p
This line used to have a mistake on it.
```

Adding Text Within a File

After deleting line three, Screen 2-5 shows the user reentering it correctly by preceding the new line with a line number and the Append command. In this case, the **2a** command places the new text after line two. A period on a line by itself takes **ed** out of the Append Mode. Then the **3p** command displays the new line. When you precede the Append command with a line number, **ed** puts the new text after the line you specify.

Substituting Text

The Substitute command substitutes one string of text for another. The format of the Substitute command is

```
address s/old-text/new-text/p
```

The **address** is either a single line number or a pair of line numbers. If you do not specify an address, **ed** assumes that the change is on the current line. If you do use an address, **ed** makes the change on the specified line(s). The **old-text** is the existing text that you want to change and the **new-text** is the text that will replace the existing text. The **p** is optional; it commands **ed** to display the changed line.

Screen 2-6

```
4s/This/Line four/p
Line four is the last line.
w
150
q
$
```

Screen 2-6 shows the substitute command changing This on line four to Line four and then displaying the changed line.

Writing the File to the Disk and Exiting from ed

While you are editing, **ed** keeps the edited text in an area called the *Work Buffer.*

When you finish editing, you must write out the contents of the Work Buffer to a disk file so that it will be saved and available when you next want it. Enter the Write command, **w**, followed by a (RETURN). **ed** verifies that the file was written out by displaying the number of characters in the file.

Enter the Quit command, **q**, to exit from **ed**. The Shell prompt appears after the **q** command. This prompt indicates that you are no longer using the **ed** utility and that the Shell, which was quietly standing by during the editing session, is again waiting for a command.

You can exit from **ed** without first writing out the contents of the Work Buffer by giving the **Q** command (on some systems, you must give two **q** commands in a row). If you use this command, all the work you did since the last **w** command will be lost; if you did not give a **w** command, the file will remain exactly as it was before you started.

Summary of ed Commands

Table 2–1 summarizes the commands that were covered in this section and introduces some new ones.

Addresses.   Zero, one, or two addresses precede an **ed** command. Frequently, no address implies the current line. One address specifies a single line. Two addresses separated by a comma specify a range of lines that includes the addressed lines.

An address can be a line number, a period (representing the current line), or a dollar sign (representing the last line in the file). You can add or subtract within an address (e.g., **.+5** means the fifth line after the current line and **$–2** means the second line before the last).

Commands.   The second column in Table 2-1 specifies the maximum number of addresses that can precede each of the commands listed in the left-hand column.

LISTING THE CONTENTS OF A DIRECTORY

If you followed the preceding example, you used **ed** to create a file named **demo** in your directory. After exiting from **ed**, you can use the **ls** (list) utility to display a list of the names of the files in your directory. The first command in Screen 2-7 shows **ls** listing the name of the **demo** file.

Table 2-1 ed Commands

Command	Max. Number of Addresses	Effect
a	1	append text after addressed line*
c	2	change addressed lines to new text*
d	2	delete addressed lines
i	1	insert text before addressed line*
l	2	list addressed lines (displays nonprinting characters)
p	2	print addressed lines (does not display nonprinting characters)
q	0	quit (does not automatically write out the file)
Q	0	quit (ignores changes)
qq	0	some systems use this instead of **Q**
r file	1	read **file**
s/old/new/[g]	2	substitute occurrences of **old**, a regular expression, with **new**, a string. If **g** (global) is not used, substitute for the first occurrence on each addressed line. Otherwise substitute for all occurrences on addressed lines.
w file	2	Write Work Buffer to **file** (no address writes the entire Work Buffer)
none	1	display addressed line
(RETURN)	2	print addressed line (does not display nonprinting characters)
! command		execute operating system **command**

*The **a**, **c**, and **i** commands leave **ed** in the Insert Mode. You can put **ed** back in the Command Mode by entering a period on a line by itself, followed by a (RETURN).

Screen 2-7

```
$ ls
demo

$ cat demo
This is the first line of text.
All of this text will become the file named demo.
This line used to have a mistake on it.
Line four is the last line.

$ rm demo
$ ls
$
```

DISPLAYING THE CONTENTS OF A TEXT FILE

The **cat** utility displays the contents of a text file. The name of the command is derived from **cat**_enate_ , which means to join together one after another. One of **cat**'s functions is to join files together in this manner. Use **cat** by entering **cat** followed by a (SPACE) and the name of the file that you want to display.

Screen 2-7 shows **cat** displaying the contents of **demo**. This screen shows the difference between the **ls** and **cat** utilities. **ls** displays the _names_ of the files in a directory and **cat** displays the _contents_ of a file.

DELETING A FILE

The **rm** (remove) utility deletes a file. Screen 2-7 shows **rm** deleting the **demo** file. After **rm** deletes the file, **ls** shows that there is nothing in the directory.

SPECIAL CHARACTERS

Special characters—those that have a special meaning to the Shell—are discussed in Chapter 5. These characters are mentioned here so that you can avoid accidentally using them as regular characters until you understand how the Shell interprets them. The standard special characters are as follows:

& ; | * ? \ ' " ` [ ] ( ) < >

In addition, % and ! are special characters to the C Shell.

Although not considered special characters, (RETURN), (SPACE), and (TAB) also have a special meaning to the Shell. (RETURN) usually ends a command line and initiates execution of the command. (SPACE) and (TAB) separate elements on the command line and are collectively known as *white space*.

Quoting Characters

If you need to use one of the characters that has a special meaning to the Shell as a regular character, you can *quote* it. When you quote a special character, you keep the Shell from giving it special meaning. The Shell treats a quoted special character as a regular character.

To quote a character, precede it with a backslash (\). One backslash must precede each character that you are quoting. If two or more special characters are used, each must be preceded by a backslash (e.g., ** must be entered as **).

Another way of quoting special characters is to enclose them between single quotation marks (e.g., ' ** '). You can quote many special and regular characters between a pair of single quotation marks (e.g., ' This is a special character: > '). In this case, the regular characters remain regular and the special characters are also interpreted as regular characters.

You can quote the delete character character (#) and the delete line character (@) by preceding either one with a backslash. Single quotation marks will not work.

SUMMARY

After reading this chapter and experimenting on your system, you should be able to log on and use the utilities and special keys listed below. Part II has more information on **ls, rm,** and **cat**.

➡ **passwd** changes your password.

➡ (CONTROL-D) or **logout** logs you off the system.

➡ The # (or another) key deletes a character on the command line.

➡ The @ (or another) key deletes the entire command line.

➡ The (DEL) (or another) key interrupts execution of the program you are running.

➡ **ed** creates or edits a text file.

➡ **ls** displays a list of files.

➡ **rm** deletes a file.

➡ **cat** displays the contents of a file on the terminal.

3

AN INTRODUCTION
TO THE UTILITIES

UNIX utility programs allow you to work with the UNIX system and manipulate the files that you create. Chapter 2 introduced the Shell, the most important UNIX utility program, and **passwd**, the utility that allows you to change your password. It also introduced some of the utilities that are used to create and manipulate files: **ed**, **ls**, **cat**, and **rm**. This chapter describes utilities that allow you to display system documentation, find out who's logged on, communicate with other users, print files, and perform other necessary functions.

Some of the utilities included in this chapter were chosen because you can learn to use them easily and they allow you to communicate with other people using the computer. Others were chosen because they form the bases for examples in later chapters. Part II of this book covers these and other utilities more concisely and completely.

man

The **man** (manual) utility displays pages from the system documentation on the terminal. This documentation is useful if you know what utility you want to use but have forgotten exactly how it works.

To find out more about a utility, give the command **man** followed by the name of the utility. The following command displays information about the **who** utility.

```
$ man who
.
.
.
$
```

The command **man man** displays information about the **man** utility.

In some installations, **man** displays one screenful of text and then displays a percent. The percent is the portion of the description that you have already viewed. If you press the (SPACE) bar, **man** displays a new screenful of information. If you press (RETURN), **man** displays one additional line. (DEL) stops **man** and gives you a Shell prompt.

who

The **who** utility displays a list of the users currently logged on. In Screen 3-1, **who** shows that hls, chas, scott, and barbara are logged on. The second column of the list shows the designation of the terminal that each person is using. The third column shows the date and time that the person logged on. To find out which terminal you are using, or to see what time you logged on, give the command **who am i**.

Screen 3-1

```
$ who
hls       console May 22 12:48
scott     tty2    May 21 09:07
barbara   tty3    May 22 12:53
chas      tty6m   May 22 10:31
$
```

The information that **who** displays is useful if you want to communicate with someone at your installation. If **who** does not show that the person is logged on, you can send that person UNIX system **mail** (page 42). If the person is logged on, you can also use the **write** utility (below) to establish communication immediately.

write

You can use the **write** utility to send messages to another user who is logged on. When the other user also uses **write** to send you messages, you establish two-way communication.

When you give a **write** command, it displays a banner on the other user's terminal saying that you are about to send a message. The format of a **write** command line is shown below.

```
write destination-user
```

The **destination-user** is the login name of the user you want to communicate with. You can find out the login name of the users who are logged on by using the **who** utility (above).

To establish two-way communication with another user, you and the other user must each execute **write**, each specifying the other's login name as the **destination-user**. **write** then copies text from one terminal to the other, on a line-by-line basis. When you want to stop communicating with the other user, press (CONTROL-D). This tells **write** to quit, displays EOF (end of file) on the other user's terminal, and returns you to the Shell. The other user must do the same.

It is helpful to establish a protocol for carrying on communication using **write**. Try ending each message with **o** (for *over*) and ending the transmission with **oo** (for *over and out*). This gives each user time to think, and to enter a complete message, without the other user wondering if the first user is finished. Because **write** copies one line at a time, if you write several short lines of text rather than one long line, the other user will frequently be reassured that you're still there.

The following example shows how one side of a two-way communication using **write** appears to Jenny. Screen 3-2 shows Jenny initiating communication by calling the **write** utility and specifying Alex as the **destination-user**. She enters a message, terminated by **o**, and waits for a reply.

Screen 3-2

```
$ write alex
Hi Alex, are you there? o
```

As soon as Alex has a chance to respond and execute **write**, **write** sends a banner to Jenny's terminal. Then, Alex sends a message indicating that he is ready to receive Jenny's message (Screen 3-3). Following the protocol that he and Jenny have established, Alex terminates his message with **o**.

Screen 3-3

```
Message from alex tty5m. . . .
Yes Jenny, I'm here. o
```

At this point, Jenny and Alex can communicate back and forth. Each time one of them types a line and presses (RETURN), the line appears on the other's terminal. When they are done, Jenny enters a final message terminated by **oo**, and then presses (CONTROL-D) (on a line by itself) to sign off (see Screen 3-4). The Shell prompt appears. Alex signs off after this and Jenny sees the EOF that results from Alex pressing (CONTROL-D). Jenny can display another Shell prompt by pressing the (RETURN) key.

Screen 3-4

```
$ write alex
Hi Alex, are you there? o
Yes Jenny, I'm here.  o
   .
   .
   .
Thank you, Alex — bye oo
[CONTROL-D]
$ Bye, Jenny oo
EOF
```

Throughout this communication, Alex and Jenny followed the convention of using **o** after each message. This is just a convention and is not recognized by **write**. You can use any convention you please, or none at all.

mesg

If Alex does not want to be interrupted, he can give the following command.

```
$ mesg n
$
```

After giving this command, another user attempting to **write** to Alex would see the following.

```
$ write alex
Permission denied.
$
```

Alex can allow messages again by entering **mesg y**.

If you want to know if someone can **write** to *you*, give the command **mesg** by itself. The **mesg** utility will respond with a **y** (for yes, messages are allowed) or **n** (for no).

mail

Using the **mail** utility, you can send UNIX system mail to other users—
whether or not they are logged on—and display mail that other users have
sent you. The Shell displays the message You have mail. if there is mail
waiting for you when you log on.

The format of the command line used to send mail is shown below.

```
mail user-list
```

The **user-list** is the login name of one or more users you want to send mail to.
After you enter this command line and press (RETURN), you will not get
a Shell prompt; you are talking to the **mail** utility. Enter the message you
want to send, terminated by a line with *just* a period on it—nothing else.
(Some versions of **mail** require you to type (CONTROL-D) on a line by itself.)
The period (or (CONTROL-D)) indicates the end of the message to **mail**. After
the UNIX system sends your mail, the Shell displays a prompt.

You can look at the letters that you have received by giving the command
mail by itself. When displaying mail, **mail** prompts you with a question
mark after it shows you each letter in your mailbox. Press (RETURN) to
display the next letter. If you press **s**, **mail** saves the letter in a file named
mbox; **d** deletes the letter.

The following example shows how Jenny sends a letter to Alex and how
Alex receives it. First, while Jenny is logged on, she uses the **mail** utility to
send a letter (Screen 3-5). She terminates her letter by entering a period on a
line by itself.

Screen 3-5

```
$ mail alex
Alex, can we change our meeting to 3:00?
.
$
```

When Alex logs on, he gets a message saying that he has mail (Screen
3-6). He uses the **mail** utility to display the letter from Jenny and responds to
the question mark prompt by pressing **d** followed by a (RETURN) to delete the
letter.

Screen 3-6

```
login: alex
Password:

Welcome to UNIX!

You have mail.

$ mail
From jenny Sun Nov 28 15:06:58 1982
Alex, can we change our meeting to 3:00?

? d
$
```

The letter from Jenny is now gone.

Some installations provide a facility for sending mail to users on other machines. If you have this facility, you can use it by preceding the user's name with a machine name and an exclamation point. The following command line sends mail to Bill on the machine named bravo. If you are using the C Shell, you must quote the exclamation point by preceding it with a backslash.

 `$ mail bravo!bill`

You can obtain a list of machine names and users that are part of your network from the system administrator.

cp

cp makes a copy of a file. It can copy any kind of file, including text and executable program files. Among other uses, you can use cp to make a backup copy of a file or a copy for experimentation.

 A cp command line specifies a source and destination file. The format is shown below.

 `cp source-file destination-file`

The **source-file** is the filename of the file that cp is going to copy. The **destination-file** is the filename that cp assigns to the resulting copy of the file.

If the **destination-file** exists *before* you give a cp command, cp over-writes it. Because cp overwrites (and destroys the contents of) an existing **destination-file**, you must take care not to cause cp to overwrite a file that you need.

The following command line makes a copy of the file named **output**. The copy is named **outputb**.

```
$ cp output outputb
$
```

Sometimes it is useful to incorporate the date in the name of a copy of a file. In the following example, the period is part of the filename—just another character.

```
$ cp memo memo.0130
$
```

Although the date has no significance to the UNIX operating system, it can help you to find a version of a file that you saved on a certain date. It can also help you avoid overwriting existing files by providing a unique filename each day.

lpr

When several people or jobs must use a single printer, the UNIX system provides a means of *queuing* printer output so that one job gets printed at a time. The lpr utility places a file in the printer queue for printing.

The following command line prints the file named **report**.

```
$ lpr report
$
```

You can send more than one file to the printer with a single command line. The following command line prints three files.

```
$ lpr memo letter text
$
```

date

The **date** utility displays the current time and date. An example of **date** is shown below.

```
$ date
Sun Feb   6 09:35:07 PST 1983
$
```

echo

The **echo** utility copies to the terminal anything you put on the command line after **echo**. An example is shown in Screen 3-7.

Screen 3-7

```
$ echo Hi
Hi

$ echo This is a sentence.
This is a sentence.

$ echo Good morning.
Good morning.
$
```

echo is a good tool for learning about the Shell and other UNIX programs. Chapter 5 uses **echo** for learning about special characters. Chapter 8 uses it for learning about Shell variables and sending messages from a Shell program to the terminal.

sort

The **sort** utility puts the contents of a file in order by lines. If you have a file named **days** that contains the names of each of the days of the week on a separate line, **sort** will display the file in alphabetical order as shown in Screen 3-8.

Screen 3-8

```
$ cat days
Monday
Tuesday
Wednesday
Thursday
Friday
Saturday
Sunday

$ sort days
Friday
Monday
Saturday
Sunday
Thursday
Tuesday
Wednesday
```

sort is useful for putting lists in order. Within certain limits, **sort** can be used to order a list of numbers. Part II goes into the features and limitations of **sort**.

SUMMARY

Below is a list of the utilities that have been introduced up to this point. Because you will be using these utilities frequently, and because they are integral to the following chapters, it is important that you become comfortable using them. The particular editor that you use is not important. If your installation has an editor that you prefer to **ed**, learn to use that editor.

- **cat** displays the contents of a file on the terminal.
- **cp** makes a copy of a file.
- **date** displays the time, day, and date.
- **echo** displays a line of text on the terminal.
- **ed** creates or edits a text file.
- **lpr** prints a text file.
- **ls** displays a list of files.
- **mail** sends or receives mail.
- **mesg** permits or denies messages sent via **write**.
- **man** displays information on utilities.
- **passwd** changes your password.
- **rm** deletes a file.
- **sort** puts a file in order by lines.
- **who** displays a list of who is logged on.
- **write** sends a message to another user who is logged on.

THE UNIX SYSTEM
FILE STRUCTURE

This chapter discusses the organization and terminology of the UNIX system file structure. It defines plain and directory files, and the rules for naming them. It shows how to create and delete directories, move through the file structure, and use pathnames to access files in different directories. This chapter also covers file access permissions that allow you to share selected files with other users. The final section describes links, which can make a single file appear in more than one directory.

THE HIERARCHICAL FILE STRUCTURE

A *hierarchical* structure takes the shape of a pyramid. One example of this type of structure is found by tracing a family's lineage: A couple has a child; that child may have several children; and each of those children may have more children. This hierarchical structure, as shown in Figure 4-1, is called a family tree.

Like the family tree it resembles, the UNIX system file structure is also called a *tree*. It is composed of a set of connected files forming a pyramid. This structure allows you to organize files so that you can easily find any particular one. In a standard UNIX system, you start with one directory.

Figure 4-1: A Family Tree

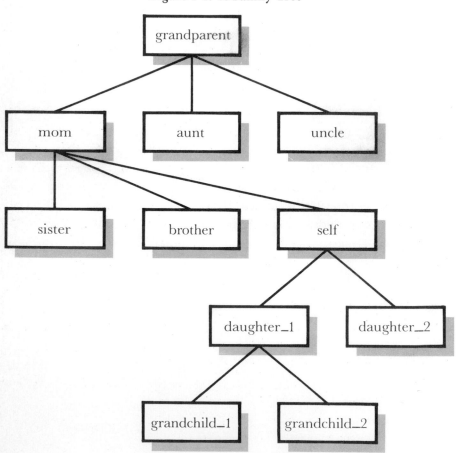

From this single directory, you can make as many subdirectories as you like, dividing subdirectories into additional subdirectories. In this manner, you can continue expanding the structure to any level according to your needs.

Using a Hierarchical File Structure

Typically, each subdirectory is dedicated to a single project. The project dictates whether a subdirectory should be further subdivided. For instance, a secretary can have a subdirectory named **correspondence**, as illustrated in Figure 4-2. This directory can contain three subdirectories: **business**, **memos**, and **personal**. The **business** directory can contain files that store each letter the secretary types. If there are a lot of letters going to one client, a subdirectory can be dedicated to that client.

The ability of the UNIX system file structure to adapt to different users' needs is one of its strengths. You can take advantage of this strength by strategically organizing your files.

Figure 4-2: A Secretary's Directory

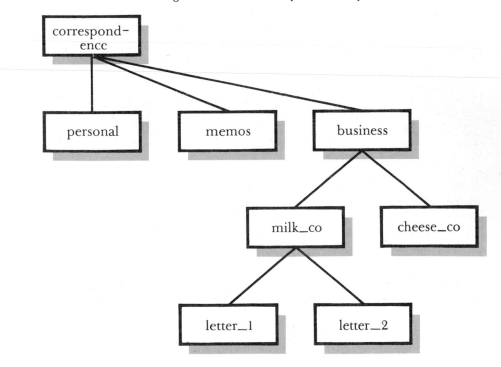

ORGANIZATION AND TERMINOLOGY OF THE UNIX SYSTEM FILE STRUCTURE

The analogy of the UNIX system file structure to a family tree is useful in describing the parts of the file structure. The tree is usually pictured upside down, with its *root* at the top. As shown in Figure 4-3, the tree "grows" downward from the root, with *branches* coming from the root and other branches. The end of a branch can be marked by a leaf or a node. *Leaves* are at the ends of branches that cannot grow other branches. *Nodes* are the points where branches can join other branches. (The illustration shows some empty nodes.) When you refer to the tree, *up* is toward the root and *down* is away from the root.

Figure 4-3: File Structure Terminology

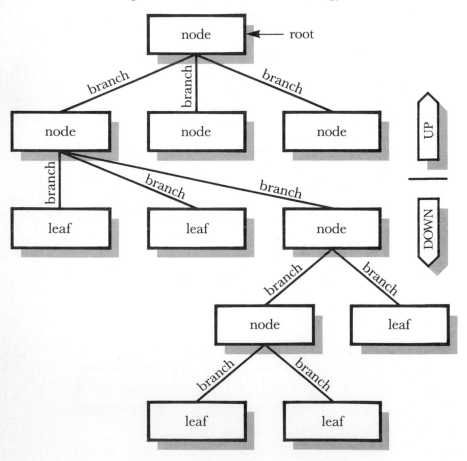

As seen in Figure 4-4, a *parent* is the node one step up (closer to the root) from a leaf or another node. A *grandparent* is two steps up the tree. The root is the only node that is the *ancestor* of all leaves and nodes on the tree.

From another perspective, a *child* is the leaf or node one step down (farther from the root) from a node. A *grandchild* is two steps down the tree. All leaves and nodes are descendants of the root.

By definition, a leaf cannot have a child, but a node can exist with or without a child. Also by definition, a child may be a leaf or a node, while a parent must be a node. (In order to be a parent, you must have a child; a leaf cannot have a child.)

Figure 4-4: Parent-Child Relationship

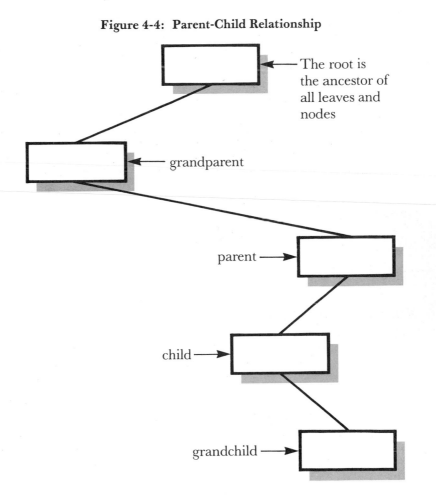

Figure 4-5: Generations

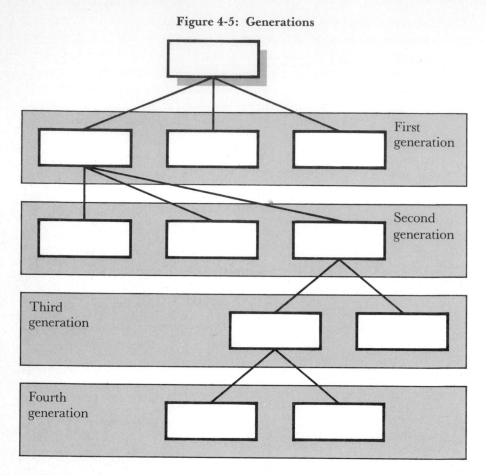

Every node and leaf belongs to one generation or another, as illustrated in Figure 4-5. If the root is generation zero, all children of the root are members of the first generation; the grandchildren of the root are members of the second generation, and so on.

Directory and Plain Files

As shown in Figure 4-6, the root, as well as every node and leaf on the tree, represents a file. The root and nodes are *directory files* (usually called *directories*), while the leaves are *plain files* (or simply *files*). Branches represent the paths between files.

Filenames. Every file has a *filename*. A filename is composed of from 1 to 14 characters. (The Berkeley UNIX system allows filenames to be up to 256

Figure 4-6: Directory and Plain Files

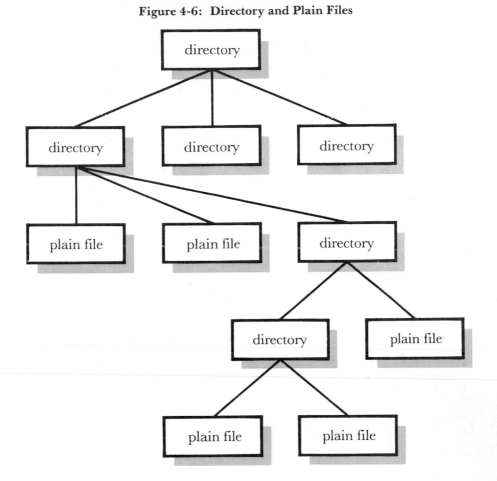

characters long.) Although you can use almost any character in a filename, you may avoid some confusion if you choose characters from the following list.

uppercase letters [A-Z]
lowercase letters [a-z]
numbers [0-9]
underscore [_]
period [.]
comma [,]

The only exception is the root directory, which is always named / and referred to by this single character. No other file can use this name.

Like children of one parent, no two files in the same directory can have the same name. Files in different directories, like children of different parents, can have the same name.

The filenames you choose should mean something. Too often, a directory is filled with important files with names such as **foobar**, **wombat**, and **junk**. A meaningless name won't help you recall what you stored in a file. The following filenames conform to the required syntax *and* convey information about the contents of the file. (Although they are not used in examples in this book, you can use uppercase letters within filenames. The UNIX operating system is, however, case-sensitive and considers files named **JAN-UARY**, **January**, and **january** as three distinct files.)

> **correspondence**
> **january**
> **davis**
> **reports**
> **1982**
> **acct_payable**

Filename extensions In the following filenames, embedded periods help describe the contents of the file. A *filename extension* is the part of the filename following a period. Some programs, such as the C programming language compiler, depend on specific filename extensions. In most cases, however, filename extensions are optional.

> **compute.c** (a C programming language source file)
> **compute.o** (the object code for the program)
> **compute** (the same program as an executable file)
> **memo.0410** (a text file)

Use extensions freely to make filenames easy to understand. If you like, you can use several periods within the same filename (for example, **notes.4.10.83**).

Invisible filenames A filename beginning with a period is called an *invisible filename* because it is not displayed by **ls**. The command **ls −a** displays *all* filenames, even "invisible" ones. Special-purpose Shell files are usually invisible so that they do not clutter a directory. Two special invisible entries, a single and double period (. and . .) , appear in every directory. These entries are discussed on page 59.

Absolute Pathnames. As shown in Figure 4-7, every file has a *pathname*. You can determine the pathname of a file by tracing a path from the

Figure 4-7: Pathnames

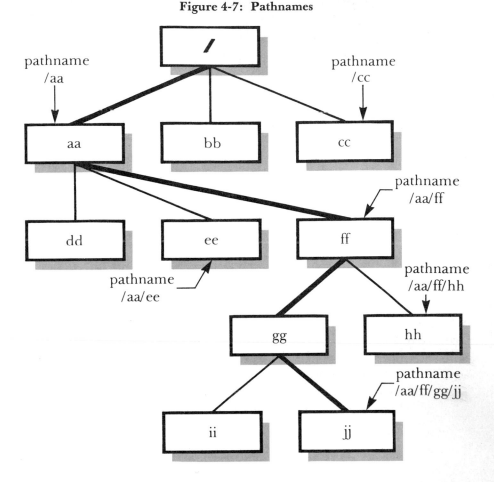

root directory, through all the intermediate directories, to the file. This path of filenames is called an *absolute pathname* because it locates a file absolutely, tracing a path from the root directory to the file.

The pathname is formed by stringing all the filenames in the path together. The names are separated by slashes and preceded by the name of the root directory. A slash can have two meanings in a pathname. As the first item in a pathname, it represents the name of the root directory, indicating that the path starts at the root. Anywhere else in a pathname, a slash represents a branch separating two filenames. By the definition of a branch, a file preceding a slash is the parent of the file following it.

The part of a pathname following the final slash is called a *simple filename*, or just a filename.

DIRECTORIES

This section covers creating, deleting, and using directories. It explains the concept of the *working* and *home directories* and their importance in relative pathnames.

The Working Directory

While you are logged on to a UNIX system, you will always be associated with one directory or another. Sometimes this association is referred to in a physical sense: "you are *in* (or *working in*) the **jenny** directory." The directory you are associated with, or are working in, is called the *working directory,* or sometimes the *current directory.* The **pwd** (print working directory) utility displays the pathname of the working directory. To access any file in the working directory, you do not need a pathname—just a simple filename. To access a file in another directory, however, you *must* use a pathname.

Your Home Directory

When you first log on to a UNIX system, the working directory is your *home* directory. To display the absolute pathname of your home directory, use **pwd** just after you log on. Screen 4-1 shows Alex logging on and displaying the names of his home directory.

Screen 4-1

```
login: alex
password:

Welcome to UNIX!

$ pwd
/usr/alex
$
```

The **ls** utility displays a list of the files in the working directory. All the files you have created up to this point are in your home directory. Because your home directory has been the only working directory you have used, **ls** has always displayed a list of all the files in your home directory.

Startup Files. Either you or the system administrator can put a *startup file,* containing Shell commands, in your home directory. The Shell executes the commands in a startup file each time you log on. With the Bourne Shell, the filename must be **.profile**, with the C Shell, **.login**. Because the files have invisible filenames, you must use the **ls –a** command if you want to see if either file is in your home directory.

A startup file frequently tells the Shell what kind of terminal you are using and executes the **stty** utility to establish your delete line and delete character keys. For more information on these and other files automatically executed by the Shell, see Chapters 8 and 9.

Creating a Directory

The **mkdir** (make directory) utility creates a directory file. It does *not* change your association with the working directory. The *argument* (the word following the name of the command) used with **mkdir** becomes the pathname of the new directory. In Screen 4-2, **mkdir** creates a directory named **literature** as a child of the working directory. (See Figure 4-8.) **ls** verifies the presence of the new directory and shows the files Alex has been working with: **names**, **temp**, and **demo**. **ls** does not distinguish between a directory file and a plain file.

Screen 4-2

```
$ mkdir /usr/alex/literature

$ ls
literature names temp demo
$
```

When you use **mkdir** as shown in Screen 4-2, enter the pathname of *your* home directory in place of **/usr/alex**.

The . and . . Directory Entries. mkdir automatically puts two entries in every directory you create. They are a single and double period, representing the directory itself and the parent directory, respectively. These entries are invisible because their filenames begin with periods.

Because **mkdir** automatically places these entries in every directory, you can rely on their presence. The . is synonymous with the pathname of the working directory and can be used in its place; . . is synonymous with the pathname of the parent of the working directory.

Figure 4-8: The File Structure Used in the Examples

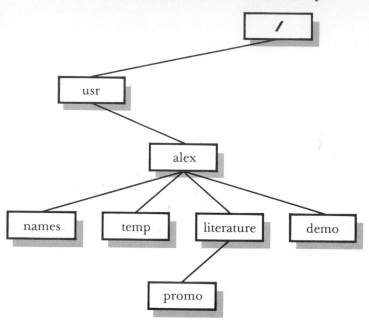

When you follow an **ls** command with a pathname of a directory, **ls** lists the contents of the directory. In Screen 4-3, the contents of the **/usr** directory is listed from **/usr/alex** by using **. .** to represent the parent directory.

Screen 4-3

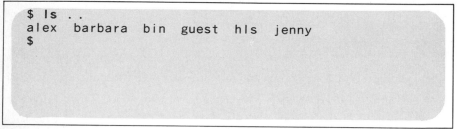

```
$ ls . .
alex  barbara  bin  guest  hls  jenny
$
```

Changing to Another Working Directory

The **cd** (change directory) utility associates you with another directory. It makes another directory the working directory—it does *not* change the contents of the working directory. In this context, it may be helpful to think of the working directory as a place marker. The first **cd** command in Screen 4-4 makes the **/usr/alex/literature** directory the working directory, as verified by **pwd**.

When used without an argument, **cd** makes your home directory the working directory, as it was when you first logged on. The second **cd** in Screen 4-4 does not have an argument and makes Alex's home directory the working directory.

Screen 4-4

```
$ cd /usr/alex/literature

$ pwd
/usr/alex/literature

$ cd

$ pwd
/usr/alex
$
```

Deleting a Directory

The **rmdir** (remove directory) utility deletes a directory file. You cannot delete the working directory or a directory containing any files. If you need to delete a directory with files in it, first delete the files (using **rm**) and then delete the directory. You do not have to delete the . and . . entries; **rmdir** automatically removes them. The following command deletes the directory that was created in Screen 4-2.

```
$ rmdir /usr/alex/literature
$
```

Relative Pathnames

A *relative pathname* traces a path from the working directory to a file. The pathname is *relative* to the working directory. Alex could have created the **literature** directory (Screen 4-2) more easily using a relative pathname, as shown below. This example assumes that his home directory (**/usr/alex**) is still the working directory.

```
$ mkdir literature
$
```

mkdir will display an error message if the **literature** directory already exists, because no two children of one parent can have the same name. The pathname used in this example is a simple filename. A simple filename is actually a relative pathname specifying a file in the working directory.

Any pathname that does not begin with the root directory (/) is a relative pathname. Like absolute pathnames, relative pathnames can describe a path through many directories.

The following commands show two ways to create the same directory, **promo**, a child of **literature** and a grandchild of Alex's home directory. (Refer back to Figure 4-8.) The first uses a relative pathname; the second uses an absolute pathname.

```
$ mkdir literature/promo
$
```

or

```
$ mkdir /usr/alex/literature/promo
$
```

Because the location of the file that you are accessing is dependent on (relative to) the working directory, always make sure you know which is the working directory before using a relative pathname. When you use an absolute pathname, it does not matter which is the working directory.

Anywhere that a UNIX utility program requires a filename or pathname, you can use an absolute or relative pathname or a simple filename. You can use any of these types of names with most utilities, including **cd**, **ls**, **mkdir**, **rm**, and **rmdir**.

Significance of the Working Directory. Typing long pathnames is tedious and increases the chances of making mistakes. You can choose a working directory for any particular task to reduce the need for long pathnames. Your choice of a working directory does not allow you to do anything you could not do otherwise—it just makes some operations easier.

Files that are children of the working directory can be referenced by simple filenames. Grandchildren of the working directory can be referenced by relative pathnames, composed of two filenames separated by a slash. When you manipulate files in a large directory structure, short relative pathnames can save much time and aggravation. If you choose a working directory that contains the files used most for a particular task, you will need to use fewer long, cumbersome pathnames.

Using Pathnames

The following example assumes that **/usr/alex** is the working directory. It uses a relative pathname to copy the file **letter** to the **/usr/alex/literature/promo** directory. The copy of the file has the simple filename **letter.0610**.

```
$ cp letter literature/promo/letter.0610
$
```

Assuming that Alex has not changed to another working directory, the following command allows him to edit the copy of the file he just made.

```
$ ed literature/promo/letter.0610
.
.
.
```

If Alex does not want to use a long pathname to specify the file, he can use **cd** to make the **promo** directory the working directory before calling **ed**.

```
$ cd literature/promo

$ pwd
/usr/alex/literature/promo

$ ed letter.0610
.
.
.
```

If Alex wants to make the parent of the working directory (**/usr/alex/literature**) the new working directory, he can give the following command which takes advantage of the **. .** directory entry.

```
$ cd . .

$ pwd
/usr/alex/literature
$
```

Important Standard Directories and Files

The UNIX system file structure is usually set up according to a convention. Aspects of this convention may vary from installation to installation. Figure 4-9 shows the usual locations of some important directories and files.

Figure 4-9: The Standard UNIX System File Structure

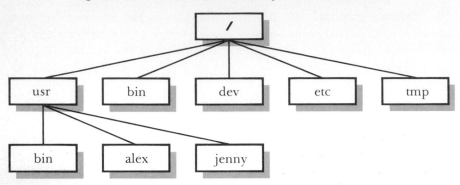

/ (root)   The root directory is present in all UNIX system file structures.

/usr   Each user's home directory is usually a subdirectory of **/usr**. Using this scheme, the absolute pathname of Jenny's home directory would be **/usr/jenny**.

/bin and **/usr/bin**   These directories contain the standard UNIX utility programs. By convention, **/bin** contains the most frequently used standard utilities, while **/usr/bin** contains more obscure utilities as well as programs that are specific to an installation.

/dev   All files that represent devices are kept in this directory.

/etc   Miscellaneous files are kept here. The most useful is the **passwd** file, containing a list of all users who have permission to use the system.

/tmp   Many programs use this directory to hold temporary files.

ACCESS PERMISSIONS

There are three types of users who can access a file: the owner of the file (*owner*); a member of the group to which the owner belongs (*group*); and everyone else (*other*). A user can attempt to access a plain file in three ways—by trying to *read* from, *write* to, or *execute* it. Three types of users, each able to access a file in three ways, equals a total of nine possible ways to access a plain file. These ways are listed below.

> The owner of a file can try to:
> read from the file
> write to the file
> execute the file

> A member of the owner's group can try to:
> read from the file
> write to the file
> execute the file

> Anyone else can try to:
> read from the file
> write to the file
> execute the file

The owner of a file controls which users have permission to access the file and in what manner they can access it. You can use **ls** with the -l option (refer to Part II) to display the access permissions associated with a file. Refer to the **chmod** utility in Part II for information on how to change access permissions.

Access permissions have slightly different meanings when used with directory files. Although a directory file can be accessed by the three types of users and can be read from or written to, it can never be executed. For this reason, execute access permission has been redefined for a directory: it means you can search through and list the contents of the directory. It has nothing to do with executing a file.

This access permission scheme lets you give other users access to the files you want to share and keep your private files confidential. You can allow other users to read from *and* write to a file (you may be one of several people working on a joint project); only to read from a file (perhaps a project specification that you are proposing); or only to write to a file (similar to an in-basket or mailbox, where you don't want someone else to read your mail). In a similar manner, you can protect entire directories from being scanned. There is an exception to the access permissions described above: the system administrator can log on as the *super user* and have full access to *all* files, regardless of owner or access permissions.

You can set two additional access privileges for executable files: *set user ID* and *set group ID*. These access privileges allow you to let someone else temporarily have your user privileges while that person is executing a file that you own. Setting the set user ID file access permission gives anyone executing the file the user identity of the owner of the file. In a similar manner, the group identity can be changed by setting the set group ID access permission.

This feature enables you to write "secure" programs that take on your identity while they are being executed. You can control how these programs access data stored in files that you own. If you allow another user to execute one of these programs, that user can indirectly access a file that you own, even though only you can access the file directly. Using this technique, you can allow certain users tightly controlled access to selected files. Shell scripts, described in Chapters 8 and 9, cannot be given this capability.

LINKS

A *link* is a pointer to a file. Every time you create a file using **ed**, **cp**, or any other means, you are putting a pointer in a directory. This pointer associates a filename with a place on the disk. When you specify a filename in a command, you are pointing to the place on the disk where the information that you want is (or will be) located.

Creating additional links to a file allows users to share a file. This can be useful if two or more users are working on a project and need to share information. (If you want to share a file with another user, it may be necessary for you to use the **chmod** utility to change the access permissions associated with the file.) A link can also be useful to a single user with a large directory structure. It is sometimes convenient to create a link so that a file appears in more than one directory. In some cases, this duplication of names can reduce the need for long pathnames.

When you first create a file, there is one link to it. You can delete the file or, using other terminology, remove the link with the **rm** utility. When the last existing link to a file is removed, the information stored in the file is no longer accessible, and the space it occupied on the disk is released for use by other files. If there is more than one link to a file, you can remove a link and still access the file from any remaining link.

The **ln** (link) utility creates an additional link to an existing file. The link appears as another file in the file structure. If the file appears in the same directory as the file with which it is linked, the links must have different filenames. This restriction does not apply if the file is in another directory.

The following command makes the link shown in Figure 4-10. It assumes that **/usr/jenny** is the working directory and creates a link to the file

Figure 4-10: Links and the File Structure: /usr/alex/letter and /usr/jenny/draft are two links to the same file

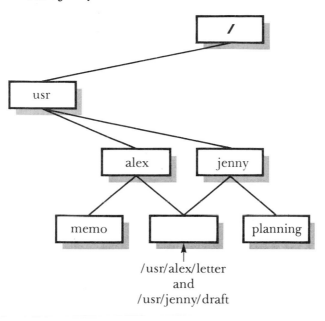

named **draft**. The link appears in the **/usr/alex** directory with the filename **letter**. In a practical situation, it may be necessary for Alex to use **chmod** to give Jenny write access permission to the **/usr/alex** directory.

```
$ ln draft /usr/alex/letter
$
```

ln creates an additional pointer to an existing file. It does *not* make another copy of the file. Because there is only one file, all of the file status information (such as access permissions, owner, and the time the file was last modified) is the same for all links. Only the filenames differ. You can verify that **ln** does not make an additional copy of a file by creating a file, making an additional link to the file using **ln**, changing the contents of the file through one of the links (use **ed**), and verifying the change through the other link. If you try the same experiment using **cp** instead of **ln** (and making a change to one of the *copies* of the file), the difference between the two utilities should become clearer. Once you make a change to a *copy* of a file, the two files are different. You can also use **ls** with the **-l** option to see that the status information is the same for two links to a file.

All links to a file are of equal value. In fact, the operating system cannot distinguish the order in which two links were made. If a file has two links, you can remove either one and still access the file through the remaining link. You can even remove the link used to create the file and, as long as there is a remaining link, still access the file through that link. Part II has more information on **ln**.

SUMMARY

The UNIX system has a *hierarchical,* or treelike, file structure that makes it possible to organize files so you can find them quickly and easily. The file structure contains *directory* files and *plain* files. Directories contain other files, including other directories, while plain files generally contain text or programs. The ancestor of all files is the *root* directory, named */*.

You can use up to 14 characters to name a file, but it is a good idea to keep the filenames simple and meaningful. *Filename extensions* can help make filenames more meaningful.

An *absolute pathname* starts with the root directory and contains all the filenames that trace a path to a given file. It starts with a slash representing the root directory and contains additional slashes in between the other filenames in the list.

When you are logged on, you are always associated with a *working directory.* Your *home directory* is your working directory from the time you first log on until you use **cd** to change directories.

A *relative pathname* is similar to an absolute pathname, but the path it traces starts from the working directory. A *simple filename* is the last element of a pathname and is a form of a relative pathname.

A *link* is a pointer to a file. You can have several links to a single file so that you can share the file with other users or have the file appear in more than one directory. Because there is only one copy of a file with multiple links, changing the file through any one link causes the changes to appear in all the links.

The following utilities were introduced in this chapter.

➡ **pwd** displays the pathname of the working directory.

➡ **mkdir** creates a directory.

➡ **cd** associates you with another working directory.

➡ **rmdir** deletes a directory.

➡ **ln** makes a link to an existing file.

5

THE SHELL

This chapter takes a close look at the Shell and explains how to use some of its features. It discusses command line syntax, how the Shell processes a command line, and how it initiates execution of a program. The chapter shows how to redirect input to and output from a program, construct pipes and filters on the command line, and run a program as a background task. The final section covers the Shell's ability to generate filenames and explains how you can use this feature in your everyday work. Everything in this chapter applies to both the C and Bourne Shells.

THE COMMAND LINE

A program is executed by giving the Shell a command in response to its prompt. The line that contains the command, including any arguments, is called the *command line*.

Command Line Syntax

Command line syntax dictates the spelling, ordering, and separation of the elements on a command line. When you press the (RETURN) key after entering a command, the first thing the Shell does is scan the command line for proper syntax. The command line syntax can be represented as:

```
command [arg1] [arg2] . . . . [argn] (RETURN)
```

The square brackets enclose optional elements. One or more (SPACE)s or (TAB)s must appear between elements on the command line.

Command Name.   All a useful command line need contain is the name of a command. An example of a minimal command line is an **ls** command without any options.

Arguments.   An *argument* is a filename, string of text, number, or some other object that a command acts on. For example, the argument to an **ed** command is the name of the file you want to edit.

The following command line shows **cp** copying the file named **temp** to **tempcopy**.

```
$ cp temp tempcopy
$
```

The **cp** utility requires two arguments on the command line. The first is the name of an existing file and the second is the name of the file that it is creating. The arguments are not optional in this case; both arguments must be present for the command to work. If you do not supply the right number or kind of arguments, **cp** displays an error message.

Options   An option is an argument that modifies the effects of a command. In many cases, you can specify more than one option, modifying the command in several different ways. Options are specific to and interpreted by the program that the command calls.

By convention, options are separate arguments that follow the name of the command. Most UNIX utility programs require options to be prefixed by a hyphen. This requirement is, however, specific to the utility and not the Shell.

The **−r** (reverse order) option causes the **ls** utility to display the list of files in reverse alphabetical order as shown in Screen 5-1. Another option, **−l** (long list), causes **ls** to display more information about each of the files it lists. It shows the name of the file in the column on the far right, while the columns to the left of the filename show the time and date the file was created, the size of the file in characters, the login name of the person who created the file, the number of links to the file, and other information that is covered in detail in the section on **ls** in Part II.

Screen 5-1

```
$ ls -r
test temp names

$ ls -l
total 3
-rw-rw-r-- 1 alex 216 Jan 3 18:09 names
-rw-rw-r-- 1 alex 223 Jan 3 20:26 temp
-rw-rw-r-- 1 alex 128 Jan 3 18:43 test
$
```

If several options are needed, they can usually be grouped into one argument that starts with a single hyphen. In this case, the characters are *not* separated by (SPACE)s. Specific rules for combining options depend on the utility. Screen 5-2 shows both the **−l** and **−r** options with the **ls** utility. The use of these options together generates a long list in reverse alphabetical order. The order you give the options in doesn't matter; **ls −lr** will produce the same results as **ls −rl**. Also, the same list would have been generated by the commands **ls −l −r**.

Screen 5-2

```
$ ls -lr
total 3
-rw-rw-r-- 1 alex 128 Jan 3 18:43 test
-rw-rw-r-- 1 alex 223 Jan 3 20:26 temp
-rw-rw-r-- 1 alex 216 Jan 3 18:09 names
$
```

Processing the Command Line

As you enter a command line, each character is examined to see if any action must be taken, as illustrated by the flowchart in Figure 5-1. When you enter a # (to delete a character) or a @ (to delete a line), the UNIX operating system immediately adjusts the command line as required. If the character

Figure 5-1: Entering a Command Line

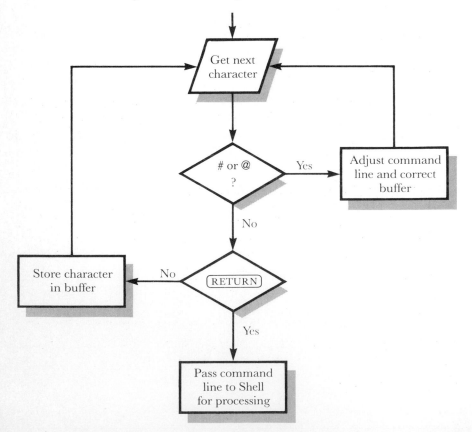

does not require immediate action, the operating system stores the character in a buffer and waits for additional characters. If the character is a (RETURN), the operating system passes the command line to the Shell for processing.

When the Shell processes a command line, as in Figure 5-2, it looks at the line as a whole and breaks it down into its component parts. Next, the Shell looks for the name of the command. It assumes that the name of the command is the first thing on the command line after the prompt (i.e., argument zero), so it takes the first characters on the command line, up to the first (SPACE), and sees if it can find a program with that name. If the Shell can't find the program, it displays the message, Command not found.

Figure 5-2: Processing the Command Line

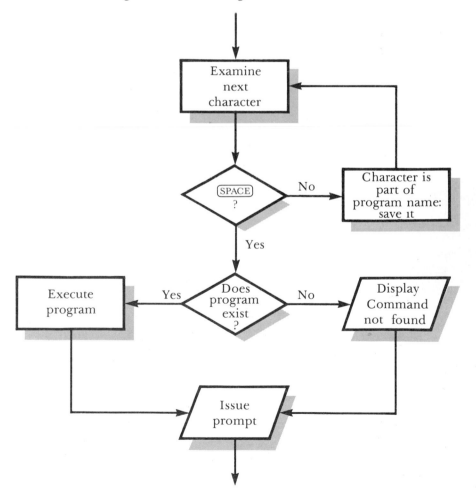

The Shell has no way of knowing whether a particular option or other argument is valid for a given program. Any error messages concerning options or arguments come from the program itself. Many UNIX utility programs ignore bad options.

Executing the Command Line

If the Shell finds a program with the same name as the command, it starts a new process. A *process* is the means by which the UNIX system executes a program. The Shell makes each command line argument, including options and the name of the program, available to the program. While the program is executing, the Shell waits in a quiescent state called *sleep*. When the program finishes executing, the Shell returns to an active state (wakes up), issues a prompt, and waits for another command.

STANDARD INPUT AND STANDARD OUTPUT

A program's *standard output* is a place it can send information, frequently text. The program never "knows" where the information it sends to its standard output is going. The information can go to a printer, a plain file, or a terminal. This section shows how the Shell directs the standard output from a program to the terminal, and how you can redirect this output to another file. It also explains how to redirect the *standard input* to a program so that it comes from a plain file instead of the terminal.

The Terminal as a File

Chapter 4 introduced plain and directory files. The UNIX system has one additional type of file, a *device file*. A device file resides in the UNIX system file structure, usually in the **/dev** directory, and represents a peripheral device such as a terminal, printer, or disk drive.

The device name that the **who** utility displays after your login name is the filename of your terminal. If **who** displays the device name **tty6**, the pathname of your terminal is probably **/dev/tty6**. Although you wouldn't normally have occasion to, you could read from and write to this file as though it were a text file. Writing to it would display what you wrote on the terminal screen and reading from it would read what you entered on the keyboard.

The Terminal as the Standard Input and Output

When you first log on, the Shell directs your programs' standard output to the device file that represents your terminal. This concept is illustrated in Figure 5-3. Directing output in this manner causes it to appear on your terminal screen.

The Shell also directs the standard input to come from the same file, so that anything you type on your terminal keyboard is input to your program.

The **cat** utility provides a good example of the way the terminal functions as the standard input and output. When you use **cat**, it copies a file to its standard output. Because the Shell directs the standard output to the terminal, **cat** displays the file on the terminal.

Figure 5-3: Standard Input and Output

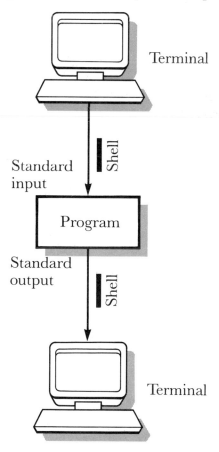

Up to this point, **cat** has taken its input from the filename (argument) you specified on the command line. If you do not give **cat** an argument (i.e., if you give the command **cat** immediately followed by a (RETURN)), **cat** receives input from its standard input.

cat can now be defined as a utility that, when called without an argument, copies its standard input file to its standard output file. On most systems, it copies one line at a time. To see how **cat** works, type **cat** (RETURN) in response to the Shell prompt. Nothing happens. Enter a line of text and a (RETURN). The same line appears just under the one you entered. **cat** is working. (Some versions do not display anything until you signal the end of the file by pressing (CONTROL-D); see below.) You typed a line of text on the file that the Shell associated with **cat**'s standard input. **cat** copied your line of text to its standard output file, which the Shell had also associated with the terminal. This exchange is shown in Screen 5-3.

Screen 5-3

```
$ cat
This is a line of text.
This is a line of text.
Cat keeps copying lines of text
Cat keeps copying lines of text
until you press CONTROL-D at the beginning
until you press CONTROL-D at the beginning
of a line.
of a line.
(CONTROL-D)
$
```

cat keeps copying until you enter (CONTROL-D) on a line by itself. (CONTROL-D) causes the Shell to send an *end of file* signal that indicates to **cat** that it has reached the end of the standard input file and that there is no more text for it to copy. When you enter (CONTROL-D), **cat** finishes execution and returns control to the Shell, which gives you a prompt.

Redirection

The Shell can redirect the standard input and/or the standard output of any program. It performs this redirection by associating the standard input or output of the program with a file other than the device file representing your terminal. Input and output can be redirected from/to any appropriate file.

This section demonstrates how to redirect input to and output from plain text files.

Redirecting the Standard Output. The *redirect output* symbol (>) indicates to the Shell that it is not to direct the program's output to the terminal, but rather to the indicated file. The format of a command line that redirects output is shown in Figure 5-4.

The **program** is any executable program (e.g., an application program or a UNIX utility program), **arguments** are optional arguments, and **filename** is the name of the plain file to which the Shell redirects the output.

Figure 5-4: Redirecting the Standard Output

```
program [arguments] > filename
```

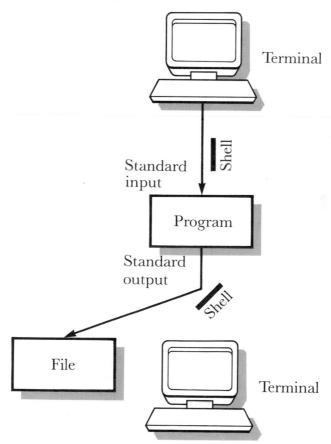

> Use caution when you redirect output. If the file already exists, the Shell overwrites it and destroys its contents.

In Screen 5-4, **cat** provides a demonstration of output redirection. This screen contrasts with Screen 5-3, where both the standard input *and* standard output were associated with the terminal. In this case, only the input comes from the terminal. Because of the redirect output symbol on the command line, the Shell associates **cat**'s standard output file with the file specified on the command line, in this case, **sample.txt**.

Screen 5-4

```
$ cat > sample.txt
This text is being entered at the keyboard.
Cat is copying it to a file.
Press CONTROL-D to indicate the
end of file.
 CONTROL-D
$
```

Now, **sample.txt** contains the text you entered. You can use **cat** with an argument of **sample.txt** to display the file. The next section shows another way to use **cat** to display the file.

As shown in Screen 5-4, redirecting the output from **cat** is a handy way to make files without using an editor. Its drawback is that, once you enter a line and press RETURN , you cannot edit the text. While you are entering a line, the # and @ keys work to delete text. This procedure is useful for making short, simple files.

Redirecting the Standard Input. Just as you can redirect **cat**'s standard output, you can redirect its standard input. The *redirect input* symbol (<) indicates to the Shell that it is not to direct input to the program to come from the terminal, but rather from the indicated file. The format of a command line that redirects input is shown in Figure 5-5.

The **program** is any executable program (e.g., an application program or a UNIX utility program), **arguments** are optional arguments, and **filename** is the name of the plain file the Shell redirects the input from.

Screen 5-5 shows **cat** with its input redirected from the **sample.txt** file that was created in Screen 5-4 and its standard output going to the terminal. This setup causes **cat** to display the sample file on the terminal.

Figure 5-5: Redirecting the Standard Input

```
program [arguments] < filename
```

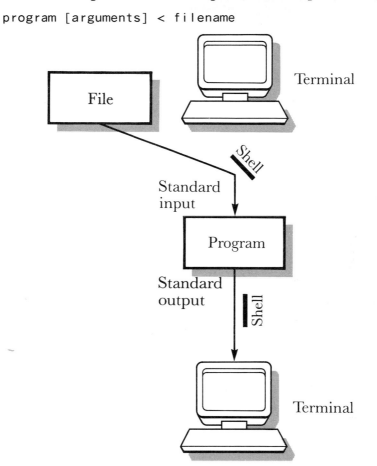

Screen 5-5

```
$ cat < sample.txt
This text is being entered at the keyboard.
Cat is copying it to a file.
Press CONTROL-D to indicate the
end of file.
$
```

The system automatically supplies an end of file signal at the end of a plain file, so no (CONTROL-D) is necessary.

Using **cat** with input redirected from a file yields the same result as giving a **cat** command with an argument. **cat** is a member of a class of UNIX utility programs that function in this manner. These utilities first examine the command line you use to call them. If you follow the name of the command with an argument, the utility takes its input from the file specified by that argument. If there is no argument, the utility takes its input from its standard input.

Appending the Standard Output to a File. The redirect output symbol causes the shell to overwrite any information in the file you redirect output to. The *append output* symbol (>>) causes the Shell to add the new information to the end of the file, leaving the information that was already there intact.

The example in Screen 5-6 shows how to create a file that contains the date and time (the output from the **date** utility) followed by a list of who is logged on (the output from the **who** utility).

Screen 5-6

```
$ date > whoson

$ cat whoson
Fri Apr 15 12:31:15 PST 1983

$ who >> whoson

$ cat whoson
Fri Apr 15 12:31:15 PST 1983
hls       console Apr 15 08:47
jenny     tty2    Apr 15 07:21
alex      tty6m   Apr 15 11:01
$
```

The first line in Screen 5-6 redirects the output from **date** to the file named **whoson**. Then **cat** displays the file. Next, the example appends the output from **who** to the **whoson** file. Finally, **cat** displays the file containing the output of both utilities.

Examples of Redirecting Input and Output. Screen 5-7 shows how to use **cat** to *catenate* (join together one after the other) several files.

Screen 5-7

```
$ cat tony
This is a letter to Tony.

$ cat alice
This is a letter to Alice.

$ cat linda
This is a letter to Linda.

$ cat tony alice linda > all

$ cat all
This is a letter to Tony.
This is a letter to Alice.
This is a letter to Linda.
$
```

The first three commands display the contents of three files, **tony**, **alice**, and **linda**. The next command shows **cat** with three filenames as arguments. When you give **cat** more than one filename, it copies the files, one at a time, to its standard output. In this case, the standard output is redirected to the file **all**. **all** receives a catenation of all three files, as shown by the final command.

The following technique is useful when you want to make the same change to several files. By making a file of editor commands that make the required change, and then redirecting input to the editor to come from this file, you can save yourself the time and trouble of editing each of the files individually.

In Screen 5-8, input is redirected to **ed** to change the word **letter** to **note** in the file **alice** (first shown in Screen 5-7). Imagine that you were using **ed** to make the change. Figure out what commands you would need to enter once you called **ed**, put those commands in a file, and run **ed** on the text file, using input that is redirected to come from the file of commands.

Screen 5-8 shows **cat** creating a file of commands, **change**. **change** contains exactly the characters you would enter on the keyboard to cause **ed** to change the word letter to note. To make this substitution, you would call up **ed**, give **ed** a Substitute command to make the change, a **w** command to write the altered file out, and finally a **q** command to quit using the editor.

Screen 5-8

```
$ cat > change
s/letter/note/
w
q
CONTROL-D
$
```

The first part of Screen 5-9 shows an editing session that uses redirected input. **ed** edits the file named **alice**. Instead of receiving commands from the keyboard, the commands are taken from the file named **change**. The two numbers appearing after the call to **ed** are the only output that **ed** generates: the number of characters that **ed** reads and writes. Only the *input* to **ed** has been redirected. The output still goes to the terminal. If a **p** command follows the **s** command in the **change** file, the output that **p** generates will appear in between the numbers.

The second part of Screen 5-9 shows the input to *and* output from **ed** being redirected. The file named **tony** is edited, with the input coming from **change**. The output is redirected to **/dev/null**, a null file. You can always send output you don't want to **/dev/null** and the system will discard it.

Screen 5-9

```
$ cat alice
This is a letter to Alice

$ ed alice < change
27
25

$ cat alice
This is a note to Alice.

$ ed tony < change > /dev/null

$ cat tony
This is a note to Tony.
$
```

Read Ahead

The logical separation of standard input and output makes it possible for you to enter information at the keyboard at the same time as the system displays different information on the screen. This feature is called *read ahead* or *type ahead*. When you type ahead on your keyboard, the operating system stores the characters that you enter until it is able to display them.

You can use type ahead at any time—you do not have to do anything special to set it up. It allows you to give commands to a program before it finishes executing the last command you gave. This feature is useful if you are in a hurry or if the system is not responding quickly. It allows you to give commands and go about your other business while the system is responding.

PIPES

The Shell uses a *pipe* to connect the standard output of one program directly to the standard input of another program. A pipe has the same effect as if you had redirected the standard output of one program to a file and then had used that file as the standard input to another program. It does away with separate commands and the intermediate file. The symbol for a pipe is a vertical bar (|). The format of a command line using a pipe is shown below.

```
program_a [arguments] | program_b [arguments]
```

This single command line uses a pipe to generate the same result as would be produced by the following sequence of command lines.

```
program_a [arguments] > temp
program_b [arguments] < temp
rm temp
```

This sequence first redirects the standard output from **program_a** to an intermediate file named **temp**. Then it redirects the standard input for **program_b** to come from **temp**. The final command line deletes **temp**.

A pipe is frequently used with a member of the class of UNIX utility programs that accept input either from a file specified on the command line or from the standard input. **lpr** (printer) is one of these utilities. When you follow **lpr** with the name of a file, **lpr** places that file in the printer queue. If you do not specify a filename on the command line, **lpr** expects input from its standard input. This allows you to use a pipe to redirect input to **lpr**.

Screen 5-10

```
$ ls > temp

$ lpr temp

$ rm temp
$


or


$ ls | lpr
$
```

The first set of commands in Screen 5-10 shows how you can use **ls** and **lpr,** in conjunction with an intermediate file, to send a list of the files in the working directory to the printer. The second set of commands sends the same list to the printer using a pipe.

Screen 5-11

```
$ who > temp

$ sort temp
barbara    tty3      May 22 12:53
chas       tty6m     May 22 10:31
hls        console   May 22 12:48
scott      tty2      May 21 09:07
$
```

The commands in Screen 5-11 redirect the output from the **who** utility to **temp** and then display this file in sorted order. The **sort** utility functions in a manner similar to **lpr.** It takes its input from the file specified on the command line or, if no file is specified, from its standard input. It sends its output to its standard output. In Screen 5-11, **temp** is specified as the input file. The output that **sort** sends to the terminal lists the users in alphabetical order.

Screen 5-12 achieves the same result using a pipe.

Screen 5-12

```
$ who | sort
barbara    tty3     May 22 12:53
chas       tty6m    May 22 10:31
hls        console  May 22 12:48
scott      tty2     May 21 09:07
$
```

FILTERS

A *filter* is a program that processes an input stream of data to produce an output stream of data. A command line that includes a filter uses a pipe to redirect the filter's input from the standard output of one program. Another pipe redirects the filter's output to the standard input of another program.

In Screen 5-13, **sort** is a filter, taking its standard input from the standard output of **who** and using a pipe to redirect its standard output to the standard input of **lpr**. The command line in Screen 5-13 sends the sorted output of **who** to the printer.

Screen 5-13

```
$ who | sort | lpr
$
```

This example demonstrates the power of the Shell combined with the versatility of UNIX utility programs. The three utilities, **who, sort**, and **lpr**, were not specifically designed to work with each other. By using the Shell to redirect input and output, you can piece standard utilities together on the command line to achieve the results you want.

RUNNING A PROGRAM IN THE BACKGROUND

When you run a program in the *background,* you do not have to wait for the program to finish before you start running another program. Running a program in the background can be useful if the program will be running a long time and doesn't need supervision. The terminal will be free so that you can use it for something else.

To run a program in the background, type an ampersand (**&**) just before the (RETURN) that ends the command line. The Shell will display a PID (process ID) number that identifies the program running in the background, and give you another prompt. You can use the PID number that the Shell displays if you need to terminate the background task. Refer to the **kill** utility in Part II for more information.

Screen 5-14 runs an **ls -l** command in the background. A pipe redirects the output from the command to the **lpr** utility, which sends it to the printer.

Screen 5-14

```
$ ls -l | lpr &
31725
$
```

If a background task sends output to the standard output and you do not redirect it, the output appears on your terminal, even if you are running another job. If a background task requests input from the standard input and you have not redirected the standard input, the Shell supplies a null string.

You will probably want to redirect the output of a job you run in the background to keep it from interfering with whatever you are doing at the terminal. Chapter 8 goes into more detail about background tasks in the section on "Command Separation and Grouping."

FILENAME GENERATION

When given abbreviated filenames that contain *special characters* (characters that have a special meaning to the Shell), the Shell can generate filenames that match the names of existing files. When one of these special characters appears in an argument on the command line, the Shell expands that argument into a list of filenames and passes the list to the program that the command line is calling. Filenames that contain these special characters are called *ambiguous file references* because they do not refer to any one specific file.

The special characters are sometimes referred to as *wild cards,* because they act like the jokers in a deck of cards. The process of expanding an ambiguous file reference is called *globbing.* Globbing allows you to quickly reference a group of files with similar names or a file whose name you don't remember in its entirety.

The ? Special Character

The question mark is a special character that causes the Shell to generate filenames. It matches any single character in the name of an existing file. The following command uses this special character in an argument to the lpr utility.

```
$ lpr memo?
$
```

The Shell globs the **memo?** argument and generates a list of the files in the working directory that have names composed of **memo** followed by any single character. The Shell passes this list to the lpr utility. lpr never "knows" that the Shell generated the filenames it was called with. If there is no filename that matches the ambiguous file reference, the Shell passes the string itself (memo?) to the program or, in some versions of the Shell, displays an error message such as No match.

Some filenames that memo? does and doesn't match are shown below.

memo? matches	memo? does not match
memoa	memoalex
memo5	memo12
memos	newmemo5
memo9	memo
	mem

You can also use a question mark in the middle of an ambiguous file reference.

may?report	may?report
matches	does not match
may4report	may14report
mayqreport	mayreport
may.report	7may4report
may_report	may4report.79

The * Special Character

The asterisk performs a function similar to that of the question mark, except that it matches *zero or more* characters in a filename. An asterisk does not match a leading period (one that indicates an invisible file).

memo*	memo*
matches	does not match
memo	amemo
memoa	mem
memo.0612	.memo.0612
memorandum	user.memo
memosally	sallymemo

a	*a*
matches	does not match
saturday	thurs
aaa	.aaa
sally.0612	memo.0612
memo.sally	report

.*	.*
matches	does not match
.login	memo.0612
.cshrc	reminder
.logout	report
.private	private

If you establish conventions for naming files, you can take advantage of ambiguous file references. For example, if you end all your text file filenames with .txt, you can reference that group of files with *.txt. Following this convention, the command below will send all the text files in the working directory to the printer.

```
$ lpr *.txt
$
```

The [ ] Special Characters

A pair of square brackets causes the Shell to glob selected filenames. Where **memo?** matches **memo** followed by any character, **memo[17a]** matches only **memo1**, **memo7**, and **memoa**. The brackets define a *character class* that includes all the characters within the brackets. The Shell expands an argument that includes a character class definition, substituting each member of the character class, *one at a time,* in place of the brackets and their contents. The Shell passes a list of filenames that match existing filenames in the working directory to the program it is calling.

Each character class definition can only replace a single character within a filename. The brackets and their contents can be thought of as a question mark that will only substitute the members of the character class.

The first of the following commands lists the names of all the files in the working directory that begin with a, e, i, o, or u. The second command displays the contents of the files named **page2.txt**, **page4.txt**, **page6.txt**, and **page8.txt**.

```
$ ls [aeiou] *
.
.
.
$ cat page[2468].txt
.
.
.
$
```

A hyphen defines a range of characters within a character class definition. For example, [6-9] represents [6789] and [a-z] represents all lowercase letters.

The following command lines show three ways to print the files named **part0**, **part1**, **part2**, **part3**, and **part5**. Each of the command lines calls **lpr** with five filenames.

```
$ lpr part0 part1 part2 part3 part5
$ lpr part[01235]
$ lpr part[0–35]
$
```

The first command line explicitly specifies the five filenames. The second and third command lines use ambiguous file references, incorporating character class definitions. The Shell expands the argument on the second command line to include all files that have names beginning with part and ending with any of the characters in the character class. The character class is explicitly defined as 0, 1, 2, 3, and 5. The third command line also uses a character class definition, except it defines the character class to be all characters in the range from 0–3 and 5.

The next two examples list the names of some of the files in the working directory. The first lists the files whose names start with a through m. The second lists files whose names end with x, y, or z.

```
$ ls [a–m]*
 .
 .
 .
$ ls *[x–z]
 .
 .
 .
$
```

Practicing with Filename Generation

The echo utility displays the arguments that the Shell passes to it. Give the following command.

```
$ echo *
```

The Shell expands the asterisk into a list of all files in the working directory and passes this list to echo, as though you had entered the list of filenames as arguments to echo. The echo utility responds to this command by displaying the list of files in the working directory.

You can use **echo** to experiment with ambiguous filenames. Try giving a command such as the following.

```
$ echo *a*
```

echo displays all the filenames in the working directory that contain an **a**.

SUMMARY

The Shell is the UNIX system command interpreter. It scans the command line for proper syntax, picking out the command name and any arguments. Options are used by many programs to modify the effects of a command. Most UNIX programs identify options by their leading hyphens.

When you give the Shell a command, it tries to find a program with the same name as the command. If it does, it executes the program. If it doesn't, it tells you that it cannot find the command.

When the Shell executes a program, it assigns a file to the program's *standard input* and *standard output.* By default, the Shell causes a program's standard input to come from, and standard output to go to, the terminal. You can instruct the Shell to *redirect* a program's standard output to any reasonable file or device. You can also redirect the standard input.

When a program runs in the *foreground,* the Shell waits for it to finish before it gives you another prompt and allows you to continue. If you put an ampersand (**&**) at the end of a command line, the Shell executes the command in the *background* and gives you another prompt immediately.

The Shell interprets special characters on a command line for *filename generation.* It uses a question mark to represent any single character and an asterisk to represent a string of zero or more characters. A reference to a file that includes one of these characters is called an *ambiguous file reference.*

6

THE vi EDITOR

The **vi** editor is used to create new text files and change existing ones. This chapter explains how to use **vi**. It describes how **vi** works, shows you how to tell **vi** what type of terminal you are using, and guides you through a brief editing session. It also goes into detail about many of the **vi** commands, and explains the use of parameters for customizing **vi** for your needs. At the end of the chapter is a summary of commands that can be used as a quick reference to **vi**.

vi (visual) is a powerful (although cryptic), interactive, visually oriented text editor. Unlike **ed**, **vi** takes advantage of the entire terminal screen by displaying the text you are editing. When you use **vi**, it is not necessary to refer to lines by line numbers—you can manually position the cursor on any line or character. **vi** keeps track of what's on the screen and refreshes the screen only when absolutely necessary. This screen management allows **vi** to display changes to the text as efficiently as possible and reduce response time, especially for users accessing the system via slower telephone lines.

vi is not a text formatting program. It does not justify margins, center titles, or provide the features of a word processing system. You can use **nroff** (Chapter 7) to format the text that you edit with **vi**. Your installation may not provide **vi**. It is generally available on Berkeley versions of the UNIX system and System V from Bell Labs.

THE WORK BUFFER

vi, like **ed**, does all its work in the *Work Buffer*. At the start of an editing session, **vi** reads the contents of the file you are editing into the Work Buffer. During the editing session, **vi** makes all changes to this copy of the file. It does not change the file until you write the contents of the Work Buffer back to the file. When editing a new file, **vi** does not create the file until it writes out the contents of the Work Buffer at the end of the editing session. Normally, when you end an editing session, **vi** automatically writes out the contents of the Work Buffer and makes the changes to the text final.

This way of doing things has advantages and disadvantages. If you accidentally end an editing session without writing out the contents of the Work Buffer, all your work will be lost. However, if you unintentionally make some major changes (such as deleting the entire contents of the Work Buffer), you can terminate the editing session without implementing the changes. **vi** will leave the file as it was before the start of the editing session.

MODES OF OPERATION

vi is part of another editor named **ex** and encompasses two of the five modes of operation of **ex**, the *Command Mode* and the *Insert Mode*. While in the Command Mode, **vi** accepts keystrokes as commands, responding to each command as you enter it. In the Insert Mode, **vi** accepts keystrokes as text, displaying the text as you enter it.

At the start of an editing session, **vi** is in the Command Mode. There are several commands, such as the Insert and Append commands, that put **vi** in the Insert Mode. When you press the (ESCAPE) key, **vi** always reverts to the Command Mode.

The Change and Replace commands combine the Command and Insert Modes. The Change command deletes the text you want to change and puts **vi** in the Insert Mode so that you can insert new text. The Replace command deletes the character(s) you overwrite and inserts the new one(s) you enter.

SPECIFYING A TERMINAL

Because **vi** takes advantage of features that are specific to various kinds of terminals, you must tell it what type of terminal you are using. The file named **termcap** contains a list of terminals and functional descriptions of how each one operates. Each entry in this file has a name; this is the name of the Termcap entry for your terminal that you inquired about at the beginning of Chapter 2.

If you are using the Bourne Shell, give the following commands to establish the type of terminal you are using. You can also place these commands in the **.profile** file in your home directory so that the UNIX system automatically executes them each time you log on. Replace **name** with the name of the Termcap entry for your terminal.

```
$ TERM=name
$ export TERM
$
```

The C Shell requires the following command. Place it in the **.login** file in your home directory for automatic execution. Again, replace **name** with the name of the Termcap entry for your terminal.

```
% setenv TERM name
%
```

AN EDITING SESSION

This section describes how to call **vi**, enter text, and exit from **vi**. All **vi** commands take effect immediately; you do not need to press (RETURN) to indicate the end of the command.

When giving **vi** a command, it is important that you distinguish between uppercase and lowercase letters. **vi** interprets the same letter as two different commands, depending on whether it is entered as an uppercase or lowercase character.

Calling vi

Call **vi** with the following command line to create a file named **practice** in the working directory.

```
$ vi practice
```

Screen 6-1

```
  ~
  ~
  ~
  ~
  ~
  ~
  ~
  ~
  ~
  "practice" No such file or directory.
```

The terminal screen will look similar to the one shown in Screen 6-1. If it doesn't, your terminal type is probably not set correctly. Try typing **:q** [RETURN] to get the Shell prompt back. Then refer to the preceding section, "Specifying a Terminal."

The **practice** file is new; there is no text in it yet. **vi** displays one of the following messages on the status (bottom) line of the terminal to indicate that you are creating and editing a new file.

```
"practice" No such file or directory.
```

or

```
"practice" ERROR
```

When you edit an existing file, **vi** displays the first few lines of the file and gives status information about the file on the status line.

Entering Text

Putting vi in the Insert Mode. Once you have gained access to vi, put vi in the Insert Mode by pressing the **i** key. vi does not respond to indicate that it is in the Insert Mode.

If you are not sure that you are in the Insert Mode, press the (ESCAPE) key; vi will return to the Command Mode if it was in the Insert Mode or beep (some terminals flash) if it was already in the Command Mode. You can put vi back in the Insert Mode by pressing the **i** key again.

Entering Text. While vi is in the Insert Mode, you can put text into the Work Buffer by typing on the terminal. If the text does not appear on the screen as you type it, you are not in the Insert Mode.

Enter the sample paragraph shown in Screen 6-2, pressing the (RETURN) key to end each line. As you are entering text, there are a couple of things to look out for. Prevent lines of text from wrapping around from the right side of the screen to the left by pressing the (RETURN) key before the cursor reaches the far right side of the screen. Also, make sure that you do not end a line with a (SPACE). Some vi commands behave strangely when they encounter a line that ends with a (SPACE).

Screen 6-2

```
vi (visual) is a powerful (although cryptic),
interactive, visually oriented text editor.
Unlike ed, vi takes
advantage of the entire terminal screen by
displaying the text you are editing.
When you
~
~
~
~
```

If you notice that you have made a mistake on the line you are entering, you can correct it before you continue. Refer to the next paragraph. You can correct other mistakes later. When you finish entering the paragraph, press the (ESCAPE) key to return vi to the Command Mode. Your screen will look like Screen 6-2.

Correcting Text as It Is Inserted. The keys that allow you to back up and correct a Shell command line (usually (CONTROL-H), @, and #) perform the same function when **vi** is in the Insert Mode. In addition, you can use (CONTROL-W) to back up over words. **vi** may not remove text from the screen as you back up over it. The text is, however, removed from the Work Buffer.

There are two restrictions on the use of these correction keys. They will only allow you to back up over text on the line you are entering (you cannot back up to a previous line) and they will only back up over text that was just entered. As an example, assume that you are in the Insert Mode entering text and you press the (ESCAPE) key to return **vi** to the Command Mode. Then you give the **i** command to put **vi** back in the Insert Mode. Now you cannot back up over text you entered the first time you were in the Insert Mode, even if the text is on the current line.

Ending the Editing Session

You can end an editing session in one of two ways—so that the changes made during the editing session are saved or not saved. Normally you will want to save the changes.

Normal Termination. Normal termination of an editing session requires that **vi** write out the edited text (the contents of the Work Buffer) before it returns control to the Shell. This method of terminating an editing session insures that the disk file reflects any changes you have made.

Make sure **vi** is in the Command Mode and use the **ZZ** command (you must use uppercase **Z**s) to write out your newly entered text from the Work Buffer to the disk and end the editing session. The only time you should not use the **ZZ** command to end an editing session is when you do not want to save the edited text.

After you give the **ZZ** command, **vi** displays the name of the file you are editing and the number of characters in the file; then it returns control to the Shell.

Abnormal Termination. On occasion, it may be necessary to terminate an editing session without writing out the contents of the Work Buffer. When you use the **:q!** (RETURN) command (the **:** moves the cursor to the status line) to terminate an editing session, **no work from the current editing session is preserved—the contents of the Work Buffer is lost**. The next time you edit or use the file, it will appear as it did before the start of the current editing session. Use this command with caution.

Screen 6-3

```
vi (visual) is a powerful (although cryptic),
interactive, visually oriented text editor.
Unlike ed, vi takes
advantage of the entire terminal screen by
displaying the text you are editing.
When you use vi, it is not necessary to refer
to lines by line numbers--you can manually
position the cursor on any line or character.
~
~
"practice" 332 characters

$
```

THE vi DISPLAY

The vi editor uses the status line and several special symbols to give you information about what is happening during an editing session.

The Status Line

vi displays status information on the bottom line—the twenty-fourth line of most terminals. This information includes error messages, information about the deletion or addition of large blocks of text, Search Strings, file status information, all commands that start with a colon, and information about the various text buffers.

The @ Symbol

vi refreshes the screen display as little and as infrequently as possible. This means that users, especially those using a UNIX system over slow telephone lines, do not have to wait through unnecessary pauses when text is deleted from the screen. On some terminals, deleted lines are replaced by an @ symbol at the left of the screen. This symbol only appears on the screen, and is never written to the Work Buffer or file. If the screen becomes cluttered with these symbols, enter (CONTROL-R) (some terminals use (CONTROL-L)) while vi is in the Command Mode to redraw the screen.

The ˜ Symbol

If the end of the file is displayed on the screen, **vi** marks lines that would appear past the end of the file with a tilde (˜) at the left of the screen. Every line on the screen, except for line 1, is marked with these symbols when you start editing a new file.

COMMAND MODE—MOVING THE CURSOR

While **vi** is in the Command Mode, you can position the cursor over any character on the screen. You can also display a different portion of the Work Buffer on the screen. By manipulating the screen and cursor position, you can place the cursor on any character in the Work Buffer.

   vi can move the cursor forward or backward through the text. As illustrated in Figure 6-1, *Forward* always means toward the bottom of the screen and the end of the file. *Backward* means toward the top of the screen and the beginning of the file. When you use a command that moves the cursor

Figure 6-1: Forward and Backward

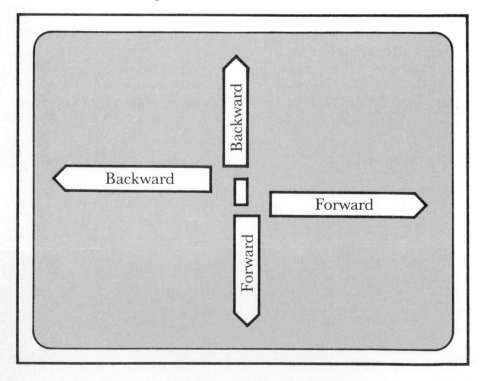

forward past the end (right) of a line, the cursor generally moves to the beginning (left) of the next line. When you move it backward past the beginning of a line, it moves to the end of the previous line.

vi allows you to move the cursor through the text by any *Unit of Measure* (i.e., character, word, line, sentence, paragraph, or screen—refer to the section at the end of this chapter on "Units of Measure"). If you precede a cursor-movement command with a number, called a *Repeat Factor,* the cursor moves that number of units through the text.

Moving the Cursor by Characters

The (SPACE) bar moves the cursor forward, one character at a time, toward the right side of the screen. The l (ell) key and the right arrow key (see Figure 6-2) do the same thing. The command 7 (SPACE) or 7l moves the cursor seven characters to the right. These keys *will not* move the cursor past the end of the current line to the beginning of the next.

The **h** key and the left arrow key are similar to the l key but work in the opposite direction.

Moving the Cursor by Words

The **w** key moves the cursor forward to the first letter of the next word, as illustrated in Figure 6-3. Groups of punctuation count as words. This com-

Figure 6-2: Moving by Characters

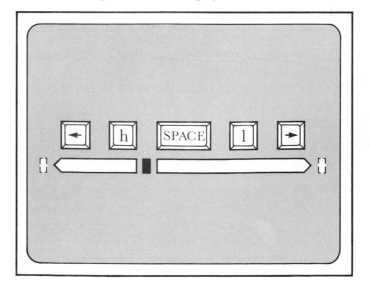

Figure 6-3: Moving by Characters and Words

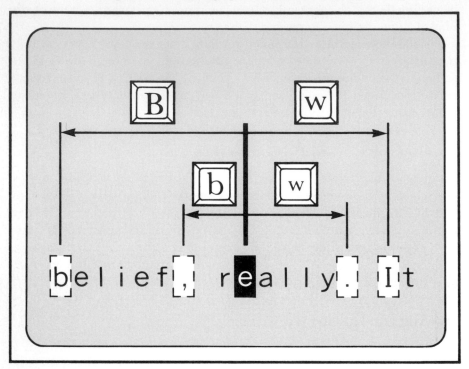

mand *will* go to the next line if that is where the next word is, unless the line ends with a (SPACE). The command **15w** moves the cursor to the first character of the fifteenth subsequent word.

The **W** key is similar to the **w** key, except that it moves the cursor by blank delimited words, including punctuation as it skips forward over words. (See "Blank Delimited Word," page 122.)

The **b** key moves the cursor backward to the first letter of the previous word. The **B** key moves the cursor backward by blank delimited words.

Moving the Cursor by Lines

The (RETURN) key moves the cursor to the beginning of the next line (see Figure 6-4), while the **j** and down arrow keys move it down one line to the character just below the current character. If there is no character immediately below the current character, the cursor moves to the end of the next line. The cursor will not move past the last line of text.

The **k** and up arrow keys are similar to the **j** key but work in the opposite direction.

Figure 6-4: Moving by Lines

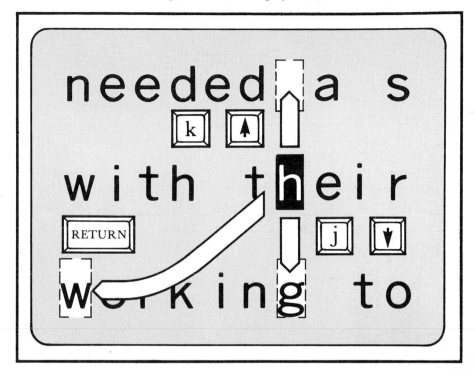

Moving the Cursor by Sentences and Paragraphs

The) and } keys move the cursor forward to the beginning of the next sentence or paragraph, respectively, as shown in Figure 6-5. The (and { keys move the cursor backward to the beginning of the current sentence or paragraph.

Moving the Cursor Within the Screen

The **H** key positions the cursor at the left end of the top, or *H*ome, line of the screen. The **M** key moves the cursor to the *M*iddle line and **L** moves it to the bottom, or *L*ower line.

Viewing Different Parts of the Work Buffer

The screen displays a portion of the text that is in the Work Buffer. You can display the text preceding or following the text on the screen by scrolling the display. You can also display a portion of the Work Buffer based on a line number.

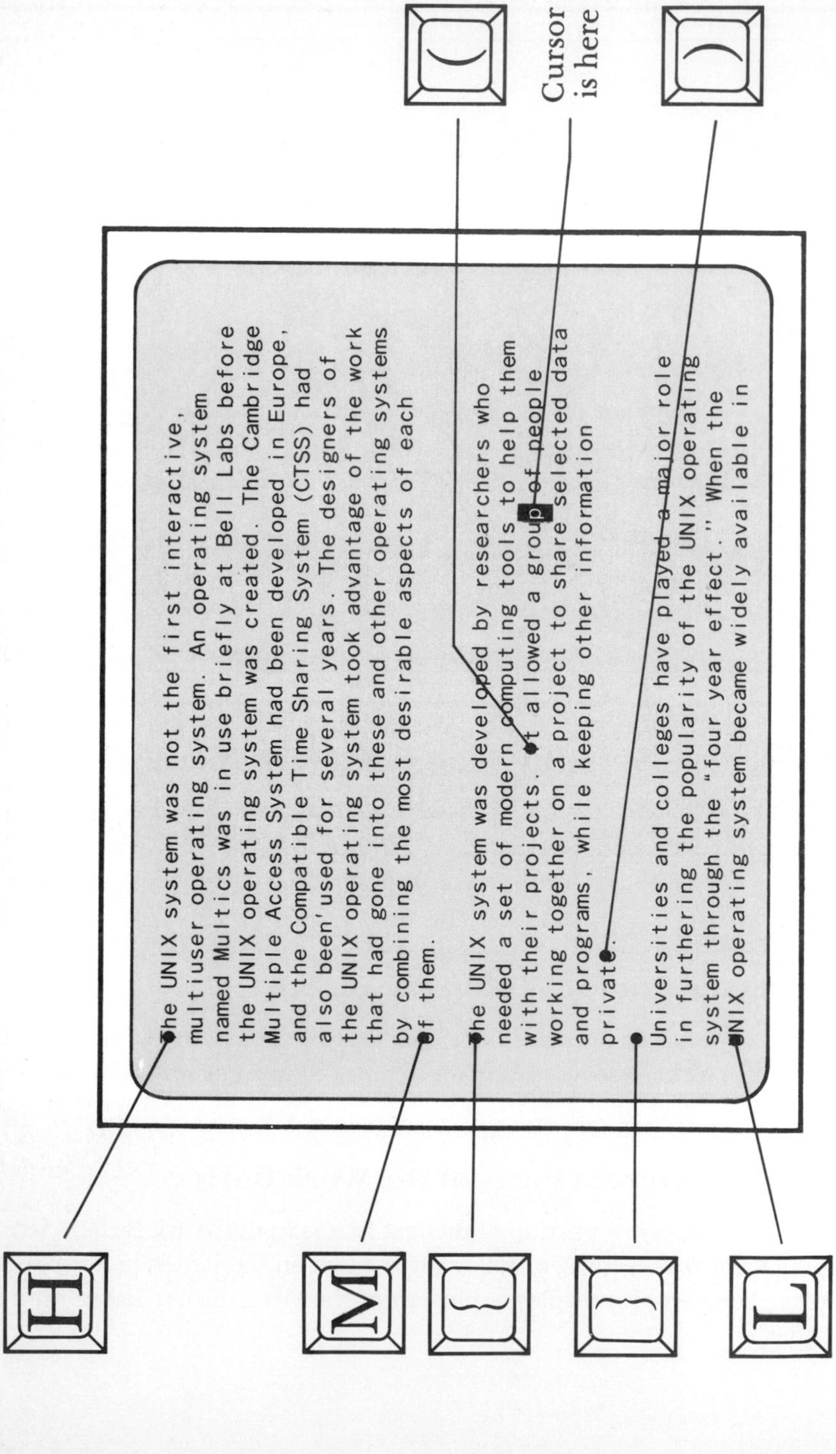

Figure 6-5: Moving the Cursor by Sentences, Paragraphs, H, M, and L

Cursor is here

The UNIX system was not the first interactive,
multiuser operating system. An operating system
named Multics was in use briefly at Bell Labs before
the UNIX operating system was created. The Cambridge
Multiple Access System had been developed in Europe,
and the Compatible Time Sharing System (CTSS) had
also been used for several years. The designers of
the UNIX operating system took advantage of the work
that had gone into these and other operating systems
by combining the most desirable aspects of each
of them.

The UNIX system was developed by researchers who
needed a set of modern computing tools to help them
with their projects. It allowed a group of people
working together on a project to share selected data
and programs, while keeping other information
private.

Universities and colleges have played a major role
in furthering the popularity of the UNIX operating
system through the "four year effect." When the
UNIX operating system became widely available in

Figure 6-6: Moving by ⬚CONTROL⬚ Characters

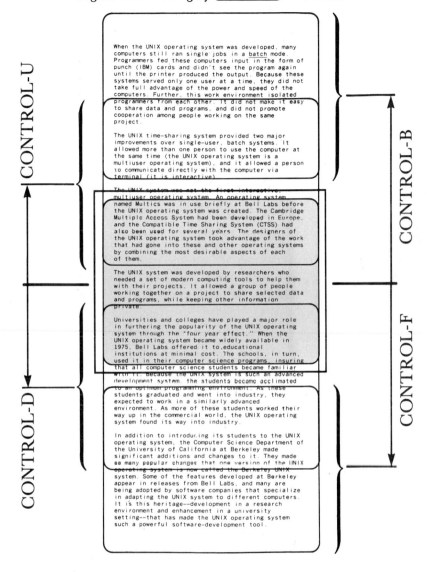

Press ⬚CONTROL-D⬚ to scroll the screen *D*own (forward) through the file so that half a screenful of new text is displayed, as shown in Figure 6-6. ⬚CONTROL-U⬚ scrolls the screen *U*p (backward) the same amount. ⬚CONTROL-F⬚ (*F*orward) or ⬚CONTROL-B⬚ (*B*ackward) displays almost a *whole* screenful of new text, leaving a couple of lines from the previous screen for continuity.

    vi displays a specific line in the Work Buffer when you enter a line number and then press the **G** (*G*oto) key. If you press **G** without a number, **vi** positions the cursor on the last line in the Work Buffer. Line numbers are implicit; your file does not need to have actual line numbers. Refer to "Line Numbers," page 120, if you want **vi** to display line numbers.

INSERT MODE

The Insert, Append, Open, and Replace commands put **vi** in the Insert Mode. While **vi** is in the Insert Mode, you can put new text into the Work Buffer. Always press the (ESCAPE) key to return **vi** to the Command Mode when you finish entering text.

The Insert Command

The **i** command puts **vi** in the Insert Mode and places the text you enter *before* the character the cursor is on (the *current character*). Although the **i** command sometimes overwrites text on the screen, the overwritten text reappears when you press (ESCAPE) and return **vi** to the Command Mode. Use the **i** command to insert a few characters or words into existing text or to insert text in a new file.

The Append Commands

The **a** command is similar to the **i** command, except that it places the text you enter *after* the current character, as shown in Figure 6-7. The **A** command places the text *after* the last character on the current line.

The Open Commands

The **o** and **O** commands open up a blank line within existing text, place the cursor at the beginning of the new (blank) line, and put **vi** in the Insert Mode. The **O** command opens a line *above* the current line; **o** opens one below. Use the Open commands when entering several new lines within existing text.

The Replace Commands

The **R** and **r** commands cause the new text you enter to overwrite (or replace) existing text. The character following an **r** command overwrites the current

Figure 6-7: The i, a, and A Commands

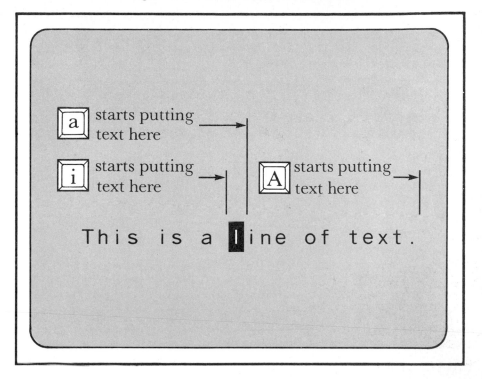

character. After that character, **vi** automatically returns to the Command Mode. You do not need to press the (ESCAPE) key.

The **R** command causes *all* subsequent characters to overwrite existing text until you press (ESCAPE) and return **vi** to the Command Mode.

COMMAND MODE—DELETING AND CHANGING TEXT

The Undo Command

The Undo command, **u**, undoes what you just did. It restores text that you have deleted or changed by mistake. The Undo command only restores the most recently deleted text. If you delete a line and then change a word, Undo restores only the changed word—not the deleted line. The **U** command restores the current line to the way it was before you started changing it, even if you have made several changes.

The Delete Character Command

The **x** command deletes the current character. You can precede the **x** command by a Repeat Factor to delete several characters on the current line, starting with the current character.

The Delete Operator

The **d** operator removes text from the Work Buffer. The amount of text that **d** removes depends on the Repeat Factor and the Unit of Measure you enter after the **d**. After the text is deleted, **vi** is in the Command Mode.

Caution: The command **d** (RETURN) illogically deletes two lines—the current line and the following one. Use the **dd** command to delete just the current line or precede **dd** by a Repeat Factor to delete several lines.

A list of some of the permissible Delete commands follows. Each of the commands, except **dd**, deletes *from* the current character.

Command	Action
d0	delete to beginning of line
dw	delete to end of word
d3w	delete to end of third word
db	delete to beginning of word
dW	delete to end of blank delimited word
dB	delete to beginning of blank delimited word
d7B	delete to beginning of seventh previous blank delimited word
dd	delete the current line
5dd	delete 5 lines starting with the current line
d)	delete to end of sentence
d4)	delete to end of fourth sentence
d(	delete to beginning of sentence
d}	delete to end of paragraph
d{	delete to beginning of paragraph
d7{	delete to beginning of seventh preceding paragraph

The Change Operator

The **c** operator replaces existing text with new text. The new text does not have to occupy the same space as the existing text. You can change a word to several words, a line to several lines, or a paragraph to a single character.

The change operator deletes the amount of text specified by the Unit of Measure that follows it, and puts **vi** in the Insert Mode. When you finish entering the new text and press (ESCAPE), the old word, line, sentence, or paragraph is changed to the new one.

When you change a word, the word is not deleted immediately. Instead, the **c** operator places a dollar sign at the end of the text that will be changed and leaves **vi** in the Insert Mode. You may appear to overwrite text, but all of it will be restored, except for the old (changed) text, when you press (ESCAPE).

A list of some of the permissible change commands follows. Each of the commands, except **cc**, changes text *from* the current character.

Command	Action
cw	change to end of word
c3w	change to end of third word
cb	change to beginning of word
cW	change to end of blank delimited word
cB	change to beginning of blank delimited word
c7B	change to beginning of seventh previous blank delimited word
cc	change the current line
5cc	change 5 lines starting with the current line
c)	change to end of sentence
c4)	change to end of fourth sentence
c(	change to beginning of sentence
c}	change to end of paragraph
c{	change to beginning of paragraph
c7{	change to beginning of seventh preceding paragraph

SEARCHING FOR A STRING

The Search Commands

vi will search backward or forward through the Work Buffer to find a specific string of text. To find the next occurrence of a string (forward), press the forward slash (/) key, enter the text you want to find (called the *Search String*), and press the (RETURN) key. When you press the slash key, a slash is displayed on the status line. As you enter the string of text, it too is displayed on the status line. When you press the (RETURN) key, **vi** searches for the string. If **vi** finds the string, it positions the cursor on the first character of the string. If you use a question mark (**?**) in place of the forward slash, **vi** searches for the previous occurrence of a string.

The **N** and **n** keys repeat the last search without making you enter the Search String again. The **n** key repeats the original search exactly, while the **N** key repeats the search in the opposite direction of the original search.

If you need to include a forward slash in a forward search or a question mark in a backward search, you must quote it by preceding it with a backslash (\).

Refer to "Ignore Case in Searches" (page 120) and "Wrap Scan" (page 121) for information about how to change search parameters.

Special Characters in Search Strings. Because the Search String is actually a regular expression (refer to Appendix A), some characters take on a special meaning within the Search String. The following paragraphs list some of these characters. The first two (∧ and $) always have their special meaning, while the rest can have their special meaning turned off. Refer to "Allow Special Characters in Searches," page 120.

The beginning of line indicator (∧)   When the first character in a Search string is a caret or circumflex, it matches the beginning of a line. The command ⁄∧ **the** finds the next line that begins with the string **the**.

The end of line indicator ($)   In a similar manner, a dollar sign matches the end of a line. The command ⁄ **!$** finds the next line ending with an exclamation point.

The any character indicator (.)   A period matches *any* character, anywhere in the Search String. The command ⁄**l . .e** finds **line**, **followed**, **like**, **included**, **all memory**, or any other word or character string that contains an **l** followed by any two characters and an **e**. To search for an actual period, use a backslash to quote the period.

The end of word indicator (\ >)   This pair of characters matches the end of a word. The command ⁄**s\>** finds the next word that ends with an **s**.

The beginning of word indicator (\ <)   This pair of characters matches the beginning of a word. The command ⁄**\<The** finds the next word that begins with **The**.

The character class definition **([])** Square brackets surrounding two or more characters match any *single* character located between the brackets. The command ∕**dis[ck]** finds the next occurrence of *either* disk or disc.

There are two special characters that you can use within a character class definition. A caret (∧) as the first character following the left bracket defines the character class to be *any but the following characters*. A hyphen between two characters indicates a range of characters.

Command	Result	Examples
∕and	finds the next occurrence of the string and	sand, and, standard, slander, andiron
∕\<and\>	finds the next occurrence of the word and	and
∕∧The	finds the next line that starts with The	The . . . There . . .
∕∧[0–9][0–9])	finds the next line that starts with a two digit number followed by a right parenthesis	77) . . . 01) . . . 15) . . .
∕\<[adr]	finds the next word that starts with an a, d or r	apple, drive, road, argument, right

SUBSTITUTING ONE STRING FOR ANOTHER

A Substitute command is a combination of a Search command and a Change command. It searches for a string just as the ∕ command does, allowing the same special characters that were discussed in the previous section. When it finds a string, the Substitute command changes it. The format of the Substitute command is shown below. As with all commands that begin with a colon, Substitute is executed from the status line.

    :[address]s∕search-string∕replace-string[∕g]

The Substitute Address

If you do not specify an address, Substitute only searches the current line. If you use a single line number as an address, Substitute searches that line. If the address is two line numbers separated by a comma, Substitute searches lines between and including the ones you specify. Refer to "Line Numbers," page 120, if you want **vi** to display line numbers.

Within the address, a period represents the current line and a dollar sign represents the last line in the Work Buffer. A percent sign represents the entire work buffer. **vi** permits address arithmetic using plus and minus signs. This address scheme is similar to the one **ed** uses. Some examples of addresses are shown below.

Address	Portion of Work Buffer addressed
5	line 5
77,100	lines 77 through 100 inclusive
1,.	the beginning of the Work Buffer through the current line
.,$	the current line through the end of the Work Buffer
1,$	the entire Work Buffer
%	the entire Work Buffer
.,.+10	the current line through the tenth following line

The Search and Replace Strings

An **s** follows the address. It indicates to **vi** that this is a Substitute command. A delimiter, marking the beginning of the Search String, follows the **s**. Although a forward slash is used in the examples in this book, you can use any character as a delimiter. You must use the same delimiter at the end of the Search String.

Next comes the Search String. It has the same format as the Search String in the / command, and may include the same special characters. Another delimiter marks the end of the Search String and the beginning of the Replace String. The Replace String is the string that will replace the Search String when it is found. The only special characters in the Replace String are the ampersand (**&**), which represents the text that was matched by the Search String, and the backslash, which is used to quote the character following it. Refer to the following examples.

To replace only the *first occurrence* of the Search String on each line within the specified address, press the (RETURN) or (ESCAPE) key after you enter the Replace String. If you want a *global* substitute—that is, if you want to replace *all* occurrences of the Search String on all addressed lines—enter a third delimiter (/) and a **g** before you press (RETURN) or (ESCAPE).

Command	Result	Examples
:s/bigger/biggest		
	replaces the string bigger on the current line with biggest	bigger→biggest
:1,.s/Chapter 1/Chapter 2/g		
	replaces every occurrence of the string Chapter 1 before or on the current line, with Chapter 2	Chapter 1→Chapter 2 Chapter 12→Chapter 22
:1,$s/ten/10/g		
	replaces every occurrence of the string ten by the string 10	ten→10 often→of10 tenant→10ant
:1,$s/\<ten\>/10/g		
	replaces every occurrence of the word ten by the string 10	ten→10
:.,.+10s/every/each/g		
	replaces every occurrence of the string every by the string each on the current line through the tenth following line.	every→each everything→eachthing

MISCELLANEOUS COMMANDS

The Join Command

The Join command, **J**, joins two lines of text. **J** joins the line below the current line to the end of the current line. It inserts a (SPACE) between what was previously two lines and leaves the cursor on this (SPACE).

You can always "unjoin" (break) a line into two lines by inserting a RETURN where you want to break the line.

The Status Command

The Status command, CONTROL-G, displays the name of the file being edited, the line number of the current line, the total number of lines in the Work Buffer, and the percent of the Work Buffer preceding the current line.

The . Command

The . (period) command repeats the most recent command that made a change. If for example, you just gave a **d2w** command (delete the next two words), the . command would delete the next two words. If you had just inserted text, the . command would repeat the insertion of the same text.

THE DELETE, YANK, AND PUT COMMANDS AND THE USE OF BUFFERS

vi has a General Purpose Buffer and 26 Named Buffers that you can use to hold text during an editing session. These buffers are useful if you want to move or copy a portion of text to another location in the Work Buffer. A combination of the Delete and Put commands removes text from one location in the Work Buffer and places it in another. The Yank and Put commands make a copy of some text at another location in the Work Buffer.

The General Purpose Buffer

The text that you most recently Changed, Deleted, or Yanked is stored in the General Purpose Buffer unless you specify a Named Buffer. The Undo command also uses the General Purpose Buffer when it restores text.

The Delete Commands. Any of the Delete commands that were described earlier in this chapter ("The Delete Operator") automatically place the deleted text in the General Purpose Buffer. Just as you can use the Undo command to put the deleted text back where it came from, you can use a Put command to put the deleted text at another location in the Work Buffer.

The Yank Commands. The Yank commands are identical to the Delete commands except that they do not delete text from the Work Buffer. **vi** places a *copy* of the yanked text in the General Purpose Buffer so that you can use Put to put another copy of it elsewhere in the Work Buffer. Use the yank operator, **y**, just as you use **d**, the delete operator.

Caution: Just as **d** (RETURN) deletes two lines, **y** (RETURN) yanks two lines. Use the **yy** command to yank the current line.

The Put Commands. The Put commands, **P** and **p**, copy text from the General Purpose Buffer into the Work Buffer.

If you delete or yank characters or words into the General Purpose Buffer, **P** inserts them before the current *character* and **p** inserts them after. If you Delete or Yank lines, sentences, or paragraphs, **P** inserts the contents of the General Purpose Buffer before the *line* the cursor is on and **p** inserts it after.

The Put commands do not destroy the contents of the General Purpose Buffer, so it is possible to place the same text at several points within the file by using one Delete or Yank command and several Put commands.

Because **vi** has only one General Purpose Buffer and **vi** changes the contents of this buffer each time you give a Change, Delete, or Yank command, **you can use only cursor positioning commands between a Delete or Yank command and the corresponding Put command**. Any other commands change the contents of the General Purpose Buffer and therefore change the results of the Put command.

The Named Buffers

You can use a Named Buffer with any of the Delete, Yank, or Put commands. There are 26 Named Buffers, each named by one of the letters of the alphabet. Each Named Buffer can store a different block of text so that each block can be recalled as needed. Unlike the General Purpose Buffer, **vi** does not change the contents of a Named Buffer unless you use a command that specifically addresses that buffer. **vi** maintains the contents of a Named Buffer throughout an editing session.

vi stores text in a Named Buffer if you precede a Delete, Yank, or Put command with a quotation mark (**"**) and a buffer name (e.g., **"kyy** puts the current line into buffer **k**). You can use a Named Buffer two ways. If you give the name of the buffer as a lowercase letter, **vi** purges the buffer before it Deletes or Yanks text into the buffer. If you use an uppercase letter, **vi** appends the newly Deleted or Yanked text to the end of the buffer. Using uppercase buffer names, you can collect blocks of text from various sections of a file and deposit them at one place in the file with a single command.

READING AND WRITING FILES

vi reads a file into the Work Buffer when you call it from the Shell. The contents of the Work Buffer is written back to the file when you give vi the **ZZ** command that terminates the editing session. This section discusses other ways of reading text into the Work Buffer and writing it out.

The Read Command

The Read command reads a file into the Work Buffer. The new file does not overwrite any text in the Work Buffer, but is positioned following the current line. The format of the Read command is shown below.

```
:r filename
```

As with other commands that begin with a colon, when you enter the colon, it appears on the status line. The **filename** is the pathname of the file that you want to read, and must be terminated by (RETURN).

The Write Command

The Write command writes part or all of the Work Buffer to a file. You can use an address to write out part of the Work Buffer and a filename to specify a file to receive the text. If you do not use an address or filename, the entire contents of the Work Buffer is written to the file being edited, updating the file you are editing. The format of the Write command is shown below.

```
:[address]w[!] [filename]
```

You can use the following format of the Write command to append text to an existing file.

```
:[address]w>> filename
```

The Address. If you use an address, it specifies the portion of the Work Buffer to be written out. The address follows the form of the address used in the Substitute command. If you do not use an address, vi writes out the entire contents of the Work Buffer.

The w and !. Because Write can destroy a large amount of work very quickly, vi demands that you enter an exclamation point following the **w** as a safeguard against accidentally overwriting a file. The only times you don't need an exclamation point are when you are writing out the entire contents of the Work Buffer to the file being edited (using no address, no filename) and when you are writing part or all of the Work Buffer to a new file. When you are writing part of the file to the file being edited, or overwriting another file, you must use an exclamation point.

The Filename.   The optional filename is the pathname of the file you are writing to. If you do not specify a filename, **vi** writes to the file you are editing.

SETTING PARAMETERS

You can adapt **vi** to your needs and habits by setting **vi** parameters. These parameters can perform many functions, such as causing **vi** to display line numbers, automatically inserting (NEWLINE) characters as needed, and establishing nonstandard searches.

You can set parameters in two different ways. You can set them while you are using **vi**, to establish the environment for the current editing session, or you can set the parameters in your **.profile** (Bourne Shell) or **.login** (C Shell) file, so that each time you use **vi** the environment has been established and you can begin editing immediately.

Setting Parameters from vi

To set a parameter while you are using **vi**, enter a colon (:), the word **set**, a (SPACE), and the parameter. The command appears on the status line as you type it and takes effect when you press (RETURN).

Setting Parameters in a Startup File

If you are using the Bourne Shell, put the following lines in the **.profile** file in your home directory.

```
EXINIT='set parm1 parm2 ...'
export EXINIT
```

Replace **parm1** and **parm2** by parameters selected from the list in the next section. **EXINIT** is a variable that **vi** reads.

If you are using the C Shell, put the following line in the **.login** file in your home directory.

```
setenv EXINIT 'set parm1 parm2 ...'
```

Again, replace **parm1** and **parm2** by parameters from the following list.

Parameters

This section contains a list of some of the most useful **vi** parameters. **vi** displays a complete list of parameters and how they are currently set when you give the command **:set all** while using **vi**.

Line Numbers. **vi** does not normally display the line number associated with each line. To display line numbers, set the parameter **numbers**. To cause line numbers not to be displayed, set the parameter **nonumbers**.

Line numbers—whether displayed or not—are not part of the file, are not stored with the file, and are not displayed when the file is printed. They only appear on the screen while you are using **vi**.

Line Wrap Margin. The line wrap margin causes **vi** to break the text that you are inserting approximately the specified number of characters from the right margin. **vi** breaks the text by inserting a (NEWLINE) character at the closest blank delimited word boundary. Setting the line wrap margin is handy if you want all your text lines to be approximately the same length. It relieves you of the burden of remembering to press (RETURN) at the end of each line of input.

Set the parameter **wrapmargin = nn** where **nn** is the number of charac-ters *from the right side of the screen* where you want **vi** to break the text. This number is not the column width of the text, but the distance from the end of the text to the right edge of the screen. Setting the wrap margin to zero turns this feature off.

Ignore Case in Searches. **vi** normally performs case-sensitive searches, differentiating between uppercase and lowercase letters. **vi** performs case-insensitive searches when you set the **ignorecase** parameter. Set **noignorecase** to restore case-sensitive searches.

Allow Special Characters in Searches. The following characters and character pairs normally have a special meaning when you use them within Search Strings. Refer to "Special Characters in Search Strings," page 112.

    . \< \> [ ]

When you set the **nomagic** parameter, these characters no longer have a special meaning. The **magic** parameter gives them back their special meaning.

The ∧ and **$** characters always have a special meaning within Search Strings, regardless of how you set this parameter.

Wrap Scan. Normally, when a search for the next occurrence of a Search String reaches the end of the Work Buffer, **vi** continues the search at the beginning of the Work Buffer. The reverse is true of a search for the previous occurrence of a Search String. The **nowrapscan** parameter stops the search at either end of the Work Buffer. Set the **wrapscan** parameter if you want searches to once again wrap around the ends of the Work Buffer.

Automatic Indention. The automatic indention feature works in conjunction with the **shiftwidth** parameter to provide a regular set of indentions for programs or tabular material. This feature is normally off. You can turn it on by setting **autoindent** (or **ai**) and off by setting **noautoindent** (or **noai**).

When automatic indention is on and **vi** is in the Insert Mode, (CONTROL-T) moves the cursor from the left margin (or an indention) to the next indention position, (RETURN) moves the cursor to the left side of the next line under the first character of the previous line, and (CONTROL-D) backs up over indention positions. (CONTROL-T) and (CONTROL-D) function in a manner analogous to (TAB) and (BACKTAB) keys, but only function before any text is placed on a line.

Shift Width. The **shiftwidth** parameter controls the functioning of (CONTROL-T) and (CONTROL-D) in Insert Mode when automatic indention is on. Set the parameter **shiftwidth=nn**, where **nn** is the spacing of the indention positions. Setting the shift width is similar to setting the (TAB) stops on a typewriter.

UNITS OF MEASURE

Many **vi** commands operate on a block of text—from a character to many paragraphs. The size of a block of text is specified by a *Unit of Measure*. You can specify multiple Units of Measure by preceding a Unit of Measure with a number, called a *Repeat Factor*. This section defines the various Units of Measure.

Character

A character is one character, visible or not, printable or not, including
(SPACE)s and (TAB)s.

Characters	
a	q
A	.
(TAB)	5
R	(SPACE)
_	>

Word

A word is an English word or its equivalent. It is a string of one or more
characters that is bounded on both sides by any combination of one or more
of the following elements: a punctuation mark, (SPACE), (TAB), numeral, or
(NEWLINE). In addition, **vi** considers each group of punctuation marks to be
a word.

Text	Word count
pear	(1 word)
pear!	(2 words)
pear!)	(2 words)
pear!) The	(3 words)
pear!) "The	(4 words)
This is a short, concise line (no frills).	(11 words)

Blank Delimited Word

A blank delimited word is the same as a word, except that it includes adjacent punctuation. Blank delimited words are separated from each other by
one or more of the following elements: a (SPACE), (TAB), or (NEWLINE).

Text	Blank delimited word count
pear	(1 blank delimited word)
pear!	(1 blank delimited word)
pear!)	(1 blank delimited word)
pear!) The	(2 blank delimited words)
pear!) "The	(2 blank delimited words)
This is a short, concise line (no frills).	(8 blank delimited words)

Line

A line is a string of characters bounded by (NEWLINE)s. It is not necessarily a single, physical line on the terminal. It is possible to enter a very long single (logical) line that wraps around (continues on the next physical line) several times. It is a good idea to avoid long logical lines by terminating lines with a (RETURN) before they reach the right side of the terminal screen. Terminating lines in this manner insures that each physical line contains one logical line and avoids confusion when you edit and format the text. Some commands do not *appear* to work properly on physical lines that are longer than the width of the screen.

Sentence

A sentence is an English sentence or the equivalent. A sentence starts at the end of the previous sentence and ends with a period, exclamation point, or question mark, followed by two (SPACE)s or a (NEWLINE).

Text	Sentence count
That's it. This is one sentence.	(one sentence: only one (SPACE) after the first period— (NEWLINE) after the second period)
That's it. This is two sentences.	(two sentences: two (SPACE)s after the first period— (NEWLINE) after the second period)
What? Three sentences? On one line?	(three sentences: two (SPACE)s after the first two question marks— (NEWLINE) after the third question mark)
This sentence takes up a total of three lines.	((NEWLINE) after the period)

Paragraph

A paragraph is preceded and followed by one or more blank lines. A blank line is actually composed of two (NEWLINE) characters in a row.

Text	Paragraph count
one paragraph	(one paragraph: blank line before and after text)
This may appear to be more than one paragraph. Just because there are two indentions does not mean it qualifies as two paragraphs.	(one paragraph: blank line before and after text)
Even though in English this is only one sentence, vi considers it to be three paragraphs.	(three paragraphs: three blocks of text separated by blank lines)

Screen

The terminal screen is a window that opens onto part of the Work Buffer. You can position this window so that it shows different portions of the Work Buffer.

Repeat Factor

A number that precedes a Unit of Measure is a Repeat Factor. Just as the "5" in "5 inches" causes you to consider "5 inches" as a single unit of measure, a Repeat Factor causes **vi** to group more than one Unit of Measure and consider it as a single Unit of Measure. For example, the command **w** moves the cursor forward one word. The command **5w** moves the cursor forward five words and **250w** moves it 250 words. If you do not specify a Repeat Factor, **vi** assumes that you mean one Unit of Measure.

SUMMARY

This summary of **vi** includes all of the commands covered in this chapter, plus some new ones.

Calling vi

Command	Function
vi filename	edit **filename** starting at line 1
vi +n filename	edit **filename** starting at line **n**
vi + filename	edit **filename** starting at the last line
vi +/pattern filename	edit **filename** starting at the first line containing pattern
vi −r filename	recover **filename** after a system crash

Moving the Cursor by Units of Measure

You must be in the Command Mode to use these commands, each of which can be preceded by a repeat factor. These commands are Units of Measure and are used in Change and Delete commands.

Command	Moves the Cursor
(SPACE), l , or right arrow	space to the right
h or left arrow	space to the left
w	word to the right
W	blank delimited word to the right
b	word to the left
B	blank delimited word to the left
$	end of line
0	beginning of line
(RETURN)	beginning of next line
j or down arrow	down one line
k or up arrow	up one line
)	end of sentence
(	beginning of sentence
}	end of paragraph
{	beginning of paragraph

Viewing Different Parts of the Work Buffer

Command	Moves the Cursor
CONTROL-D	forward ½ screenful
CONTROL-U	backward ½ screenful
CONTROL-F	forward one screenful
CONTROL-B	backward one screenful
nG	to line **n**
H	to the top of screen
M	to the middle of screen
L	to the bottom of screen

Adding Text

All the following commands leave **vi** in the Insert Mode (except **r**). You must press ESCAPE to return it to the Command Mode.

Command	Insert Text
i	before cursor
I	before first nonblank character on line
a	after cursor
A	at end of line
o	on next line down (open up a line)
O	on next line up (open up a line)
r	replace current character (no ESCAPE needed)
R	replace characters, starting with current character (overwrite until ESCAPE)

Deleting and Changing Text

In the following list, UM represents a Unit of Measure that can be preceded by a Repeat Factor. RF is a number that is a Repeat Factor.

Command	Effect
RFx	delete the number of characters specified by **RF**, starting with the current character
RFX	delete the number of characters specified by **RF**, starting with the character following the current character
dUM	delete text specified by **UM**
RFdd	delete the number of lines specified by **RF**
D	delete to end of line

The following commands leave **vi** in the Insert Mode. You must press (ESCAPE) to return it to the Command Mode.

Command	Effect
RFs	substitute the number of characters specified by **RF**
cUM	change text specified by **UM**
RFcc	change the number of lines specified by **RF**
C	change to end of line

Searching for a String

In the following list, rexp represents a regular expression that can be a simple string of characters.

Command	Effect
/rexp (RETURN)	search forward for **rexp**
?rexp (RETURN)	search backward for **rexp**
n	repeat original search exactly
N	repeat original search, opposite direction
/(RETURN)	repeat original search forward
?(RETURN)	repeat original search backward

String Substitution

The format of a substitute command is shown below.

```
:[address]s/search-string/replace-string[/g]
```

where:

address	is one line number or two line numbers separated by a comma. A **.** represents the current line, **$** represents the last line, and **%** represents the entire file.
search-string	is a regular expression that can be a simple string of characters.
replace-string	is the replacement string.
g	indicates a global replacement (more than one replacement per line).

Special Commands

: ! command	fork a Shell and execute **command**
! ! command	fork a Shell, execute **command**, place output in file starting at the current line
: e ! file	edit **file**, discarding changes to current file (use **w** first if you want to keep the changes)

7

THE nroff TEXT FORMATTER

The **nroff** utility formats text. This chapter shows how to use **nroff** to prepare documents. It discusses the theory of filling and justifying lines, describes the structure of an input file, and shows how to use **nroff** commands. Most of the commands described in this chapter are part of the **−ms** macro package. The summary at the end of the chapter covers plain **nroff** commands, **−ms** commands, and **−me** commands.

Input to **nroff** is a file of text created using an editor such as **vi**. Output from **nroff** is paginated, formatted text that can be sent to a terminal, printer, or plain file. Commands imbedded in the input file determine what the output text looks like.

nroff has default values for all margins, line lengths, indentions, and spacing of text on a page. If your input file contains text without imbedded commands, **nroff** uses these default values to format the output text. You can use as few or as many commands as the complexity of the formatting job requires.

nroff can accomplish many formatting tasks. Among its capabilities, **nroff** can

fill lines
right-justify lines
hyphenate words
center text
generate footnotes
automatically number headings
number pages
put the date on each page
put headers on each page
put footers on each page
produce numbered lists

The output from **nroff** is designed to go to a terminal or line printer. A related formatter, **troff**, sends its output to a phototypesetter. Two prepro-cessors work with either of these formatters. The **eqn** preprocessor assists you in formatting equations while **tbl** is used to format tables.

Instructing **nroff** to format a file can be tedious and unnecessarily com-plex. To make the job easier, **nroff** allows you to define and use *macros*. A macro is a short command that **nroff** expands into a longer sequence of commands. Even with this facility, you would ordinarily need an in-depth knowledge of **nroff** to format a document of moderate complexity.

Because so many people's formatting needs are similar, **nroff** provides several predefined packages of macros. Using one of the existing *macro pack-ages* can make a job easier, so that you can concentrate on the content, rather than the format, of a document. This chapter concentrates on **nroff** used in conjunction with the **−ms** macro package.

USING nroff WITH THE —ms PACKAGE

You can distinguish **—ms** commands from regular **nroff** commands because all **—ms** commands use uppercase letters while **nroff** commands use only lowercase letters. Regular **nroff** commands and **—ms** commands can be mixed in a file that is processed by **nroff** *and* the **—ms** macro package.

The following command line indicates to **nroff** that you want to use the macro package.

```
$ nroff —ms file
.
.
.
```

The **—ms** is the option that selects the macro package and the **file** is the name of the input file that you want to format. This command line sends the formatted text to the standard output. Unless you redirect it, the text appears on the terminal. If your installation has the **more** utility, you can use it to view one screenful of text at a time.

```
$ nroff —ms file | more
.
.
.
```

You can inspect **nroff** output before sending it to the printer by redirecting it and using **cat** or **more**.

```
$ nroff —ms file > hold
$ cat hold
.
.
.
$
```

If the output is what you want, you can send it to the printer using **lpr**.

```
$ lpr hold
$
```

You can also direct the output to the **lpr** utility without inspecting it.

```
$ nroff —ms file | lpr
$
```

THEORY OF FILLING AND JUSTIFYING LINES

The ability to *fill* and *justify* lines is the most important feature of any formatter. It is this process that gives the output text its finished appearance. A filled line of output text is brought as close to the right margin as is possible without padding the line with (SPACE)s; a filled and justified line is padded so that it reaches the right margin.

Input file

```
The ability to fill and justify lines is the
most important
feature of any formatter.
```

Filled output text

```
The ability to fill and
justify lines is the
most important feature
of any formatter.
```

Filled and justified output text

```
The ability to fill and
justify  lines  is  the
most  important feature
of any formatter.
```

Filling a Line

The format of the output text is not dependent upon the length of lines in the input file. **nroff** considers the input file as a stream of words. To produce a line of output text, **nroff** takes words from the input stream and keeps adding them to the output line until it gets to a word that brings the line past the right margin. If **nroff** can hyphenate and include part of this word on the line, it does. Otherwise it saves this word for the next line of output text. At this point, the line is *filled* . It cannot hold the entire next word, or part of the next word if it was hyphenated, without exceeding the right margin. When each of the output lines is filled, the right edge of the output text is ragged. It is said to have a *ragged right* margin.

Justifying Text

All the lines in justified text come exactly to (are flush with) the right margin. The only exception is the last line of a paragraph, which is never justified. Justified text is said to have a *flush right* margin. Unless you instruct **nroff** otherwise, it fills and justifies all lines.

Before a line can be justified, it must be filled. To justify text, **nroff** expands single (SPACE)s between words in the filled line, one at a time, to double, triple, or add more (SPACE)s as it brings the right end of the line to the right margin. (Some versions also increase the space between letters of words by fractions of (SPACE)s.)

THE INPUT FILE

You can prepare the input file with an editor such as **ed** or **vi**. Each line in the input file contains either an **nroff** command or text. This section covers both types of lines.

When you use the **−ms** macro package, the input file cannot begin immediately with text. You must place an initializing command, such as **.PP**, on the first line of the input file.

Command Lines

A line in the input file containing an **nroff** command begins with a period or an apostrophe. This chapter does not discuss command lines that begin with an apostrophe. They are mentioned here so that you can avoid giving **nroff** a command by mistake. A line beginning with a (SPACE) also has a special meaning to **nroff**. These lines are discussed in the section of this chapter covering "Breaks."

Because **nroff** considers a line in the input file that begins with a period, an apostrophe, or a (SPACE) to be a command line, lines of text cannot begin with any of these characters.

Commands. **nroff** commands follow immediately after a period at the beginning of a line in the input file. A command is composed of one or two letters or a number and a letter. Plain **nroff** commands use lowercase letters;

−ms macro package commands use uppercase letters. A list of sample commands follows.

```
.LP
.IP
.bp
.I
.DA
.ce
.2C
```

Command arguments Some commands require additional information on the same line with the command. (SPACE)s separate these pieces of information, or arguments, from the command and from each other.

There are two kinds of arguments—measurements and text. A measurement gives some information to **nroff**, but is not printed. When text appears after a command, **nroff** places it in the output text in some special manner.

The following command takes a number as an argument. It centers the next three lines from the input file. The three is a measurement that tells **nroff** how many lines to center.

```
.ce 3
```

The next command takes text as an argument. It underlines the word that follows it on the same line. The **I** stands for *italic*. **nroff** underlines the text because it can't produce italic type.

```
.I important
```

The next command uses both types of arguments. The hanging indented paragraph command places the text that follows it at the left margin and indents the rest of the paragraph the number of (SPACE)s specified by the second argument. The first argument contains a (SPACE), so it is enclosed within quotation marks so that **nroff** does not mistake it for more than one argument.

```
.IP "Section 5:" 15
```

Text Lines

All lines in the input file that are not command lines are text lines. **nroff** forms these lines into the output text according to the specifications of the command lines.

PARAGRAPHS

An **nroff** paragraph is a block of output text with one or more blank lines above and below it. **nroff** fills and justifies the lines of a paragraph unless you instruct it not to. The four styles of paragraphs that the **–ms** macros provide are described below.

The Standard Paragraph

A **.PP** command in the input file causes **nroff** to format the text following the command as a *standard paragraph* , a paragraph that starts with an indented line. All the rest of the lines occupy the full line length. A **.PP** command also serves as an initializing command and must be placed at the beginning of the input file. An example of the use of the **.PP** command follows.

Input file

```
.PP
This is a standard paragraph.
The first line is indented; the rest
come out to the left margin.
When you want to start a new paragraph,
you have to give nroff another paragraph
command.
.PP
This is the start of another standard
paragraph.
Again, the first line is indented
and subsequent lines come all the
way to the left margin.
```

Output text

```
        This is  a   standard  paragraph.   The  first  line  is
indented;  the  rest  come out to the left margin.  When you
want to start a  new  paragraph,  you  have  to  give  nroff
another paragraph command.

        This  is  the  start  of  another  standard  paragraph.
Again,  the first line is indented and subsequent lines come
all the way to the left margin.
```

The Left Block Paragraph

nroff produces a *left block paragraph* when you give it an **.LP** command. This type of paragraph is the same as a standard paragraph, except that the first line is not indented. The first line of a left block paragraph is flush left with the other lines. An example of a left block paragraph follows.

Input file

```
.LP
This is an example of a left block
paragraph.
All the lines, including the first,
come all the way over to the left
margin.
Just as with other types of paragraphs,
you must start a new paragraph with
a paragraph command.
```

Output text

```
This is an example of  a  left  block  paragraph.   All  the
lines,  including  the  first,  come all the way over to the
left margin.  Just as with other types  of  paragraphs,  you
must start a new paragraph with a paragraph command.
```

Indented Paragraphs

An **.IP** command produces an *indented paragraph*. There are three types of indented paragraphs.

A *plain indented paragraph* is similar to a left block paragraph, except that *all* its lines are indented from the left margin. All the lines are the same length. An **.IP** command with no arguments generates a plain indented paragraph.

A *hanging indented paragraph* is similar to a plain indented paragraph except that it has an item on the first line at the left margin. An **.IP** command with a single argument generates a hanging indented paragraph. Refer to the example below.

A hanging indented paragraph will have a *nonstandard indention* when you use a number as the second argument to an **.IP** command. The number is the number of (SPACE)s that nroff indents the paragraph. All subsequent **.IP** commands will use this indention until nroff encounters a **.PP** or **.LP** command. Refer to the example below.

Input file

```
.LP
This is a left block paragraph.
In this example, it serves as a reference
point, showing where the left margin
is.
.IP
This is an indented paragraph.
All the lines are indented from
the left margin.
It is used to set a block of text
off from a body of text.
.IP 1.
This is an example of a hanging indent
in a numbered list.
The text is all indented from the
left margin except for an item on
the first line.
nroff places this item at the left
margin.
.IP (a)
```

```
This is a short hanging indent.
.IP "paragraph 1:" 14
This is a nonstandard hanging indent.
The 14 following the hanging item
indicates that nroff is to indent
the body of text 14 characters in
from the left margin.
.IP "word 5:"
This paragraph is also indented 14
characters.
A nonstandard indent is only canceled
by a standard or block left paragraph
command.
```

Output text

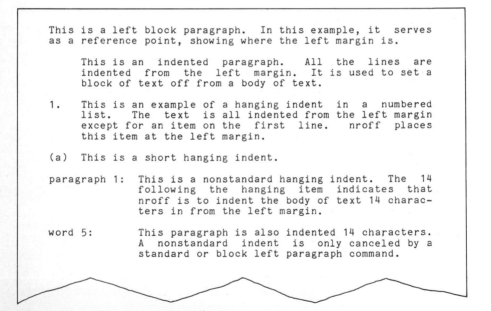

```
This is a left block paragraph.  In this example, it  serves
as a reference point, showing where the left margin is.

    This is an  indented  paragraph.   All  the  lines  are
    indented  from  the  left  margin.  It is used to set a
    block of text off from a body of text.

1.  This is an example of a hanging indent  in  a  numbered
    list.   The  text  is all indented from the left margin
    except for an item on the  first  line.   nroff  places
    this item at the left margin.

(a)  This is a short hanging indent.

paragraph 1:  This is a nonstandard hanging indent.  The  14
              following  the  hanging  item  indicates  that
              nroff is to indent the body of text 14 charac-
              ters in from the left margin.

word 5:       This paragraph is also indented 14 characters.
              A  nonstandard  indent  is  only canceled by a
              standard or block left paragraph command.
```

The Block Quote Paragraph

A *block quote paragraph*, produced by a **.QP** command, is indented from both the left *and* right margins, making all the lines the same length. This type of paragraph sets a quotation off from a body of text.

Input file

```
.LP
This is a left block paragraph that
is to be used as a reference.
It sets off the block quote paragraph
so that you can more clearly see
the intended effect.
.QP
This is a block quote paragraph.
It is indented from both the right
and left margins.
All lines are indented an equal amount.
```

Output text

```
      This is a left block paragraph that  is  to  be  used  as  a
      reference.   It  sets  off the block quote paragraph so that
      you can more clearly see the intended effect.

          This is a block quote paragraph.  It  is  indented
          from   both  the  right and left margins.  All lines
          are indented an equal amount.
```

BREAKS

This section covers commands that end lines and pages, leave blank lines, and center text. When you command **nroff** to end a line, it stops filling the line and does not justify it. What happens next depends on which command you use. All the commands in this section are plain **nroff** commands, not **–ms** macro commands.

The End Line Command

The simplest end line command is the **.br** (break) command. It does nothing except end (or break) a line. Subsequent text begins on the next line.

Input file

```
This is an example of the simplest
kind of break, or end line, command.
nroff can be halfway through filling
a line, but when you give a
.br
break command, it ends the line it
was filling and continues on the
next line.
```

Output text

```
This is an example of the simplest kind  of  break,  or  end
line,  command.  nroff  can  be  halfway  through filling a
line, but when you give a
break command, it ends the line it was filling and continues
on the next line.
```

The Implicit End Line Command

Any line in the input file that begins with a (SPACE) automatically ends the current line of output text. The new line begins with a (SPACE). If you begin a line in the input file with five (SPACE)s, the new line in the output text will begin with five (SPACE)s. This feature allows you to indent a paragraph without an explicit command.

This command is of limited use, but it is important to understand how it functions so that you do not use it unintentionally.

Input file

```
This is an example of how a line of
input text, beginning with a SPACE,
 causes the line being output to end
and a new line to start.
The new line starts with a SPACE.
```

Output text

```
This is an example of how a line of  input   text,   beginning
with a SPACE,
 causes the line being output to  end  and  a  new  line  to
start.  The new line starts with a SPACE.
```

The Space Command

The **.sp** (space) command ends the output line and skips the number of lines you specify before **nroff** continues to produce output text.

Input file

```
This is an example of an end line
command that leaves a number of blank
lines after it ends a line.
.sp 3
This .sp command left three lines
because it was followed by a 3.
```

Output text

```
        This is an example of an end  line  command  that  leaves  a
        number of blank lines after it ends a line.


        This .sp command left three lines because  it  was  followed
        by a 3.
```

The Center Text Command

Without an argument, the **.ce** (center) command centers the line that follows it in the input file. When followed by a number, the **.ce** command centers that number of lines from the input file.

Input file

```
This is a demonstration of the .ce
end line command.
It ends the line and
.ce
centers
the line following the command.
When you follow this command with
an argument, it will
.ce 3
center
as many
lines as you specify.
After the .ce command finishes centering
lines, nroff goes back to filling lines.
```

Output text

```
    This is a demonstration of the .ce  end  line  command.   It
    ends the line and
                        centers
    the line following the command.  When you follow  this  com-
    mand with an argument, it will
                        center
                        as many
                   lines as you specify.
    After the .ce command finishes centering lines,  nroff  goes
    back to filling lines.
```

The Begin Page Command

The **.bp** (begin page) command ends the line of output text that **nroff** is filling and puts subsequent text on the next page.

SETTING THE LEFT MARGIN

nroff places the left margin at the extreme left of the printed output. You can use the **.RS** command to move the left margin to the right of this point by increments of five (SPACE)s. More than one **.RS** command moves the left margin more than five (SPACE)s to the right.

The **.RS** command generates a line break. **nroff** places text following an **.RS** command on the next line starting at the new left margin.

Input file

```
This line shows the default position
of the left and right margins.
.RS
The .RS command moves the left margin
five SPACEs to the right.
.RS
.RS
Two .RS commands move it ten SPACEs
further.
```

```
The lines get shorter and
shorter so that the right margin
does not change.
```

Output text

```
This line shows the default position of the left  and  right
margins.
        The .RS command moves the left margin  five  SPACEs  to
        the right.
                Two .RS commands move it ten SPACEs  further.
                The lines get shorter and shorter so that the
                right margin does not change.
```

An **.RE** command reverses the effect of an **.RS** command, moving the left margin five (SPACE)s to the left each time you use it. The **.RE** command cannot move the left margin to the left of its starting point. The following example continues the previous one and assumes that the left margin is still 15 (SPACE)s to the right of its starting point.

Input file

```
This text continues from the previous
example.
The left margin is indented 15 SPACES.
.RE
The .RE command moves the left margin
five SPACES to the left
.RE
each time it is used.
.RE
When you have given nroff the same
number of .RE and .RS commands, the
left margin will be back where
it started.
```

Output text

```
                    This text continues from the   previous   exam-
                    ple.   The   left margin is indented 15 SPACEs.
            The .RE command moves the left margin five   SPACEs
            to the left
        each time it is used.
When you have given nroff the same number  of  .RE  and  .RS
commands, the left margin will be back where it started.
```

Following is an example of how to combine indented hanging paragraphs and changes in the left margin to form a hierarchical list.

Input file

```
.IP I.
Paragraphs
.RS
.IP 1.
The Standard Paragraph
.RS
.IP a.
Input file
.IP b.
Printed output
.RE
.IP 2.
The Left Block Paragraph
.RS
.IP a.
Input file
.IP b.
Printed output
.RE
.RE
.IP II.
Breaks
.RS
.IP 1.
The End Line Command
```

Output text

```
   I.    Paragraphs
         1.    The Standard Paragraph
               a.    Input file
               b.    Printed output
         2.    The Left Block Paragraph
               a.    Input file
               b.    Printed output
  II.    Breaks
         1.    The End Line Command
```

ADJUSTING THE RIGHT MARGIN

The **.na** (no adjust right margin) command causes **nroff** to fill, but not justify, each line of output text. The **.ad b** (adjust both margins) command causes **nroff** to revert to justifying lines. Refer to the display commands if you do not want to fill *or* justify lines.

Input file

```
nroff normally fills and justifies lines.
Filling and justifying means that each
line, unless it is broken, comes all the way
to the right margin.
Justified text looks balanced and neat.
.br
.na
Give nroff an .na command if you want it
```

```
to fill but not to justify the text.
This can be useful when you want to use nroff
to type a letter but you want the letter to
look as though it was typed by hand.
.br
.ad b
The .ad b command puts nroff back
in its default mode.
It causes nroff to fill and justify lines
of text.
Once again, each line comes all the way to the
right margin.
```

Output text

```
    nroff normally fills and justifies lines.  Filling and  jus-
tifying means that each line, unless it is broken, comes all
the way to the right margin.  Justified text looks  balanced
and neat.
Give nroff an .na command if you want it to fill but not to
justify the text.  This can be useful when you want to use
nroff to type a letter but you want the letter to look as
though it was typed by hand.
The .ad b command puts nroff back in its default  mode.   It
causes nroff to fill and justify lines of text.  Once again,
each line comes all the way to the right margin.
```

SECTION HEADINGS

Section headings are underlined titles. They start at the left margin and are generally less than one line long. A section heading command begins a section heading. Any type of paragraph command or a second section heading command terminates a section heading.

There are two types of section headings. A standard section heading is initiated by an **.SH** command and a numbered section heading is initiated by an **.NH** command. An example of a standard section heading follows.

Input file

```
.SH
Section Heading
.LP
A section heading is underlined.
It can be as long as you want.
It is terminated by a paragraph command
or another section heading command.
```

Output text

```
Section Heading

A section heading is underlined.  It can be as long  as  you
want.   It  is  terminated by a paragraph command or another
section heading command.
```

A numbered section heading is a section heading preceded by a number indicating the level of the heading. A fourth level heading could be preceded by a number such as 3.2.4.1, while a second level heading could be preceded by 1.5.

An **.NH** command, followed by a level number, generates a numbered section heading. The level number can range from one to five. **nroff** produces a level one heading if you do not specify a level number. Each subsequent **.NH** command automatically increments the appropriate section number, as shown in the following example.

Input file

```
.NH
Parts
.NH 2
Screws
.NH 3
Sheet Metal Screws
.NH 3
Wood Screws
.NH 4
Phillips Head
.NH 4
Slotted Head
.NH 3
Specially Hardened Screws
.NH 2
Nails
.NH 2
Glass
```

Output text

```
1.  Parts

1.1.  Screws

1.1.1.  Sheet Metal Screws

1.1.2.  Wood Screws

1.1.2.1.  Phillips Head

1.1.2.2.  Slotted Head

1.1.3.  Specially Hardened Screws

1.2.  Nails

1.3.  Glass
```

EMPHASIS

The **.I** (italic) command underlines output text for emphasis. **nroff** accepts the **.I** command with or without an argument. Without an argument, it underlines more than one word. The **.R** (roman) command stops the underlining.

With an argument, the **.I** command underlines a single word—the word you give as an argument. You do not need an **.R** command when you use the **.I** command with an argument.

Input file

```
This is an example of the use of
the .I command.
It
.I will
underline text.
If you want to underline more than
a single word,
.I
do not give the .I command an argument.
.R
Use the .R command to return to text
that is not underlined.
```

Output text

```
This is an example of the use of the .I   command.   It  will
underline text.  If you want to underline more than a single
word, do not give the .I command an argument.   Use   the   .R
command to return to text that is not underlined.
```

PAGE LAYOUT

When used with the –ms macros, nroff automatically lays out each page of output text with the page number at the top and the date at the bottom. This section covers the commands that change this layout, add running titles, and produce footnotes.

The Date

The date normally appears centered at the bottom of each page of output. If you don't want the date in the output text, use an .ND (no date) command near the beginning of the input file. If you want a date other than today's date, use a .DA command such as the following.

```
.DA March 19, 1953
```

Headers and Footers

nroff uses six variable strings to hold six running titles for each page. The titles are positioned at the left, center, and right of the bottom of every page and the left, center, and right of the top of all but the first page. nroff uses the page number between hyphens (–5–) as the top center running title and today's date as the bottom center running title.

The names of the six running title variables are shown below. The default values are given in parentheses.

LH left header
CH center header (page number)
RH right header

LF left footer
CF center footer (today's date)
RF right footer

You can alter the contents of these strings by giving a .ds (define string) command with the name and desired contents of the string as arguments. The following command causes FIRST DRAFT to be printed at the lower right of each page.

```
.ds RF FIRST DRAFT
```

The following command causes **nroff** to set the center header to a null string and not print the page number at the top center of the pages.

```
.ds CH
```

Page Numbers

You can place the page number in any of the headers or footers. Use a percent sign within the string to represent the page number. The first of the following commands places the page number at the upper right of each page, after the word **page**. The second command places the page number at the lower left, followed by a period.

```
.ds RH page %
```

```
.ds LF %.
```

The following example summarizes the use of the **nroff** commands covered in this section.

Input file

```
.PP
.ds LH left head
.ds RH right head
.ds LF left foot
.ds RF page %
.PP
This example demonstrates the use of the headers and footers.
The headers do not appear on page one, but can be found on all
subsequent pages.
.PP
The date automatically appears as the center head.
A paragraph command is used to separate the paragraphs and a .bp
command ends the page.
.bp
.PP
This is the start of another page.
Because it is not the first page, the headers appear at the top of
it.
.PP
The page number automatically appears as the center head and also
appears as the right foot because it was specified at the beginning
of the input file.
```

Output text

This example demonstrates the use of the headers and
footers.   The headers do not appear on page one, but can be
found on all subsequent pages.

The date automatically appears as the center head.   A
paragraph command is used to separate the paragraphs and a
.bp command ends the page.

Output text (continued)

```
    left head                       - 2 -                        right head

          This is the start of another page.  Because it  is  not
     the first page, the headers appear at the top of it.

          The page number automatically  appears  as  the  center
     head  and  also  appears  as  the  right foot because it was
     specified at the beginning of the input file.

















    left foot                   June 8, 1983                       page 2
```

KEEPS, FOOTNOTES, AND DISPLAYS

Keeps, footnotes, and displays are blocks of text that are normally treated as integral units. A keep is a block of text that **nroff** does not break between pages. A footnote is a block of text that **nroff** puts at the bottom of a page. A display is a block of text that **nroff** does not fill or justify.

Keeps

A keep is a block of text that **nroff** keeps on one page. It can be a chart, table, or paragraph that must appear intact. You can define a keep by placing the appropriate **nroff** commands before and after the block of text in the input file.

Ending a Keep. Use the **.KE** command to mark the end of any type of keep. If you forget to end a keep, the output text that **nroff** produces will not be what you intended.

Standard Keeps. When **nroff** finds in the input file a block of text that you have specified as a standard keep, it places the text on the current page only if there is room for the entire block. If there is no room, **nroff** starts a new page and places the block of text there.

Mark the beginning of a standard keep with a **.KS** command and the end with a **.KE** command. There is an example of a standard keep following the discussion of footnotes.

Floating Keeps. A floating keep is similar to a standard keep; it is a block of text that **nroff** keeps on one page. However, if there is no room for a floating keep on the current page, **nroff** sets aside the block of text that is defined as the keep. **nroff** then finishes filling the page with text from the input file that follows the keep. When the page is full, **nroff** places the keep at the top of the next page and continues with the text from the previous page.

The placement of a floating keep can change the order of the output text. It is useful for a table or chart that is not context-sensitive, when you do not want a blank space at the bottom of a page.

A floating keep starts with a **.KF** command and ends with a **.KE** command.

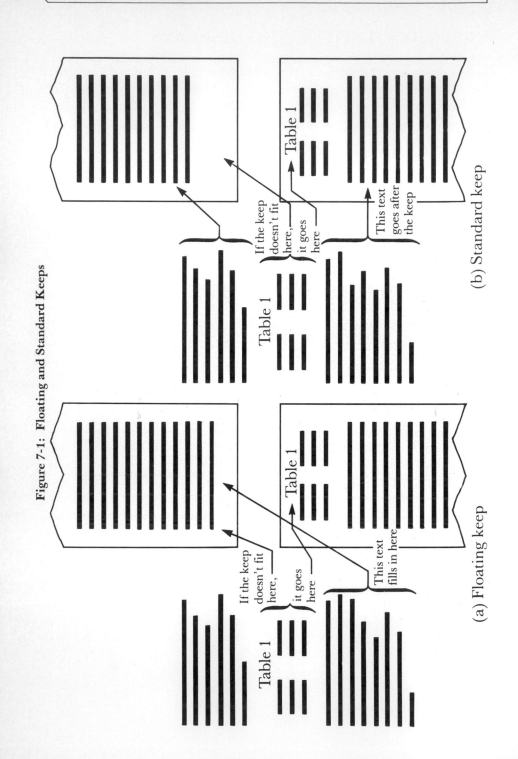

Figure 7-1: Floating and Standard Keeps

If the keep doesn't fit here, it goes here

Table 1

This text goes after the keep

(b) Standard keep

If the keep doesn't fit here, it goes here

Table 1

This text fills in here

(a) Floating keep

Footnotes

A footnote is a reference to a block of text that is located at the bottom of the page. You can place a footnote in the input file immediately after the reference to which it refers. **nroff** positions the footnote properly at the bottom of the page.

A footnote begins with an **.FS** command and ends with an **.FE** command. Refer to the following example.

Input file

```
.PP
.ds LH TITLE OF THIS PAPER
.ds CH
.ds CF - % -
.PP
This is the body of the text on the page.
This is the body of the text on the page.
This is the body of the text on the page.
This is the body of the text on the page.
.PP
This is the body of the text on the page.
This is the body of the text on the page.
This is the body of the text on the page.*
.FS
*This is a footnote.
It is placed at the bottom of the page.
.FE
This is the body of the text on the page.
.PP
This is the body of the text on the page.
This is the body of the text on the page.
This is the body of the text on the page.
This is the body of the text on the page.
.PP
       .

       .

       .

This is the body of the text on the page.
This is the body of the text on the page.
This is the body of the text on the page.
```

```
This is the body of the text on the page.
This is the body of the text on the page.
.PP
.KS
This is a special paragraph that
is not to be split between two pages.
The regular keep command insures
that the text is not divided.
If the text between the .KS and .KE
commands will not fit entirely on
the current page, nroff will put it,
as a block, on the next page.
.KE
.PP
This is the body of the text on the page.
This is the body of the text on the page.
This is the body of the text on the page.
This is the body of the text on the page.
.PP
This is the body of the text on the page.
This is the body of the text on the page.
This is the body of the text on the page.
This is the body of the text on the page.
.PP
This is the body of the text on the page.
This is the body of the text on the page.
This is the body of the text on the page.
This is the body of the text on the page.
```

Output text

```
        This is the body of the text on the page.  This is  the
body  of the text on the page.  This is the body of the text
on the page.  This is the body of the text on the page.

        This is the body of the text on the page.  This is  the
body  of the text on the page.  This is the body of the text
on the page.* This is the body of the text on the page.

        This is the body of the text on the page.  This is  the
body  of the text on the page.  This is the body of the text
on the page.  This is the body of the text on the page.




                             .
                             .
                             .




        This is the body of the text on the page.  This is  the
body  of the text on the page.  This is the body of the text
on the page.  This is the body of  the  text  on  the  page.
This is the body of the text on the page.


        _____
*This is a footnote.  It is placed at the bottom of the
page.



                           - 1 -
```

Output text (continued)

```
TITLE OF THIS PAPER

This is a special paragraph that is not to be split  between
two  pages.   The regular keep command insures that the text
is not divided.  If the text between the .KS  and  .KE  com-
mands  will not fit entirely on the current page, nroff will
put it, as a block, on the next page.

     This is the body of the text on the page.  This is  the
body  of the text on the page.  This is the body of the text
on the page.  This is the body of the text on the page.

     This is the body of the text on the page.  This is  the
body  of the text on the page.  This is the body of the text
on the page.  This is the body of the text on the page.

     This is the body of the text on the page.  This is  the
body  of the text on the page.  This is the body of the text
on the page.  This is the body of the text on the page.




                          - 2 -
```

Displays

A display is a table, chart, or other block of text that **nroff** transfers unchanged from the input file to the output text. **nroff** will not fill or justify a display, but copies it from the input file to the output text on a line-by-line basis.

As with all blocks of text, you must mark the beginning and end of each display with a command. There are three types of displays, each beginning with its own variation of the display command. All displays end with a **.DE** command.

nroff has two sets of display commands. One set treats each display as a keep. These commands are used in the examples in this section. The other set does not attempt to keep the text within a display on a single page. The names of these display commands are mentioned in the text.

Standard Display. A standard display copies each line from the input file to the output text, indenting all lines five (SPACE)s from the left margin. Begin a standard display that you want to keep on a single page with a **.DS** command. This display ends with a **.DE** command, as do all displays. A standard display that does *not* keep the text together on a page begins with an **.ID** command.

The following example shows how a standard display works. **nroff** does not compress any of the (SPACE)s from the input file and it does not fill or justify the lines. Each line in the output text is just as it appeared in the input file, except that **nroff** has placed five (SPACE)s before it.

Input file

```
.DS
This is
     a
     standard display.
All the lines are indented
from the
left margin.
.DE
```

Output text

```
        This is
            a
            standard display.
        All the lines are indented
        from the
        left margin.
```

Flush Left Display. A flush left display is similar to a standard display, except that **nroff** does not indent the lines in the output text. Begin a flush left display that you want to keep on a single page with a **.DS L** command. Use an **.LD** command if you want a flush left display that does *not* keep the text together on one page.

Input file

```
.DS L
This
is a flush
        left
            display.
All the lines
are
flush with the left margin.
.DE
```

Output text

```
    This
    is a flush
            left
                display.
    All the lines
    are
    flush with the left margin.
```

Centered Display. nroff centers each line in the output text of a centered display.

A centered display that **nroff** keeps on a single page begins with a **.DS C** command. A **.CD** command begins a centered display without a keep.

Input file

```
.DS C
This is
a
centered display.
All the lines
are
centered.
.DE
```

Output text

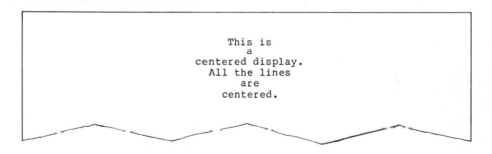

```
            This is
               a
       centered display.
        All the lines
             are
         centered.
```

CHANGING DIMENSIONS

This section tells you how to change dimensions for vertical spacing of text and paragraphs, line length of text and footnotes, indention of standard and quoted paragraphs, and margins at the top and bottom of the page. The −ms macros store all these dimensions in number registers. Uppercase letters are used as register names to indicate that the registers are used by the −ms macros. You can change the value of a number register by using an nroff command (**.nr**) followed by the name of the register you want to change and the new value. The following command changes the line length to four inches.

```
.nr LL 4i
```

When you change the value of a register using **–ms** commands, nroff does not respond immediately. For example, the line length command shown above does not take effect until after the next paragraph command. Use the plain nroff commands listed in the chapter summary if you want an immediate change.

Different units of measure are used for different dimensions. Some dimensions, such as line length, use inches; others use characters or points. The place each change takes effect and the unit of measure that each command expects are covered in the following paragraphs.

Vertical Spacing: Text and Paragraphs

Effect   When nroff starts processing the input file, it generates single-spaced output text. This is the vertical spacing of the text. You can change to double- or triple-spaced output by changing the value of the text vertical spacing register.

nroff places one blank line before each paragraph. This is the vertical spacing of the paragraphs. You can change this to two or three blank lines by changing the value of the paragraph vertical spacing register.

Unit of measure   nroff measures vertical spacing in points. The symbol for points is **p**. Each line of single-spaced text occupies 12 points.

When the change takes effect   When you change the vertical spacing of the text or of the paragraphs using an **–ms** macro, the change does not take effect until the next paragraph command.

Names of the registers   The name of the register that stores the text vertical spacing measurement is **VS**. nroff stores the paragraph vertical spacing measurement in the **PD** register.

Examples   The following commands change the text vertical spacing to double space, triple space, and then back to the default—single space.

```
.nr VS 24p
.nr VS 36p
.nr VS 12p
```

The following commands change the paragraph vertical spacing to two lines, three lines, and back to the default — one line.

```
.nr PD 24p
.nr PD 36p
.nr PD 12p
```

Line Length: Text and Footnotes

Effect   A default full-length line of output text is six inches long. A footnote is five and one-half inches long. You can change these dimensions by changing the values of the line length and footnote length registers.

Unit of measure   nroff measures line and footnote length in inches. The symbol for inches is **i**.

When the change takes effect   When you change the line length, the change takes effect at the next paragraph. A change in the footnote length takes effect at the next footnote reference (**.FS** command).

Names of the registers   nroff stores the line length in the **LL** register and the footnote length in the **FL** register.

Examples   The first two commands change the line length to four and then to three and one-half inches. The next commands change the footnote length to six and one-half inches and three inches.

```
.nr LL 4i
.nr LL 3.5i

.nr FL 6.5i
.nr FL 3i
```

Paragraph Indention

Effect   nroff indents the first line of a standard paragraph and the entire body of an indented paragraph five (SPACE)s from the left margin. It indents the entire body of a block quote paragraph five (SPACE)s from both the left and right margins. The values of the standard paragraph indention register (standard and indented paragraphs) and the block quote paragraph indention register control these dimensions.

Unit of measure   The unit of measure for indention is the character. The symbol for characters is **n**.

When the change takes effect   When you change either of the paragraph indention registers, the change takes effect at the next corresponding paragraph command.

Names of the registers   The name of the standard paragraph indention register is **PI**; the block quote paragraph indention register is **QI**.

Examples   The first two commands change the indention for standard and indented paragraphs to ten characters and then to 17 characters. The next two change the amount of indention for block quote paragraphs to 20 and then to 25 characters (from both the left and right margins).

```
.nr PI  10n
.nr PI  17n

.nr QI  20n
.nr QI  25n
```

Top and Bottom Margins

Effect   nroff starts with a top and bottom margin of one inch on each page. You can change the size of these margins by changing the values of the top margin and bottom margin registers.

Unit of measure   The top and bottom margins are measured in inches. The symbol for inches is **i**.

When the change takes effect   Changes to either the top or bottom margin take effect on the next page.

Names of the registers   nroff stores the values of the top and bottom margins in the **HM** and **FM** registers respectively.

Examples   The first two commands change the top margin to three inches and the bottom margin to four inches. The next two commands change the top margin to two and one-half inches and the bottom margin to one-half inch.

```
.nr HM 3i
.nr FM 4i

.nr HM 2.5i
.nr FM 0.5i
```

SUMMARY

This summary reviews the commands covered in this chapter, plus some additional ones. After describing how to call **nroff**, the summary describes plain **nroff** commands. These commands work with or without a macro package. In general, when macro and plain **nroff** commands are combined in the same input file, the plain commands will take effect sooner than the macro commands.

Following the plain commands, the **–ms** macro package commands are reviewed. Finally, commands for a different macro package, **–me**, are introduced. Although you can use plain **nroff** commands with the **–me** package, you cannot mix commands from the **–ms** and **–me** macro packages.

Calling nroff

The following command lines use **nroff** with the **–ms** macro package to format the file named **ntext**. If you are using the **–me** macro package, replace **–ms** with **–me** on the command line. If you are not using a macro package, omit **–ms** from the command line altogether. The command line below displays the output text on the terminal.

```
$ nroff —ms ntext
 .
 .
 .
```

The next command line uses a pipe to send the output text to the printer. The job is executed in the background.

```
$ nroff —ms ntext | lpr &
$
```

Plain nroff Commands

All commands must start at the left margin of the input file. A command line
starts with a (SPACE), an apostrophe, or a period.

Breaks

Command	Break line and . . .
.br	break line, nothing else
.sp n	leave **n** blank lines
.ce	center next line
.ce n	center next **n** lines
.bp	begin new page

Margins

Command	Effect
.na	do not justify lines
.ad b	justify lines
.nf	do not fill lines
.fi	fill lines
.in[±]xi	adjust left margin to the right (+) or left (−) **x** inches (if + or − is not used, set the indent absolutely to **x** inches)
.ti [±]xi	for the next line only, adjust left margin as above

Headings

Command	Effect
.tl 'left'center'right'	produce a three part heading (see page 171)

Changing Dimensions

Command	Effect
.ls 1	single space text
.ls 2	double space text
.ls 3	triple space text
.ll [±]xi	adjust line length to the right (+) or left (−) **x** inches (if + or − is not used, set the line length absolutely to **x** inches)

Hyphenation

Command	Effect
.nh	turn off hyphenation
.hy	turn on hyphenation

−ms Macro Commands

All commands must start at the left margin of the input file. A command line starts with a (SPACE), an apostrophe, or a period.

Paragraphs

Command	Type of Paragraph
.PP	standard, first line indented
.LP	left block, all lines flush left
.IP	indented, all lines indented
.IP arg	hanging indent, **arg** at left margin
.IP arg1 n	nonstandard hanging indent, **arg1** at left margin, **n** defines number of characters for indent
.QP	block quote, all lines indented left and right

Margins

Command	Effect
.RS	move left margin 5 (SPACE)s to the right
.RE	move left margin 5 (SPACE)s to the left

Headings

Command	Effect
.SH	following text is an underlined section heading
.NH	following text is a numbered, underlined section heading
.NH n	following text is a numbered, underlined section heading at level **n**
.ND	no date
.ds LH arg	**arg** is left header (all pages but the first)
.ds CH arg	**arg** is center header (all pages but the first)
.ds RH arg	**arg** is right header (all pages but the first)
.ds LF arg	**arg** is left footer (all pages)
.ds CF arg	**arg** is center footer (all pages)
.ds RF arg	**arg** is right footer (all pages)

Keeps, Footnotes, and Displays

Command	Effect
.KE	end any keep
.KS	start standard keep
.KF	start floating keep
.FS	start footnote
.FE	end footnote
.DE	end any display
.DS	start standard display with keep
.ID	start standard display, no keep
.DS L	start flush left display with keep
.LD	start flush left display, no keep
.DS C	start centered display with keep
.CD	start centered display, no keep

Changing Dimensions

Command	Effect
.nr VS 12p	single spaced text
.nr VS 24p	double spaced text
.nr VS 36p	triple spaced text
.nr PD 12p	single spaced paragraphs
.nr PD 24p	double spaced paragraphs
.nr PD 36p	triple spaced paragraphs
.nr LL xi	set line length to **x** inches
.nr FL xi	set footnote length to **x** inches
.nr PI xn	set paragraph indention to **x** characters
.nr QI xn	set block quote paragraph indention to **x** characters
.nr HM xi	set header margin to **x** inches
.nr FM xi	set footer margin to **x** inches

Underlining

Command	Effect
. l	underline following text
.R	turn off underlining
. l arg	underline **arg**

–me Macro Commands

All commands must start at the left margin of the input file. A command line starts with a (SPACE), an apostrophe, or a period.

The following list of commands applies to the **–me** macro package. As with the **–ms** macro package, the commands can be combined with regular nroff commands. Commands from the two macro packages cannot be combined in a single input file.

Paragraphs

Command	Type of Paragraph
. pp	standard, first line indented
. l p	left block, all lines flush left
. i p	indented, all lines indented
. i p arg	handing indent, **arg** at left margin
. i p arg1 n	nonstandard hanging indent, **arg1** in left margin, **n** defines number of characters for indent

Headings. The **–me** macro package produces three-part headings. The argument to a heading command is a string of the form ′left′center′right′. The string between the first two delimiters (′) is positioned flush with the left margin; the string between the second and third delimiters is centered; the final string is positioned flush with the right margin.

Command	Effect
.he ′left′center′right′	three part header printed on every page
.fo ′left′center′right′	three part footer printed on every page
.oh ′left′center′right′	three part header printed on odd numbered pages
.of ′left′center′right′	three part footer printed on odd numbered pages

Command	Effect
.eh 'left'center'right'	three part header printed on even numbered pages
.ef 'left'center'right'	three part footer printed on even numbered pages
.hx	no header or footer on next page only

Block Quotes, Footnotes, and Displays

Command	Effect
.(q	begin block quote, all lines indented left and right
.)q	end block quote
.(f	start footnote (** represents footnote number)
.)f	end footnote (** represents footnote number)
.)b	end any display (with keep)
.(b	start standard display, with keep
.(b L	start flush left display, with keep
.(b C	start centered display, with keep
.)l	end any display (no keep)
.(l	start standard display, no keep
.(l L	start flush left display, no keep
.(l C	start centered display, no keep
.)z	end any display (floating keep)
.(z l	start standard display, floating keep
.(z	start flush left display, floating keep
.(z C	start centered display, floating keep

8

THE BOURNE SHELL AS A PROGRAMMING LANGUAGE

The Bourne Shell is both a command interpreter and a high-level programming language. As a command interpreter, it processes commands that you enter in response to its prompt. When you use the Shell as a programming language, it processes groups of commands stored in files called *Shell scripts*. This chapter explains how to write and execute Shell scripts, and explores aspects of Shell programming such as variables, control structures, processes, executable files, and signals. Although this chapter is primarily about the Bourne Shell, much of the theory explained in it, and the sections on "Executable Files" and "Command Separation and Grouping," also apply to the C Shell.

Shell scripts allow you to group command lines together so that a single command can execute them. These files of commands make it possible for any user to initiate a complex series of tasks, or to execute a repetitive procedure simply and quickly. You can redirect input and output within a Shell script to combine standard UNIX utility programs to fulfill your specific needs.

EXECUTABLE FILES

An executable file is one that you or another user has permission to execute. It typically contains a compiled program (e.g., **ed, who,** or an application program) or a Shell script. This section discusses how to use the **chmod** utility to make a Shell script executable.

Shell Scripts

The **com1** file (below) is an example of a Shell script. It contains a legal Shell command line. As it stands, you cannot execute the **com1** file because you do not have execute access permission to it.

```
$ cat com1
echo 'This is the output of com1.'

$ com1
com1: cannot execute
$
```

The Shell does not recognize **com1** as an executable file, and issues an error message when you try to execute it. Your system may display a different message than the one shown above.

Execute Access

In order to execute a Shell script, you must have execute access permission to the file containing the script. Execute access is similar to read or write access—only it tells the Shell that the user, group, or public has permission to execute the file. It also implies that the contents of the file is executable.

The **chmod** utility changes the access privileges associated with a file. Below, **ls** displays permission of **com1** before and after **chmod** gives the owner execute access privilege to the file.

```
$ ls -l com1
-rw⃞rw-r-- 1 alex        36 Aug 22 10:55 com1

$ chmod u+x com1

$ ls -l com1
-rw⃞rw-r-- 1 alex        36 Aug 22 10:55 com1

$ com1
This is the output of com1.
$
```

The first **ls** displays a hyphen as the fourth character, indicating that the owner does not have execute access permission to the file. **chmod** uses two arguments to give the owner execute access permission. The **u+x** indicates that **chmod** is to add (+) execute access permission (x) for the owner (u). The second argument is the name of the file. The second **ls** shows an **x** in the fourth position, indicating that the owner now has execute access permission.

Finally, the Shell executes the file when its name is given as a command. If other users are going to execute the file, group or public access privileges must also be changed. For more information on access permissions, refer to **ls** and **chmod** in Part II, and "Access Permissions" in Chapter 4.

VARIABLES

The Shell uses string variables (variables that are able to take on the value of a string of characters) to represent numbers as well as text. There are three types of variables: *user variables, Shell variables,* and *Shell read-only variables.* You can declare, initialize, read, and change user variables from the command line or from a Shell script. The Shell declares and initializes Shell variables, but you can read and change them. The Shell declares and initializes read-only Shell variables, which you can read, but not change.

User Variables

You can declare any sequence of nonblank characters as the name of a variable. The first line in the example below declares the variable **person** and initializes it with the string alex. **The equal sign must not be preceded or followed by a** (SPACE).

```
$ person=alex

$ echo person
person

$ echo $person
alex
$
```

The second line shows that **person** does not represent alex. The string person is echoed as person. The Shell only substitutes the value of a variable when you precede the name of the variable with a dollar sign. The final command (above) displays the value of the variable **person**.

As shown in the following examples, you must quote a string with imbedded (SPACE)s in order to assign it to a variable.

```
$ person='alex and jenny'

$ echo $person
alex and jenny
$
```

Variable Substitution

The echo utility copies its arguments to the standard output. The command **echo $person** displays the value of the variable **person**. echo does not display $person because the Shell does not pass $person to echo as an argument. Because of the leading dollar sign, the Shell recognizes that $person is the name of a variable, *substitutes* the value of the variable, and passes that value to echo. echo displays the value of the variable, not its name, never knowing that you called it with a variable. The Shell would have passed echo the same command line, and echo would have displayed the same string, if you had given the command **echo alex and jenny**.

You can prevent the Shell from substituting the value of a variable by quoting the leading dollar sign. Double quotation marks will not prevent the substitution.

```
$ echo $person
alex and jenny

$ echo \$person
$person

$ echo '$person'
$person

$ echo "$person"
alex and jenny
$
```

Read-only User Variables

The next example declares the variable **person** to be read-only. You must assign a value to a variable *before* you declare it to be read-only, as you cannot change its value after the declaration. When you attempt to change the value of a read-only variable, the Shell displays an error message.

```
$ readonly person

$ person=helen
person: is read only

$ readonly
readonly person
$
```

A Readonly command without an argument displays a list of read-only variables.

Read-only Shell Variables

A read-only Shell variable is similar to a read-only user variable, except that the Shell assigns it a value.

Name of the Calling Program. The Shell stores the name of the command that you use to call a program in the variable named **$0**. It is variable number zero because it appears before the first argument on the command line.

```
$ cat abc
echo 'The name of the command used'
echo 'to execute this Shell script was' $0

$ abc
The name of the command used
to execute this Shell script was abc
$
```

The Shell script above uses **echo** to verify the name of the program you are executing. The **abc** file must be executable (use **chmod**) before this example will work.

Arguments. The Shell stores the first nine command line arguments in the variables **$1, $2, . . ., $9**.

```
$ cat display_args
echo 'The first five command line'
echo 'arguments are' $1 $2 $3 $4 $5

$ display_args jenny alex helen
The first five command line
arguments are jenny alex helen
$
```

The Shell script above displays the first five command line arguments. The variables representing arguments that were not present on the command line, **$4** and **$5**, have a null value.

The variable **$*** represents all the command line arguments, as the **display-all** program demonstrates.

```
$ cat display_all
echo $*

$ display_all helen jenny alex barbara
helen jenny alex barbara
$
```

The variable **$#** contains the number of arguments on the command line. This string variable represents a decimal number. You can use the **expr** utility (see Part II) to perform computations involving this number.

```
$ cat num_args
echo 'This Shell script was called with'
echo $# 'arguments.'

$ numargs helen alex jenny
This Shell script was called with
3 arguments.
$
```

Shift   The Shift command promotes each of the command line arguments. The second argument (which was represented by **$2**) becomes the first (now represented by **$1**), the third becomes the second, up through the last argument becoming the next to last.

You can access only the first nine command line arguments (as **$1** through **$9**) from a Shell script. The Shift command gives you access to the tenth command line argument by making it the ninth, and makes the first unavailable. Successive Shift commands make additional arguments available. There is, however, no "Unshift" command to bring back the arguments that are no longer available.

```
$ cat demo_shift
echo 'arg1=' $1 'arg2=' $2 'arg3=' $3
shift
echo 'arg1=' $1 'arg2=' $2 'arg3=' $3
shift
echo 'arg1=' $1 'arg2=' $2 'arg3=' $3

$ demo_shift alice helen jenny
arg1= alice arg2= helen arg3= jenny
arg1= helen arg2= jenny arg3=
arg1= jenny arg2= arg3=
$
```

The example above calls the **demo_shift** program with three arguments. The program displays the arguments and shifts them repeatedly, until the third argument (**jenny**) becomes the first argument.

Shell Variables

The Shell declares and initializes variables that determine the prompt you receive, the home directory that **cd** uses, and the search path the Shell follows when you give it a command. You can assign new values to these variables from the command line or from the **.profile** file in your home directory.

HOME.   By default, your home directory is your working directory when you first log on. The system administrator determines your home directory when you establish your account, and stores this information in the **/etc/passwd** file. When you log on, the Shell gets the pathname of your home directory from this file and assigns it to the variable **HOME**.

When given without an argument, **cd** makes the directory whose name is stored in **HOME** the working directory. If you change the value of **HOME** to a different directory pathname, **cd** will make the new directory the working directory.

```
$ echo $HOME
/usr/jenny

$ cd
$ pwd
/usr/jenny

$ HOME=/usr/jenny/literature
$ cd
$ pwd
/usr/jenny/literature
$
```

The example above shows the value of the **HOME** variable and the effect of the **cd** utility. After you execute **cd** without an argument, the pathname of the working directory is the same as the value of **HOME**. After assigning a different pathname to **HOME**, **cd** makes the working directory correspond to the new pathname.

PATH.   When you give the Shell a command, it searches through the file structure for the program you want to execute. The Shell looks in several directories for a file that has the same name as the command and for which you have execute access permission. The **PATH** Shell variable controls this search path. The first directory the Shell normally searches is the working directory. If the program is not there, the search continues with the **/bin** and the **/usr/bin** directories. These directories usually contain executable programs. If the Shell does not find the program in any of these directories, the Shell reports that it cannot find the program.

If you use the absolute pathname of a program as a command, the Shell does not use **PATH**. If the executable file does not have the exact pathname that you specify, the Shell reports that it cannot find the program.

The **PATH** variable specifies the directories in the order the Shell is to search them. Each must be separated from the next by a colon. The following command causes the search for an executable file to start with the working directory [specified by a null string (nothing) preceding the first colon]. If the Shell fails to find the file in the working directory, it consults the **/user/jenny/bin**, **/bin**, and **/user/bin** directories.

```
$ PATH=:/usr/jenny/bin:/bin:/usr/bin
$
```

If each user is given a unique search path, each user can execute a different program by giving the same command. Because the search stops when it is satisfied, you can use the name of a standard UNIX utility program for your own program by including the program in one of the first directories that the Shell searches.

PS1. The Shell prompt lets you know that the Shell is waiting for you to give it a command. The Bourne Shell prompt used in the examples throughout this book is a dollar sign followed by a (SPACE). Your prompt may differ. The Shell stores the prompt as a string in the **PS1** variable. When you change the value of this variable, the appearance of your prompt changes. The following example shows how to change the prompt to two right braces followed by a (SPACE).

```
$ PS1='}} '

}} echo test
test
}}
```

PS2. Prompt string two is a secondary prompt and is stored in **PS2**. On the first line of the following example, an unclosed quoted string follows an **echo** command. The Shell assumes that the command is not finished and, on the second line, gives the default secondary prompt (>). This prompt indicates that the Shell is waiting for the user to continue the command. The Shell waits until it sees the apostrophe that closes the string, and then executes the command.

```
$ echo 'demonstration of prompt string
> two'
demonstration of prompt string
two

$ PS2='secondary prompt: '

$ echo 'this demonstrates
secondary prompt: prompt string two'
this demonstrates
prompt string two
$
```

The second command in the preceding example changes the secondary prompt to secondary prompt: followed by a (SPACE). A multiline echo command demonstrates the new prompt.

IFS. You can always use a (SPACE) or (TAB) to separate fields on the command line. When you assign **IFS** (inter-field separator) the value of another character, you can also use this character to separate fields.

The **num_args** program (page 179) reports the number of arguments it was called with. Below, it demonstrates how setting **IFS** can affect interpretation of a command line.

```
$ num_args a:b:c:d
This Shell script was called with
1 arguments.

$ IFS=:

$ num_args a:b:c:d
This Shell script was called with
4 arguments.
$
```

The first time **num_args** is executed, the Shell interprets the string a:b:c:d as a single argument. After **IFS** is set to : the Shell interprets the same string as four separate arguments.

Reading User Input

The Read command enables a Shell script to read input from its standard input. The following program shows how Read works.

```
$ cat read1
echo -n 'Go ahead: '
read firstline
echo 'You entered:' $firstline

$ read1
Go ahead: This is the line I'm entering.
You entered: This is the line I'm entering.
$
```

The first line of the **read1** program prompts you to enter a line of text. The second line reads the text into the variable **firstline**. The third line verifies the action of the Read command by displaying the value of **firstline**.

The **read2** Shell script shown below prompts for a command line and then reads it into the variable **command**. The Shell script then executes the command line by placing **command** on a line by itself. When the Shell executes the Shell script, it replaces the variable with its value and executes the command line as though it were part of the Shell script.

```
$ cat read2
echo -n 'Enter command: '
read command
$command
echo 'Thanks'

$ read2
Enter command: echo Please display this message.
Please display this message.
Thanks

$ read2
Enter command: who
alex      tty5m    Oct 30 07:50
scott     tty7     Oct 20 11:54
Thanks
$
```

The first time **read2** is executed, it reads a command line that calls the echo utility. The Shell executes the command and then displays Thanks. Next, **read2** reads a command line that executes the **who** utility.

PROCESSES

A process is the means by which the UNIX system executes a command. When you give a command, you initiate a process. The operating system can also initiate processes.

Process Structure

In the same manner as the file structure, the process structure is hierarchical. It has parents, children, and even a *root*. A parent process *forks* (or *spawns*) a child process which in turn can fork other processes. The UNIX operating system begins execution with a single process, PID number 1. This process holds the same position in the process structure as the root directory does in the file structure. It is the ancestor of all processes. It forks a **login** process for each terminal. Each of these processes becomes a Shell process when a user logs on.

Executing a Command

When you give the Shell a command, it usually forks a child process to execute the command. While the child process is executing the command, the parent process *sleeps*. While a process is sleeping, it does not use any computer time; it remains inactive, waiting to wake up. When the child process finishes executing the command, it dies. The parent process (which is running the Shell) wakes up and prompts you for another command.

When you request that the Shell run a process in the background (by ending a command with an **&**), the Shell forks a child process without going to sleep and without waiting for the child process to run to completion. The parent process, executing the Shell, reports the PID number of the child and prompts for another command. The child process runs in the background, independent of its parent.

Process Identification

The UNIX system assigns a unique process identification (PID) number at the inception of each process. As long as a process is in existence, it keeps the same PID number. During one session, the same process is always executing the login Shell. When you fork a new process—for example, when you use an editor, the new (child) process has a different PID number than its parent process. When you return to the login Shell, it is still being executed by same process, and has the same PID number, as when you logged on.

The Shell stores the PID number of the process that is executing it in the **$$** variable. In the following interaction, **echo** displays the value of this variable and then uses the **ps** utility to confirm its value. The line of the **ps** display with −**sh** in the CMD column refers to the process running the Shell. The column headed by PID lists the process number.

```
$ echo $$
14437

$ ps
  PID TTY TIME CMD
14565 14  0:02 ps
14437 14  0:06 -sh
```

The PID numbers of the Shell are the same in both cases because they both identify the same process. In the first case, the Shell substitutes its own PID number for $$. The Shell makes this substitution *before* it forks a new process to execute **echo**. Thus, **echo** displays the PID number of the Shell that called it, not of the process that is executing it. In the second case, the **ps** utility lists all of your processes, including the one that is executing the Shell.

The next interaction shows that the process running the Shell forked (is the parent of) the process running **ps**. When you call **ps** with the −**l** option, it displays more information. The column headed PPID lists the PID number of the *parent* of each of the processes. From the PID and PPID columns, you can see that the process running the Shell (PID 14437) is the parent of the process running **ps** (PID 14566). The parent PID number of **ps** is the same as the PID number of the Shell.

```
$ ps -l
F S UID   PID  PPID CPU PRI NICE  ADDR  SZ WCHAN TTY TIME CMD
1 R 107 14566 14437  97  20   20   5e7  11        14  0:02 ps -l
1 S 107 14437     1   0  30   20   59a  10  e2b6  14  0:06 -sh
$
```

When you give another **ps −l** command, you can see that the Shell is still being run by the same process, but that it forked another process to run **ps**.

```
$ ps -l
F S UID   PID  PPID CPU PRI NICE  ADDR  SZ WCHAN TTY TIME CMD
1 R 107 14708 14437  91  20   20   3ae  11        14  0:02 ps -l
1 S 107 14437     1   0  30   20   4e4  10  e2b6  14  0:07 -sh
$
```

The **$!** variable has the value of the PID number of the last process that you ran in the background. The next example executes **ps** as a background task and then uses **echo** to display the value of **$!**.

```
$ ps &
14727
  PID TTY TIME CMD
14727 14  0:02 ps
14437 14  0:07 -sh

$ echo $!
14727
$
```

When you execute a program in the background, the Shell displays the PID number of the background process and then gives you a prompt. Above, this PID number is confirmed by **ps** and again by the **echo $!** command.

Exit Status

When a process terminates, it passes an *exit status* to its parent process. The exit status is also referred to as a *condition code* or *return code*. The Shell stores the exit status of the last command in the Shell read-only variable **$?**.

By convention, a nonzero exit status represents a false value and means that the command failed. A zero is true and means that the command was successful.

You can specify the exit status that a Shell script is to return by using an Exit command, followed by a number, to terminate the script. The number specifies the exit status, as shown in the following example.

```
$ cat es
echo 'This program returns an exit'
echo 'status of 7.'
exit 7

$ es
This program returns an exit
status of 7.

$ echo $?
7

$ echo $?
0
$
```

The **es** Shell script displays a message and then terminates execution with an Exit command that returns an exit status of seven. echo displays the value of the exit status of **es**. The second echo displays the value of the exit status of the first echo. The value is zero because echo was successful.

Invocation

There are five ways to execute a program under the UNIX operating system. Each method is slightly different from the others and has its own uses. The **chmod** utility has been explored as a method of making a Shell script executable. Using Shell scripts, this section demonstrates the four other methods. Except for **sh** and ., these techniques can also be used with binary executable files, such as those generated by the C compiler.

sh. You can fork a new Shell and command it to execute a script by using sh. Because sh expects a command file, you do not need to have execute access permission to the file. The example below uses **id**, a command file that displays the PID number of the process that called it. **id** displays the PID number of the Shell that sh forked. echo displays the PID number of the first Shell. The difference in these PID numbers demonstrates that sh forked a new Shell.

```
$ cat id
echo 'id PID =' $$

$ sh id
id PID = 28953

$ echo $$
28907
$
```

As with any utility, the Shell forks a new process to execute sh (see Figure 8-1). The program that sh executes is another Shell. This second Shell forks yet another process that executes the program you specify. Above, sh causes the Shell to fork a secondary Shell that forks a process that runs **id**. While the program is running, the second Shell sleeps. When execution is complete, the forked process dies, waking the second Shell. Then this Shell dies, waking the original Shell which issues a prompt.

The . and Exec Commands. There are two ways to execute a program without forking a new process. The . command executes a Shell script as

Figure 8-1: sh Flowchart

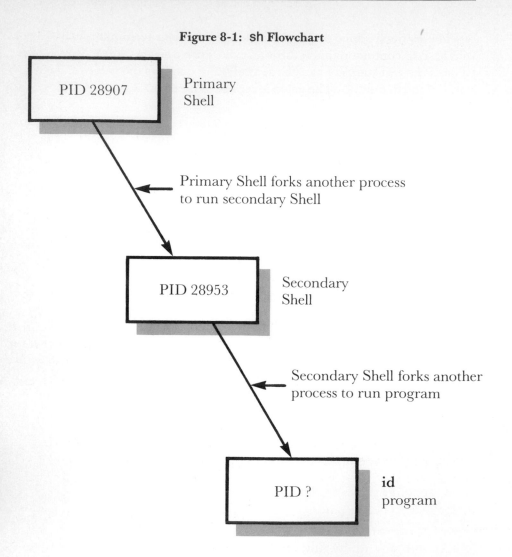

part of the current process. When the new program finishes execution, the current process continues to execute the original program. The Exec command executes the new program in place of the current process and never goes back to the original program.

While the . command does not require that you have execute access permission to the program it executes, Exec does.

The Shell script below displays its PID number and then calls the **id** Shell script (see the previous example) by using a . command. When **id** finishes execution, the . command returns control to the calling Shell script, which displays an appropriate message.

```
$ cat testpgm4
echo $0 'PID =' $$
. id
echo 'This line is executed.'

$ testpgm4
testpgm4 PID = 28907
id PID = 28907
This line is executed.
$
```

By examining the PID numbers, you can see that the . command did not fork a new process to execute **id**.

```
$ chmod u+x id

$ cat testpgm3
echo $0 'PID =' $$
exec id
echo 'This line is never executed.'

$ testpgm3
testpgm3 PID = 28894
id PID = 28894
$
```

After giving the owner execute access permission to **id**, the Shell script above calls it using an **exec** command. **testpgm3** never executes the line following the call to **id** because Exec never returns control to **testpgm3**.

Command Substitution. You can execute a command by enclosing it between grave accent marks (`). The command, including the accent marks, is replaced by the output of the command.

The Shell script below assigns the output of the **pwd** utility to the variable **dir** and displays a message containing this variable.

```
$ cat dir
dir=`pwd`
echo 'You are using the' $dir 'directory.'

$ dir
You are using the /usr/jenny directory.
$
```

The next example contains a variation of the previous one. In this Shell script, the output of the **pwd** command is not assigned to a variable. It is incorporated where it is needed in the **echo** command.

```
$ cat dir2
echo 'You are using the ''pwd'' directory.'

$ dir
You are using the /usr/jenny directory.
$
```

Environment and Exporting Variables

Within a given process, you can declare, initialize, read, and change variables. But a variable is local to a process. When a process forks a child process, the parent does not pass the value of a variable on to the child.

The **extest1** Shell script assigns a value of american to the variable named **cheese**. Then it displays the name of the file being executed (**$0**), its PID number (**$$**), and the value of **cheese**. **extest1** then calls **display**, which attempts to display the same information. When **display** finishes, it returns control to the parent process executing **extest1**, which again displays the value of **cheese**. **extest1** is executed below.

```
$ cat extest1
cheese=american
echo $0 $$ $cheese
display
echo $0 $$ $cheese

$ cat display
echo $0 $$ $cheese

$ extest1
extest1 12247 american
display 12249
extest1 12247 american
$
```

display never receives the value of **cheese** from **extest1**, while **extest1** never loses the value. When a process attempts to display the value of a variable that has not been declared, as is the case in **display**, it displays nothing—the value of an undeclared variable is that of a null string.

extest2 and **change** (see next page) are very similar to **extest1** and **display**. The difference is in **change**, which declares and initializes **cheese** in the child process.

```
$ cat extest2
cheese=american
echo $0 $$ $cheese
change
echo $0 $$ $cheese

$ cat change
echo $0 $$ $cheese
cheese=swiss
echo $0 $$ $cheese

$ extest2
extest2 12252 american
change 12254
change 12254 swiss
extest2 12252 american
$
```

change first displays the (null) value of the as-yet undeclared variable **cheese**. Then it declares the variable by assigning **swiss** to **cheese**, and displays this value. This **cheese** variable is local to the child process that is executing **change**. As can be seen above, the parent process preserves the value of its **cheese** variable.

Export. You can pass the value of a variable to a child process by using the Export command. This command places the value of the variable in the calling environment for the child process. This *call by value* gives the child process a *copy* of the variable for its own use.

Although the child can change the value of the variable, any changes it makes only affect its own copy and not the parent's copy.

```
$ cat extest3
export cheese
cheese=american
echo $0 $$ $cheese
change
echo $0 $$ $cheese

$ extest3
extest3 12258 american
change 12260 american
change 12260 swiss
extest3 12258 american
$
```

Above, the child process inherits the value of **cheese** as **american** and, after displaying this value, changes *its copy* to **swiss**. When control is returned to the parent, the parent's copy of **cheese** still retains its original value, american.

If you need several routines to share variables, you can use the method demonstrated below.

```
$ cat extest4
cheese=american
echo $0 $$ $cheese
. change
echo $0 $$ $cheese

$ extest4
extest4 12264 american
extest4 12264 american
extest4 12264 swiss
extest4 12264 swiss
```

Calling **change** using the **.** command executes it as part of the calling process, not a child process. The PID number remains the same throughout the display. When the value of **cheese** is altered in **change**, it remains changed when control returns to **extest4**.

The value of **$0**, the name the process was called with, doesn't change when another Shell script is executed by the **.** command. The name stays the same because, although a different program is being executed, the same process is executing it.

COMMAND SEPARATION AND GROUPING

When you are giving the Shell commands interactively or writing a Shell script, you must separate commands from one another. This section reviews the ways that were covered in Chapter 5 and introduces a few more.

The (NEWLINE) Character

The (NEWLINE) character is a unique command separator because it initiates execution of the command preceding it. You have seen this throughout this book, each time you press the (RETURN) key at the end of a command line.

The | and & Characters

Other command separators are the pipe symbol (|) and the background task symbol (**&**). These command separators *do not* start execution of a command, but *do* change some aspect of how the command functions. They alter where the input or output comes from or goes to, or determine whether the Shell executes the task in the background or foreground.

If **a**, **b**, and **c** are commands, then the following command line initiates a job that is comprised of three tasks. The Shell directs the output from task **a** to task **b**, and **b**'s output to **c**. Because the Shell runs the entire job in the foreground, you don't get a prompt back until all three tasks have run to completion.

```
$ a| b| c
```

The next command line executes tasks **a** and **b** in the background and task **c** in the foreground. You get a prompt back as soon as **c** is finished.

```
$ a& b& c
```

The command line below executes all three tasks as background jobs. You get a prompt immediately.

```
$ a& b& c&
```

You can use a pipe to send the output from one subtask to the next, and run the whole job as a background task. Again, the prompt comes back immediately.

```
$ a| b| c&
```

The semicolon is a command separator that *does not* initiate execution of a command and *does not* change any aspect of how the command functions. You can execute a series of commands sequentially by entering them on a single command line and separating each from the next by a semicolon. You must terminate the command line with a (RETURN) to initiate execution of the sequence of commands. This has the same effect as if you had entered each command in turn, following each with a (RETURN).

```
$ a; b; c
```

The command line above yields the same results as the following three command lines.

```
$ a
$ b
$ c
```

Command Grouping

You can use parentheses to group commands. The Shell treats each group of commands as a job, forking child processes as needed to execute tasks.

Assume that **a**, **b**, **c**, and **d** are commands. The following command line executes commands **a** and **b** sequentially in the background while executing **c** in the foreground. The Shell prompt returns when **c** finishes execution.

```
$ (a; b)& c
```

The example above differs from a previous example (**a& b& c**) because tasks **a** and **b** are not initiated concurrently, but sequentially.

In a similar manner, the following command line executes **a** and **b** sequentially in the background and, at the same time, executes **c** and **d** sequentially in the background. The prompt returns immediately.

```
$ (a; b)& (c; d)&
```

You can see a demonstration of sequential and concurrent processes run in both the foreground and background. Create a group of executable files named **a**, **b**, **c**, and **d**. Have each file echo its name over and over as file **a** (below) does.

```
$ cat a
echo -n 'aaaaaaaaaaaaaaaaaaaaaaaaa'
echo -n 'aaaaaaaaaaaaaaaaaaaaaaaaa'
echo -n 'aaaaaaaaaaaaaaaaaaaaaaaaa'
echo -n 'aaaaaaaaaaaaaaaaaaaaaaaaa'
echo -n 'aaaaaaaaaaaaaaaaaaaaaaaaa'
$
```

Execute the files sequentially and concurrently, using the example command lines from this and the previous section. When you execute two of these Shell scripts sequentially, their output follows one another. When you execute two of them concurrently, their output is interspersed as control is passed back and forth between the tasks. The results will not always be identical because the UNIX system schedules jobs slightly differently each time they run. Two sample runs are shown below.

```
$ a&b&c&
16717
16718
16719
$ aaaaaaaaaaaaaaaaaaaaaaaaaaaaccccccccccccccccccccccccccccccccc
ccccccccccccccccccccccccccccccccccccccccccccccccccccccccccccccc
ccccccccccccccccccccccccccccccaaaaaaaaaaaaaaaaaaaaaaaaaaaaaaaaa
aaaaaaaaaaaaaaaaaaaaaaaaaaaaaaaaaaaaaaaaaaaaaaaaaaaaaaaaaaaaaaa
aaaaaaaaaaaabbbbbbbbbbbbbbbbbbbbbbbbbbbbbbbbbbbbbbbbbbbbbbbbbbbb
bbbbbbbbbbbbbbbbbbbbbbbbbbbbbbbbbbbbbbbbbbbbbbbbbbbbbbbbbbbbbbbb
bbbbbbbbbbbbbbbbbbb
```

```
$ a&b&c&
16738
16739
16740
$ ccccccccccccccccccccccccccccccccccccccccccccccccccccccccccccc
ccccccccccccccccccccccccccccccccccccccccccccccccccccccccccccccc
ccccccbbbbbbbbbbbbbbbbbbbbbbbbbbbbbbbbbbbbbbbbbbbbbbbbbbbbbbbaaa
aaaaaaaaaaaaaaaaaaaaaaaaaaaaaaaaaaaaaaaaaaaaaaaaaaaaaaaaaaaaaaa
aaaaaaaaaaaaaaaaaaaaaaaaaaaaaaaaaaaaaaaaaaaaaaaaaaaaaaaaaaaaaaa
aabbbbbbbbbbbbbbbbbbbbbbbbbbbbbbbbbbbbbbbbbbbbbbbbbbbbbbbbbbbbbb
bbbbbbbbbbbbbbbbbbb
```

CONTROL STRUCTURES

A Shell control structure alters the flow of control within a Shell script. The Shell provides simple two-way branch If statements, multiple branch Case statements, as well as For, While, and Until statements.

If Then

The format of the If Then control structure is shown below. The **bold** words in the format description are the keywords by which the Shell identifies a particular control structure. The other words are the items that you supply to cause the structure to have the desired effect.

```
if test-command
    then commands
fi
```

Figure 8-2: If Then Flowchart

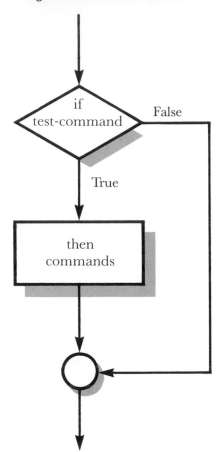

As seen in Figure 8-2, the If statement tests the status that the **test-command** returns, and transfers control based on this status. When you spell i f backward, it's f i ; the Fi statement appropriately marks the end of the If structure.

The program shown on the following page prompts you and reads in two words. Then it uses an If structure to evaluate the result returned by the **test** utility when it compares the two words. test returns a status of true if the two words are the same and false if they are not.

```
$ cat if1
echo -n 'word 1: '
read word1
echo -n 'word 2: '
read word2
if (test "$word1" = "$word2")
    then echo 'Match'
fi
echo 'End of program.'

$ if1
word1: peach
word2: peach
Match
End of program.
$
```

In the example, the command tested by the If is enclosed in parentheses for clarity. If this command returns a true status (= 0), the Shell executes the commands between the Then and Fi statements. If the command returns a false status (not = 0), the Shell passes control to the statement after Fi.

If Then Else

The introduction of the Else statement turns the If structure into a two-way branch as seen in Figure 8-3. If the command that is tested returns a true status, the If structure executes the commands between the Then and Else statements and diverts control to the statement after Fi. If the command returns a false status, the commands following the Else statement are executed.

The format of the If Then Else control structure is shown below.

```
if test-command
      then commands
      else commands
fi
```

Figure 8-3: If Then Else flowchart

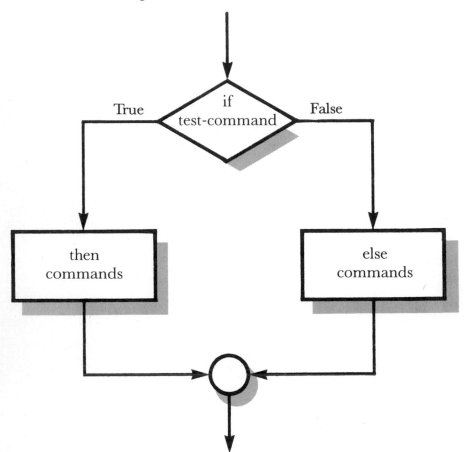

The following expanded word-match program demonstrates an If Then Else Fi structure. The leading (SPACE)s on the lines within the If structure are put there to make the program easier to read. If does not require them.

```
$ cat if2
echo -n 'word 1: '
read word1
echo -n 'word 2: '
read word2
if (test "$word1" = "$word2")
     then echo 'Match'
     else echo 'No match'
fi
echo 'End of program.'

$ if2
word 1: peach
word 2: pear
No match
End of program.
$
```

If Then Elif

The Elif statement combines the Else and If statements and allows you to construct a nested set of If Then Else structures.

The following example shows an If Then Elif Then Else Fi structure. This Shell script compares three words. In the first If statement, the **test** utility determines whether all three words are the same. If they are, the program executes the command following the next Then statement and passes control to the statement after Fi, terminating execution of the Shell script.

If the three words are not the same, the structure passes control to the first Elif which begins a series of tests to see whether any pair of words is the same. As the nesting continues, if any one of the If statements is satisfied, the structure passes control to the next Then statement and subsequently to the statement after Fi. Each time an Elif statement is not satisfied, the structure passes control to the next Elif statement.

```
$ cat if3
echo -n 'word 1: '
read word1
echo -n 'word 2: '
read word2
echo -n 'word 3: '
read word3
if (test "$word1" = "$word2" -a "$word2" = "$word3")
        then echo 'Match: word 1, 2, & 3'
    elif (test "$word1" = "$word2")
        then echo 'Match: words 1 & 2'
    elif (test "$word1" = "$word3")
        then echo 'Match: words 1 & 3'
    elif (test "$word2" = "$word3")
        then echo 'Match: words 2 & 3'
    else echo 'No match'
fi
$
```

The format of the If Then Elif control structure is shown below.

```
if test-command
        then commands
    elif test-command
        then commands
    else commands
fi
```

Figure 8-4: If Then Elif Flowchart

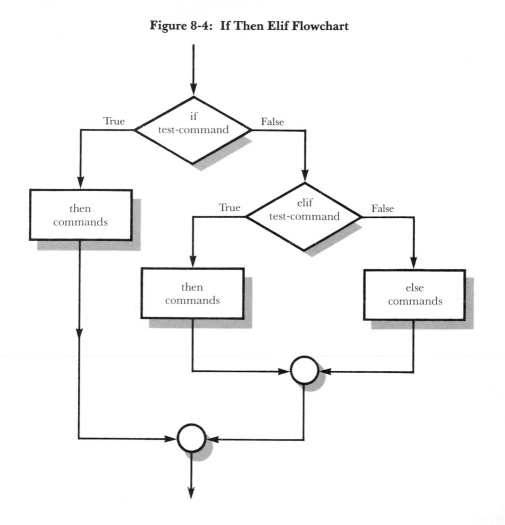

For In

The For In structure has the following format.

```
for loop-index in argument-list
    do
    commands
    done
```

This structure assigns the value of the first item in the **argument-list** to the **loop-index** and executes the **commands** between the Do and Done statements. The Do and Done statements mark the beginning and end of the For loop.

Figure 8-5: For In Flowchart

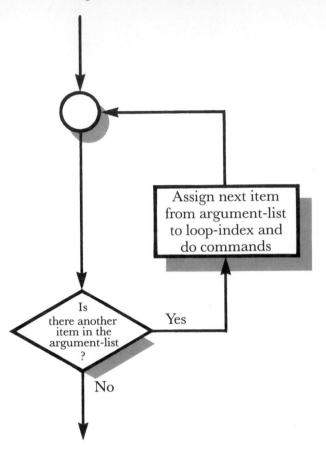

After the structure passes control to the Done statement, it assigns the value of the second item in the **argument-list** to the **loop-index** and repeats the **commands**. The structure repeats the **commands** between the Do and Done statements—once for each of the items in the **argument-list**. When the structure exhausts the **argument-list**, it passes control to the statement following the Done statement.

The For In structure shown on the following page assigns apples to the variable **fruit** and then displays the value of **fruit**, which is apples. Next, it assigns oranges to **fruit** and the process is repeated. When the argument list is exhausted, the structure transfers control to the statement following Done. Because there is no statement after Done, the Shell script terminates execution.

```
$ cat fruit
for fruit in apples oranges pears bananas
        do
        echo $fruit
        done

$ fruit
apples
oranges
pears
bananas
$
```

For

The For structure has the following format.

```
for loop-index
    do
    commands
    done
```

The For structure is very often used to loop through the command line parameters ($1, $2, . . .), performing a series of commands involving each of the parameters in turn. When the keyword in and the **argument-list** are omitted, the **loop-index** automatically takes on the value of each of the command line parameters, one at a time.

The Shell script below shows a For structure displaying each of the command line arguments. The first line of the Shell script for args implies for args in $*, where $* is expanded into a list of command line arguments. The balance of the script mimics the standard For structure.

```
$ cat for_test
for args
        do
        echo $args
        done

$ for_test candy gum chocolate
candy
gum
chocolate
$
```

While

The While structure (see Figure 8-6) has the following format:

```
while test-command
     do
     commands
     done
```

   While the **test-command** returns a true exit status, the series of **commands** delimited by the Do and Done statements continues to be executed. Before each loop through the **commands**, the structure executes the **test-command**. When the exit status of the **test-command** is false, the structure passes control to the statement following the Done statement.

Figure 8-6: While Flowchart

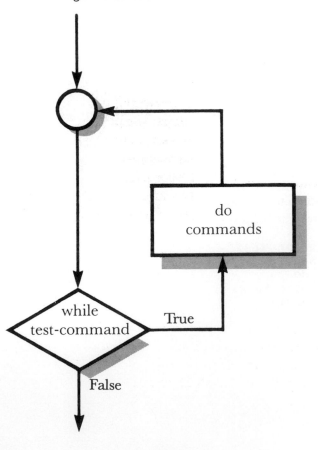

The Shell script shown below first initializes the variable **number** to 0. The character value of zero is used—Shell variables can only take on values of character strings. The **test** utility then determines whether the value of the variable **number** is less than ten. The **test** utility has an exit status of true as long as **number** is less than ten. While **test** returns true, the commands will be executed.

The first command following Do displays the string represented by **number**. The next command uses the **expr** utility to increment the value of **number** by one. **expr** converts its arguments to numbers, adds them, converts the result to characters and echoes them to the standard output. The grave accent marks cause the command which they enclose to be replaced by the output of the command. This value is then assigned to the variable **number**. The next statement is Done, which returns control to the While statement. Then the loop starts over again.

```
$ cat count
number=0
while (test $number −lt '10')
      do
        echo −n $number
        number=`expr $number + 1`
      done
echo

$ count
0123456789
$
```

Until

The **Until** structure is shown below.

```
Until test−command
      do
      commands
      done
```

The Until and While structures are very similar. They only differ in the sense of the test at the top of the loop. As shown in Figure 8-7, Until continues to loop *until* the **test-command** returns a true or nonerror condition. While loops *while* the **test-command** continues to return a true or nonerror condition.

Figure 8-7: Until Flowchart

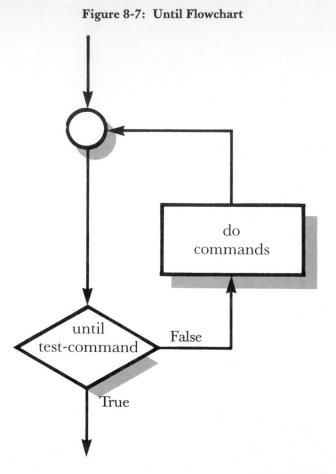

The program shown below demonstrates an Until structure that includes a Read command. When the user enters the correct name, the test command is satisfied and the structure passes control out of the loop.

```
$ cat until1
secretname='jenny'
name='noname'
echo 'Try to guess the secret name!'
echo
until (test $name = $secretname)
      do
      echo -n 'Your guess: '
      read name
      done
echo 'Very good.'
```

```
$ until1
Try to guess the secret name!

Your guess: helen
Your guess: barbara
Your guess: jenny
Very good.
$
```

Case

The Case structure is shown below.

```
case test-string in
      pattern-1) commands-1;;
      pattern-2) commands-2;;
      pattern-3) commands-3;;
         .
         .
         .

esac
```

As illustrated in Figure 8-8, the Case structure provides a multiple branch decision mechanism. The path that is chosen depends on a match between the **test-string** and one of the **patterns**.

The following Case structure uses the value of the character that the user enters as the test string. This value is represented by **letter.** If the test string has a value of **A**, the structure executes the command following **A)**. If the test string has a value of **B** or **C**, the appropriate command is executed. The asterisk indicates any string of characters and is used as a catchall, in case a match is not found. The second sample execution of **case1** shows the user entering a lowercase **b**. Because this does not match the uppercase **B** in the case statement, the program tells you there is no match.

```
$ cat case1
echo -n 'Enter A, B, or C: '
read letter
case $letter in
      A) echo 'You entered A';;
      B) echo 'You entered B';;
      C) echo 'You entered C';;
      *) echo 'You did not enter A, B, or C';;
esac
```

Figure 8-8: Case Flowchart

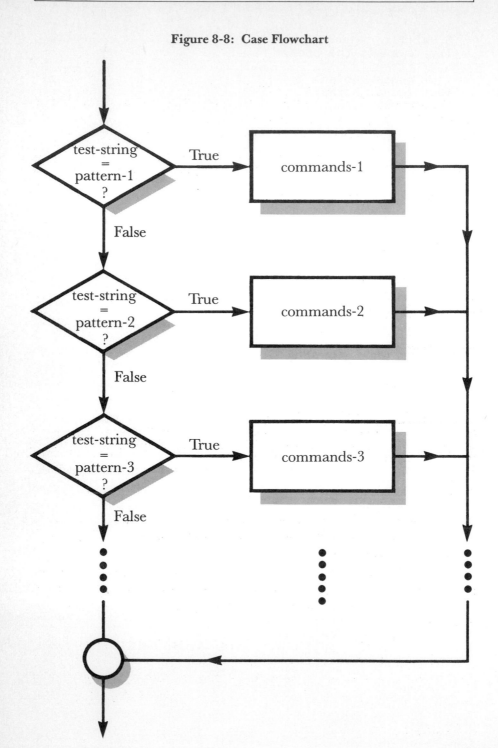

```
$ case1
Enter A, B, or C: B
You entered B

$ case1
Enter A, B, or C: b
You did not enter A, B, or C
$
```

The pattern in the Case structure is analogous to that of an ambiguous file reference. You can use the following special characters and strings.

*	An asterisk matches any string of characters. You can use it for the default case.
?	A question mark matches any single character.
[...]	Square braces define a character class. Any characters enclosed within square braces are tried, one at a time, in an attempt to match a single character. A hyphen specifies a range of characters.
|	A vertical bar separates alternate choices that will satisfy a particular branch of the Case structure.

The next program is a variation of the previous one. This script accepts upper- and lowercase letters.

```
$ cat case2
echo -n 'Enter A, B, or C:   '
read letter
case $letter in
      a|A) echo 'You entered A.';;
      b|B) echo 'You entered B.';;
      c|C) echo 'You entered C.';;
      *) echo 'You did not enter A, B, or C.';;
esac

$ case2
Enter A, B, or C: b
You entered B.
$
```

The Here Document

A Here document allows you to redirect input to a process from within the Shell script that calls the process. It is called a Here document because it is *here,* immediately accessible in the Shell script, instead of *there,* in another file.

The following program, named **update**, contains a Here document. The two less-than symbols on the third line indicate to the Shell that a Here document follows. The symbols are followed by one or more characters that delimit the Here document. This example uses plus signs. Everything between these two delimiters is sent to the process as its standard input. It is as though you had redirected the standard input to the **ed** utility from a file, except that the file is imbedded in the Shell script.

```
$ cat update
today=`date`
ed $1 <<+
1d
i
$today
.
w
q
+
echo 'Update complete.'
$
```

On the first line of the program above, the character string that the **date** utility returns is assigned to the variable **today**. The Shell script calls the **ed** utility with the file that was specified on the command line. The first line of the file is deleted and the string contained in the variable **today** is inserted in its place. **ed** is commanded to write out the file (**w**) and quit (**q**), returning control to the Shell script. Finally, the Shell script sends a message to the user indicating that the process is complete.

Below, the Update utility changes the date in the **testf** file. **ed** displays the number of characters that it reads in and writes out before the Shell script displays the message Update complete.

```
$ cat testf
Fri Oct 29 12:34:55 PDT 1982
line 2
line 3 (end)

$ update testf
49
49
Update complete.

$ cat testf
Sun Oct 31 07:44:31 PST 1982
line 2
line 3 (end)
$
```

The next program is a more sophisticated version of Update. It uses a For loop to update each of the files given on the command line, and redirects the output from **ed** (the number of characters read and written) to the null device. It also does away with the **today** variable by inserting the output of the **date** utility where it is needed.

Other than the Do and Done instructions, the For loop is not indented because the Here document must contain exactly the input that **ed** needs. If the period that terminates the insert mode had been preceded by (SPACE)s, it would not have terminated the insert mode.

```
$ cat update2
for file
       do
ed $file > /dev/null <<+
1d
i
`date`
.
w
q
+
echo 'Update of' $file 'complete.'
       done
echo 'End of update.'
$
```

SIGNALS

A signal is a report to a process about a condition. The UNIX system uses signals to report bad system calls, broken pipes, illegal instructions, and other conditions. This discussion covers the three signals that are useful when you work with Shell scripts. They are the *terminal interrupt* signal (number 2), the *kill* signal (number 9), and the *software termination* signal (number 15).

You can use the Trap command to trap a signal. When a program traps a signal, it takes whatever action you specify. It can close files or finish any other processing as needed, display a message, terminate execution immediately, or ignore the signal altogether. The format of a Trap command is shown below.

```
trap 'commands' signal-number
```

The **signal-number** is the number of the signal that the Trap command will catch. It must be present. The **commands** part is optional. If it is not present, the trap is reset to its initial condition, which is to exit from the program. If the **commands** part is present, the Shell executes the **commands** when it catches the signal. After the **commands** are executed, the Shell resumes executing the program where it left off.

You can interrupt the program you are running in the foreground by pressing the (DEL) key. Pressing this key sends signal number two, a terminal interrupt signal, to the program. Execution of the program is terminated if it does not trap this signal. The following program demonstrates the use of the Trap command to trap signal number two.

```
$ cat inter
trap 'echo PROGRAM INTERRUPTED; exit' 2
while (true)
      do
      echo 'Program running.'
      done
```

The first line of **inter** sets up a trap for signal number two. When the signal is caught, the Shell executes the two commands between the apostrophes in the trap command. echo displays the following message: PROGRAM INTERRUPTED. Then Exit returns control to the Shell, which displays a prompt. If the Exit command were not there, control would return to the While loop after the message was displayed.

You can send a software termination signal to a background process by using kill without a signal number. A trap command, set up to catch signal number 15, will catch this signal. Refer to the kill utility in Part II for more information.

You can send a kill signal to a process by using kill with signal number nine. The Shell cannot trap a kill signal.

SUMMARY

The Shell is both a *command interpreter* and a *programming language.* As a command interpreter, the Shell executes commands that you enter in response to its prompt. When you use it as a programming language, the Shell executes commands from files called *Shell scripts.*

Either way, the Shell executes commands by means of processes. Each process has a unique process id (PID) number. When you give the Shell a command, it generally *forks* a new process that executes the command. The

Shell has some commands that are built in. It does not fork a new process to execute these commands.

Built-in Command	Function
.	execute a program as part of the current process
` `	execute a program in line
exec	execute a program in place of the current process
export	place the value of a variable in the calling environment
read	reads a line from the standard input
shift	promotes each of the command line arguments
trap	trap a signal

You can execute a Shell script (or a compiled program) by giving yourself execute access permission to the file (using chmod) and using the name of the file as a command. If you precede the filename of a Shell script with an sh command, you do not need execute access permission to the file.

The Shell allows you to define *variables*. When you give the Shell a command, it examines the command line for words that begin with unquoted dollar signs. It assumes that such words are variables and substitutes a value for each of them. You can declare and initialize a variable by assigning a value to it.

The Shell also defines some variables. These variables are listed below. Read-only variables are preceded by a dollar sign because you can only reference them in this manner—you cannot assign a value to them.

Variable	Contents
$0	name of the calling program
$n	value of the nth command line argument
$*	all of the command line arguments
$#	count of the command line arguments
$$	PID number of the current process
HOME	pathname of your home directory
IFS	inter-field separator
PATH	search path for commands
PS1	prompt string 1
PS2	prompt string 2

The Shell provides the *control structures* listed below so that you can alter the flow of control within a Shell script.

```
if then
if then else
if then elif
for in
for
while
until
case
```

Some of the special characters that the Shell recognizes are listed below. These characters separate and group commands, initiate execution in either the foreground or background, and redirect a program's standard input and output.

Special Character	Function
RETURN	initiates execution of a command
;	separates commands
( )	groups commands for execution
&	executes a command in the background
|	pipe
>	redirect standard output
>>	append standard output
<	redirect standard input
<<	here document

9

THE C SHELL

The C Shell performs the same function as the Bourne Shell: it provides an interface between you and the UNIX operating system. It is an interactive command interpreter as well as a high-level programming language. At any one time you will be using the Bourne Shell or the C Shell, not both, although it is possible to switch back and forth between the two. This chapter contrasts the C Shell with the Bourne Shell, paying particular attention to those facets of the C Shell that are absent from the Bourne Shell. Although Chapter 8 is not specifically about the C Shell, it discusses many important concepts that are common to both Shells and provides a good background for this chapter.

C Shell variables are much more versatile than those of the Bourne Shell. The C Shell processes arrays of numbers and strings, and evaluates logical and numerical expressions. You can customize the C Shell to make it more tolerant of mistakes and easier to use. By setting the proper Shell variables, you can make the C Shell warn you when you appear to be accidentally logging off or overwriting a file. The Alias mechanism makes it easy to change the names of existing commands and create new ones. The History mechanism allows you to edit and rerun previous command lines.

ENTERING AND LEAVING THE C SHELL

Not all versions of the UNIX system have the C Shell program. If your version does have this program, and you are not already using it, you can execute the C Shell by giving the command **csh**. If you are not sure which Shell you are using, use the **ps** utility to find out (the Berkeley UNIX system requires that you use the **−g** option). It will show that you are running **csh** (the C Shell) or **sh** (the Bourne Shell).

If you want to use the C Shell as a matter of course, the system administrator can set up the **/etc/passwd** file so that you are using the C Shell immediately when you log on. On some systems, you can give a **chsh csh** command to effect the same change. Use **chsh sh** if you want to go back to using the Bourne Shell.

The first character in a Shell script that you want to run under the C Shell must be a sharp sign (#). Refer to the section of this chapter on "Shell Scripts."

There are several ways to leave a C Shell. The way that you use it is dependent on two factors: whether the Shell variable **ignoreeof** is set and whether you are using the Shell that you logged on to or another Shell that you created after you logged on. If you are not sure how to exit from a C Shell, press (CONTROL-D). You will either exit or receive instructions on how to exit.

If you have not set **ignoreeof**, and it has not been set for you in your **.cshrc** startup file (see page 58), you can exit from any Shell using (CONTROL-D) (the same procedure you used to exit from the Bourne Shell).

If **ignoreeof** is set, (CONTROL-D) will not work. It causes the Shell to display a message telling you how to exit. You can exit from a C Shell (other than the login Shell) by giving an **exit** command. A **logout** command allows you to exit from the login Shell. More information on **ignoreeof** can be found in the section of this chapter on "Shell Variables."

HISTORY

The history mechanism maintains a list of recently used command lines, also called *events*. The **history** variable (page 233) determines the number of events preserved in this list. Typically, you will want to preserve 10 to 15 events. If you attempt to preserve too many events, you may run out of memory.

The C Shell assigns a sequential *event number* to each of your command lines. If you wish, the C Shell can display this number as part of its prompt (see page 236). The history mechanism preserves events whether or not you use a numbered prompt.

Give the following command manually, or place it in your **.cshrc** startup file to establish a history list of the ten most recent events.

```
% set history = 10
%
```

Give the command **history** to display the events in the history list. When you first set the **history** variable, the history list will just record the events back to the command line you used to set it.

```
32 % history
      23  ls −l
      24  cat temp
      25  rm temp
      26  vi memo
      27  lpr memo
      28  vi memo
      29  lpr memo
      30  mail jenny < memo
      31  rm memo
      32  history
 33 %
```

Reexecuting Events

You can reexecute any event in the history list. Even if there is no history list, you can always reexecute the previous event. There are three ways to reference an event: by its absolute event number, its number relative to the current event, or by the text it contains.

All references to events begin with an exclamation point. One or more characters follow the exclamation point to specify an event.

Reexecuting the Previous Event. You can always reexecute the previous event by giving the command !!. Below, Event 4 reexecutes Event 3.

```
3 % ls -l text
-rw-rw-r-- 1 alex          5 Feb 27 12:51 text

4 % !!
ls -l text
-rw-rw-r-- 1 alex          5 Feb 27 12:51 text
5 %
```

Using Event Numbers. A number following an exclamation point refers to an event. If that event is in the history list, the C Shell executes it. A negative number following an exclamation point refers to the event that occurred that number of events prior to the current event. Both of the following commands execute Event 3.

```
7 % !3
ls -l text
-rw-rw-r-- 1 alex          5 Feb 27 12:51 text

8 % !-5
ls -l text
-rw-rw-r-- 1 alex          5 Feb 27 12:51 text
9 %
```

Using Event Text. When a string of text follows an exclamation point, the C Shell searches for and executes the most recent event that *began* with that string. If the string is enclosed between question marks, the most recent event *containing* that string is executed. The final question mark is optional if a (RETURN) would immediately follow it.

```
53 % history
        48 cat letter
        49 cat memo
        50 lpr memo
        51 mail jenny < memo
        52 ls -l
        53 history

54 % !l
ls -l
.
.
.
55 % !lp
lpr memo
```

```
56 % !?letter?
cat letter
.
.
.
57 %
```

Words Within Events

You can select any word or series of words from an event. The words are numbered starting with zero, representing the first command on the line, and continuing with one, representing the first word following the command, through n, representing the last word on the line.

A colon and the word number following the event specification specify the word. You can specify a range of words by separating two word numbers with a hyphen. The first word following the command (word number one) can be specified by a caret (∧) and the last word by a dollar sign.

```
72 % echo apple grape orange pear
apple grape orange pear

73 % echo !72:2
echo grape
grape

74 % echo !72:∧
echo apple
apple

75 % !72:0 !72:$
echo pear
pear

76 % echo !72:2-4
echo grape orange pear
grape orange pear

77 % !72:0-$
echo apple grape orange pear
apple grape orange pear
78 %
```

If an event contains a single command, the word numbers correspond to the argument numbers. If an event contains more than one command, this correspondence is not true for commands after the first. Event 78, below, contains two commands, separated by a semicolon so that the Shell executes them sequentially. The semicolon is the fifth word.

```
78 % !72 ; echo helen jenny barbara
echo apple grape orange pear ; echo helen jenny barbara
apple grape orange pear
helen jenny barbara

79 % echo !78:7
echo helen
helen

80 % echo !78:4-7
echo pear ; echo helen
pear
helen
81 %
```

Modifying Previous Events

On occasion, you may want to reexecute an event, changing some aspect of it. Perhaps you entered a complex command line with a typo or incorrect pathname. Or you may want to reexecute a command, specifying a different argument. You can modify an event, or a word of an event, by following the event or word specifier with a colon and a modifier. The following example shows the substitute modifier correcting a typo in the previous event.

```
145 % ct /usr/jenny/memo.0506 /usr/alex/letter.0506
ct: Command not found.

146 % !!:s/ct/cat
cat /usr/jenny/memo.0506 /usr/alex/letter.0506
 .
 .
 .
147 %
```

As a special case, an abbreviated form of the substitute modifier, shown below, can be used to change the most recent event.

```
% ∧old∧new
```

performs the same function as

```
% !!:s/old/new
```

Thus, Event 146 could have been entered as shown below.

```
146 %∧ct∧cat
cat /usr/jenny/memo.0506 /usr/alex/letter.0506
.
.
.
147 %
```

Following is a list of modifiers.

Modifier		Effect
h	head	Remove the last element of a pathname.
r	root	Remove the filename extension.
t	tail	Remove all elements of a pathname except the last.
&	repeat	Repeat the previous substitution.
p	print	Do not execute the modified event.
q	quote	Quote the modifications so that no further modifications take place.
s/old/new/	substitute	Substitute **new** for **old**.

The **s** modifier substitutes the new string for the old. Placing a **g** before the **s** (**gs/old/new/**) causes a global substitution, replacing all occurrences of the old string. The **/** is the delimiter in these examples, but you can use any character. The final delimiter is optional if a (RETURN) would immediately follow it. As with the **ed** and **vi** substitute commands, the history mechanism replaces an ampersand (**&**) in the new string with the old string. A null old string (**s//new/**) is replaced with the previous old string or string within a command that was searched for with ?string?.

The following examples demonstrate the use of history modifiers.

```
66 % echo /usr/jenny/letter.0406 /usr/jenny/memo.prv
/usr/jenny/letter.0406 /usr/jenny/memo.prv

67 % !!:h
echo /usr/jenny /usr/jenny/memo.prv
/usr/jenny /usr/jenny/memo.prv

68 % echo !66:2:h
echo /usr/jenny
/usr/jenny

69 % echo !66:2:t
echo memo.prv
memo.prv

70 % echo !66:1:r
echo /usr/jenny/letter
/usr/jenny/letter

71 % echo !66:1:p
echo /usr/jenny/letter.0406
72 %
```

Event 66 displays two filenames. Event 67 recalls the previous event, modified by **h**. Because the command did not specify a word from the event, word one was modified and the entire previous event recalled. Events 68 through 70 recall and modify specific words from Event 66. In these cases, only the specified words are recalled. Event 71 uses the **p** modifier to display, but not execute, the resulting command.

ALIAS

The C Shell Alias mechanism makes standard commands perform non-standard functions, and allows you to define new commands. Alias performs a string substitution on the command line according to your specifications. Alias does not function within a Shell script. The format of an Alias command is shown below.

```
alias [entered-command [executed-command]]
```

The **entered-command** is the command that you enter in response to the C Shell prompt. The **executed-command** is the string that Alias substitutes for the **entered-command**.

The following example shows how to use an Alias. The Alias command in Event 6 causes the C Shell to substitute l s − l every time you give an **ls** command. This substitution is demonstrated in Event 7.

```
5 % ls
one three two

6 % alias ls ls −l

7 % ls
total 3
−rwxrw−r−−   1 jenny           17 Mar 5 11:36 one
−rw−rw−r−−   1 jenny           42 Mar 5 11:14 three
−rwxrw−r−−   1 jenny           11 Mar 5 11:35 two

8 % ls three
−rw−rw−r−−   1 jenny           42 Mar 5 11:14 three

9 % alias w who

10 % alias
ls        ls −l
w         who

11 % alias ls
ls        ls −l

12 % unalias ls

13 % alias
w         who
14 %
```

When you give an Alias command without any arguments (Event 10), the C Shell displays a list of all the Aliases. When given with one argument (Event 11), the Alias for that argument is displayed. An Unalias command (Event 12) removes an Alias from the list of Aliases.

Implementation of Alias

When you enter a command line, the C Shell breaks it into commands. Next, the C Shell substitutes an Alias for each command that has one. After it makes these substitutions, the C Shell substitutes Aliases over and over again until there are no Aliases left. Alias flags a self-referencing Alias to prevent an infinite loop.

```
82 % alias a b
83 % alias b c
84 % alias c echo finished
85 % alias
a        b
b        c
c        echo finished
86 % a
finished
87 %
```

Events 82, 83, and 84 define a series of Aliases that reference each other; Event 85 uses Alias without any arguments to display all of the Aliases. The C Shell executes event 86 as follows:

1. **a** is replaced by its Alias **b**
2. **b** is replaced by its Alias **c**
3. **c** is replaced by its Alias echo finished
4. there are no further Aliases, so the Shell executes the **echo** command

Argument Substitution

Alias substitutes command line arguments using the same scheme as History, with a single exclamation point representing the current event. Modifiers are the same as those used by History (page 217). The exclamation points are quoted in the following example so that the Shell does not interpret them, but passes them on to Alias.

```
21 % alias last echo \!:$
22 % last this is just a test
test
23 % alias fn2 echo \!:2:t
24 % fn2 /usr/jenny/test /usr/alex/temp /usr/barbara/new
temp
25 %
```

Event 21 defines an Alias for **last** that echoes the last argument. Event 23 defines an Alias for **fn2** that echoes the simple filename, or tail, of the second argument on the command line.

VARIABLES

The C Shell, like the Bourne Shell, only uses string variables. The C Shell can however, work with these variables as numbers. You must use the **expr** utility to perform arithmetic operations on numbers in the Bourne Shell. The arithmetic functions of **expr**, and many more, are built into the C Shell.

The term *numeric variable* is used in this section to describe a string variable that contains a number and is used by the C Shell in arithmetic or logical-arithmetic computations. Remember, however, that no true numeric variables exist.

A C Shell variable name consists of 1 to 20 characters, chosen from the same set of characters as a filename.

Variable Substitution

Three commands are used to declare and manipulate variables: Set, @, and Setenv. Set assumes that a variable is a nonnumeric string variable. The @ command only works with numeric variables. Both Set and @ declare local variables. Setenv declares a variable *and* places it in the calling environment of all child processes. Using Setenv is similar to Exporting a variable in the Bourne Shell (see page 190 for a discussion of local and global variables).

Once the value—or merely the existence—of a variable has been established, the C Shell substitutes the value of that variable when it sees the variable on a command line or in a Shell script. The C Shell, like the Bourne Shell, recognizes a word that begins with a dollar sign as a variable. If the dollar sign is quoted by preceding it with a backslash (\$), the Shell will not perform the substitution. When a variable is within double quotation marks, the substitution occurs even if the dollar sign is quoted. If the variable is within single quotation marks, the substitution will not occur, regardless of whether the dollar sign is quoted or not.

String Variables

The C Shell treats string variables in a manner very similar to that of the Bourne Shell. The major difference is in their declaration and assignment.

The C Shell uses an explicit command, Set (or Setenv), to declare and/or assign a value to a string variable.

```
1 % set name = fred

2 % echo $name
fred

3 % set
argv    ()
home    /u3/jenny
name    fred
Shell   /bin/csh
status  0

4 % set name

5 % echo $name

6 % unset name

7 % set
argv    ()
home    /u3/jenny
Shell   /bin/csh
status  0
8 %
```

Event 1 declares the variable **name** and assigns the string **fred** to it. Unlike the Bourne Shell, *the C Shell requires* (SPACE)*s around the equal sign.* Event 2 displays this value. When you give a Set command without any arguments, it displays a list of all the declared variables and their values. When you give a Set command with only the name of a variable and no value, it sets the variable to the null string. Refer to Events 4 and 5, above. Events 6 and 7 show that the Unset command removes a variable from the list of declared variables.

Arrays of String Variables

Before you can access individual elements of an array, you must declare the entire array. To declare an array, you must assign a value to each element of the array.

```
 8 % set colors = (red green blue orange yellow)

 9 % echo $colors
red green blue orange yellow

10 % echo $colors[3]
blue

11 % echo $colors[2-4]
green blue orange

12 % set shapes ('' '' '' '' '' '' '' '' '' '')

13 % echo $shapes

14 % set shapes[4] = square

15 % echo $shapes[4]
square
16 %
```

Event 8 declares the array of string variables named **colors** to have five elements, and assigns values to each of these elements. If you do not know the values of the elements at the time you declare an array, you can declare an array containing the necessary number of null elements. See Event 12.

An entire array is referenced by the name of the array preceded by a dollar sign (Event 9). A number in square brackets following a reference to the array refers to an element of the array (Events 10, 14, and 15). Two numbers in square brackets, separated by a hyphen, refer to two or more adjacent elements of the array (Event 11). See "Special Forms of User Variables," page 232.

Numeric Variables

The @ command assigns a value to a numeric variable. Single numeric variables can be declared by the @ command, just as nonnumeric variables are declared by the Set command. If you give @ a nonnumeric argument, it displays an Expression syntax. error message.

Many of the expressions that the @ command can evaluate and the operators that it recognizes are derived from the C programming language. The format of a declaration or assignment using the @ command is shown below.

```
@ variable-name operator expression
```

The **variable-name** is the name of the variable that is being declared or assigned a value. The **operator** is one of the C assignment operators: = , + = , - = , * = , /=, or %= . The **expression** is an arithmetic expression that can include most C operators; refer to "Expressions," following. Parentheses can be used within the expression for clarity or to change the order of evaluation. Parentheses must be used around parts of the expression that contain any of the following characters: <, >, &, or | .

Expressions. An expression can be composed of constants, variables, and the following operators (listed in order of decreasing precedence).

Parentheses

( )	change the order of evaluation

Unary operators

~	one's complement
!	logical negation

Arithmetic operators

%	remainder
/	divide
*	multiply
−	subtract
+	add

Shift operators

>>	right shift
<<	left shift

Relational operators

>	greater than
<	less than
>=	greater than or equal to
<=	less than or equal to
!=	not equal to (compare strings)
==	equal to (compare strings)

Bitwise operators

&	and
∧	exclusive or
|	inclusive or

Logical operators

&&	and
||	or

Expressions follow these rules:

1. A number that begins with a 0 (zero) is considered to be an octal number.
2. A missing or null argument is evaluated as zero.
3. All results are decimal numbers.
4. Except as noted (!= and ==), the operators act on numeric arguments.
5. Each element of an expression must be separated from another by a (SPACE), unless the other element is an &, |, <, >, (, or).

Expressions can also return a value based on the status of a file. The format of this type of expression is shown below.

```
-n filename
```

where **n** is selected from the following list.

n	Meaning
d	The file is a directory file.
e	The file exists.
f	The file is a plain file.
o	The user owns the file.
r	The user has read access to the file.
w	The user has write access to the file.
x	The user has execute access to the file.
z	The file is zero bytes long.

If the specified file does not exist or is not accessible, the expression is evaluated as zero. Otherwise, if the result of the test is true, the expression has a value of one; if it is false, it has a value of zero.

```
16 % @ count = 0

17 % echo $count
0

18 % @ count = ( 5 + 2 )

19 % echo $count
7

20 % @ result = ( $count < 5 )

21 % echo $result
0

22 % @ count += 5

23 % echo $count
12

24 % @ count++

25 % echo $count
13
26 %
```

Event 16 declares the variable **count** and assigns a value of zero to it. Event 18 shows the result of an arithmetic operation being assigned to a variable. Event 20 uses @ to assign the result of a logical operation involving a constant and a variable to **result**. The value of the operation is false (= 0) because the variable **count** is not less than 5. Event 22 is a compressed form of the following assignment statement.

```
% set count = count + 5
%
```

Event 24 uses a postfix operator to increment **count**.

Arrays of Numeric Variables. An array of numeric variables must be declared by the Set command before you can use the @ command to assign values to the elements of the array. The Set command can assign any values to the elements of a numeric array, including zeros, other numbers, and null strings.

Assigning a value to an element of a numeric array is similar to assigning a value to a simple numeric variable. The only difference is that you must specify the element, or index, of the array. The format is shown below.

```
@ variable-name[index] operator expression
```

The **index** must be either a numeric constant or a variable. It cannot be an expression. The **index** indicates the element of the array that is being addressed. The first element has an index of one.

```
26 % set ages = (0 0 0 0 0)

27 % @ ages[2] = (15)

28 % @ ages[3] = ($ages[2] + 4)

29 % echo $ages[3]
19
30 %
```

Elements of a numeric array behave just as though they were simple numeric variables. The only difference is that you must use Set to declare a numeric array. Event 26 declares an array with five elements, each having a value of zero. Events 27 and 28 assign values to elements of the array and Event 29 displays the value of one of the elements.

Braces

You can use braces to distinguish a variable from surrounding text without the use of a separator (e.g., a (SPACE)).

```
100 % set prefix = Alex

101 % echo $prefix is short for ${prefix}ander.
Alex is short for Alexander.
102 %
```

Without braces in the above example, **prefix** would have to be separated from ander with a (SPACE) so that the Shell would recognize **prefix** as a variable. This would cause Alexander to become Alex ander.

Special Forms of User Variables

The number of elements in an array is stored in a special variable as shown below.

$#variable-name

You can determine whether a variable has been declared or not by testing a variable of the following format.

$?variable-name

This variable has a value of one if a variable name has been declared. Otherwise it has a value of zero.

```
205 % set days = (mon tues wed thurs fri)

206 % echo $#days
5

207 % echo $?days
1

208 % unset days

209 % echo $?days
0
210 %
```

Event 206 displays the number of elements in the **days** array that was set in Event 205. Event 207 shows that **days** has been declared because **$?days** echoes as one (= true). Events 208 and 209 show what happens when **days** is Unset.

Shell Variables

This section lists the Shell variables that are either set by the Shell or set by the user and used by the Shell. The section is divided into two parts. The first contains variables that take on significant values (e.g., the PID number of a background process). The second part lists variables that act as switches — *on* if they are declared, *off* if they are not.

Shell Variables That Take on Values

$argv   This Shell variable contains the command line arguments from the command that invoked the Shell. **argv[0]** contains the name of the calling program, **argv[1]** contains the first command line argument, and so on. You can change any element of this array except **argv[0]**. All of the arguments can be referenced together as **argv[*]**. References to **argv** can be abbreviated as **$ * ** (short for **$argv[*]**) and **$n** (short for **$argv[n]**).

$#argv   The Shell sets this variable to the number of elements in **argv**.

$cdpath   This variable affects the operation of the **cd** utility. It takes on the value of a list of absolute pathnames (similar to the **path** variable) and is usually set in the **.login** file with a command line such as the one shown below.

```
set cdpath = (/usr/jenny/reports /usr/jenny/letters)
```

When you specify a simple filename as an argument to a **cd** command, **cd** always searches the working directory for a subdirectory with the same name as the argument. If the subdirectory does not exist and **cdpath** is not set, **cd** issues an error message. If **cdpath** is set, **cd** continues its search and tries to find an appropriately named directory in the **cdpath** list. If it does, that directory becomes the working directory.

$child   The Shell sets this variable in the parent process when you execute a detached, or background, process. The variable **child** takes the value of the PID of the child process. The Shell unsets this variable when the child process terminates.

$history   You can use this variable to control the size of your History list. As a rule of thumb, its value should be kept under 15. If you assign too large a value, the Shell can run out of memory. Refer to "History," page 217.

$home   This variable is similar to the HOME variable in the Bourne Shell. It has the value of the pathname of the home directory of the user. The **cd** command refers to this variable, as does the filename expansion of ˜ (see "Filename Generation," page 88).

$path   This variable is similar to the PATH variable in the Bourne Shell. Unless it is set, you can execute a file only if it is in the working directory or if you specify its full pathname.

$prompt   This variable is similar to the **PS1** variable in the Bourne Shell. If it is not set, the prompt will be % [# for the system administrator (super user)]. The Shell expands an unquoted exclamation point in the prompt string to the current event number. A typical command line which sets the value of **prompt**, found in the **.cshrc** file, is shown below.

```
set prompt = '! % '
```

The exclamation point is quoted so that the Shell does not expand it before it is assigned to the variable **prompt**.

$shell   This variable contains the pathname of the Shell.

$status   This variable contains the exit status returned by the last command.

$$ As in the Bourne Shell, this variable represents the PID number of the current Shell.

Shell Variables That Act as Switches

The following Shell variables act as switches; their values are not significant. If the variable has been declared, the Shell takes the specified action. If not, the action is not taken or is negated. You can set these variables in your **.cshrc** file, in a Shell script, or from the command line.

$echo   When you call the C Shell with the **−x** option, it sets the **echo** variable. You can also set **echo** using a Set command. In either case, when **echo** is declared, the C Shell displays each command before it is executed.

$ignoreeof   When you set the **ignoreeof** variable, you cannot exit from the Shell using (CONTROL-D). This can prevent you from accidentally logging off. When this variable is declared, you must use Exit or Logout to leave a Shell.

$noclobber   The **noclobber** variable prevents you from accidentally overwriting a file when you redirect output. It also does not allow you to create a file if you attempt to append output to a nonexistent one. To override **noclobber**, add an exclamation point to the symbol you use for redirecting or appending output (i.e., > ! and >> !).

When **noclobber** is *not* declared, these command lines have the following effects.

Command Line	Effect
x > fileout	The standard output from process **x** is directed to **fileout**. If **fileout** exists, it is overwritten.
x >> fileout	The standard output from process **x** is directed to **fileout**. If **fileout** exists, new output is appended to the end of it. If **fileout** does not exist, it is created.

When **noclobber** *is* declared, the command lines have different effects.

Command Line	Effect
x > fileout	The standard output from process **x** is directed to **fileout**. If **fileout** exists, the C Shell displays an error message.
x >> fileout	The standard output from process **x** is directed to **fileout**. If **fileout** exists, new output is appended to the end of it. If **fileout** does not exist, the C Shell displays an error message.

$noglob When **$noglob** is declared, the C shell will not expand ambiguous filenames. You can use *, ?, ~, and [] on the command line or in a Shell script without quoting them.

$nonomatch When **nonomatch** is declared, the C Shell passes an ambiguous file reference that does not match a filename to the program that is being called. The file reference is passed in its unexpanded form. When **nonomatch** is not declared, the C Shell generates a nomatch error message and does not execute the command.

$verbose The C Shell declares the **verbose** variable when you call it with the **-v** option. You can also declare it using the Set command. In either case, **verbose** causes the C Shell to display the words of each command after a History substitution. (Refer to "History," page 217.)

FILENAME GENERATION

The C Shell generates filenames the same way the Bourne Shell does, with two added features. Refer to Chapter 5 for more information on "Filename Generation."

The C Shell uses an additional special character, a tilde (˜), for filename generation. By itself, ˜ expands into the pathname of your home directory. When followed by a user name, it expands into the pathname of the home directory of that user. The following example shows how to copy the file named **idea.txt** into Helen's home directory (Helen's user name is hls).

```
152 % cp idea.txt ˜hls
153 %
```

You can turn off the filename-expansion feature of the C Shell by setting the **noglob** variable. When **noglob** is set, the Shell treats *, ?, [,], and ˜ as regular characters.

C SHELL SCRIPTS

Just as the Bourne Shell can execute a file of Bourne Shell commands, the C Shell can execute a file of C Shell commands. The concepts of writing and executing programs in the two Shells are similar. However, the methods of declaring and assigning values to variables and the syntax of control structures are different.

Executing a C Shell Script

The first nonblank character in a C Shell script must be a sharp sign (#). If the Shell script starts with any other character, it will be executed by the Bourne Shell. This syntax allows Shell scripts written for both shells to be executed from a C Shell command line. It means that when you switch from the Bourne Shell to the C Shell, all your Bourne Shell scripts will still execute properly and you can write new C Shell scripts as needed. The C Shell considers all Shell script lines that begin with a sharp sign to be comments.

Automatically Executed Shell Scripts

While the Bourne Shell automatically executes one file (the **.profile** file in your home directory) when you log on, the C Shell executes three files at different times during a session.

.login   When you log on and start a session, the C Shell executes the contents of the **.login** file that is located in your home directory. This file should contain commands that you want to execute once, at the beginning of each session. The environment is established from this Shell script: you can use Setenv to declare global variables here. You can also declare the type of terminal that you are using and any parameters that you want to set for **vi** in your **.login** file. A sample **.login** file follows.

```
setenv TERM vt100
setenv EXINIT 'set wrapmargin=10'
stty erase -lcase kill -tabs
echo "This is who's on the machine:"
who
```

This file establishes the type of terminal that you are using by setting the TERM variable. In this case, the Termcap entry for the terminal is vt100. The variable EXINIT, used by **vi**, is also declared and assigned a value. (There is more information about the Setenv command in the section of this chapter titled "Variables.") The sample **.login** file then executes the **stty** utility, displays a message, and executes the **who** utility so that you know who else is using the machine.

.cshrc The C Shell executes the **.cshrc** file that is located in your home directory each time you invoke a new C Shell, as when you log on or execute a C Shell script. You can use this file to establish variables and parameters that are local to a specific Shell. Each time you create a new Shell, the C Shell reinitializes these variables for the new Shell. A sample **.cshrc** file follows.

```
set noclobber
set ignoreeof
set history = 10
set prompt = '! % '
set path = (. /u3/jenny/bin /bin /usr/bin)
alias h history
alias ls ls -l
```

This sample **.cshrc** file sets several Shell variables and establishes two Aliases.

.logout The C Shell executes the **.logout** file in your home directory when you log off the system, normally when you finish your session.

CONTROL STRUCTURES

The C Shell uses many of the same control structures as the Bourne Shell. In each case the syntax is different, but the effects are the same. This chapter summarizes the differences between the control structures in the two Shells. There is a more complete discussion of control structures in Chapter 8.

If

The format of the If control structure is shown below.

```
if (expression) simple-command
```

The If control structure only works with simple commands, not pipes or lists of commands. You can use the If Then control structure (opposite page) to execute more complex commands.

```
# routine to show the use of a simple If
# control structure
#
if ($#argv == 0) echo 'There are no arguments.'
```

The example program above checks to see if it was called without any arguments. If the expression (enclosed in parentheses) evaluates to true—that is, if there were zero arguments on the command line, the If structure displays a message to that effect.

Goto

The format of a Goto statement is shown below.

```
goto label
```

A Goto statement transfers control to the statement beginning with label:. The following example demonstrates the use of Goto.

```
#
if ($#argv == 2) goto goodargs
echo "Please use two arguments."
exit
goodargs:
 .
 .
 .
```

Interrupt Handling

The Onintr statement transfers control when a Shell script is interrupted. The format of an Onintr statement is shown below.

```
onintr label
```

Control is transferred to the statement beginning with label : when you press the (DEL) key during execution of a Shell script.

This statement gives you a way to terminate a script gracefully when it is interrupted. You can use it to insure that upon interruption, a Shell script updates and closes its files before returning control to the Shell.

The following program demonstrates Onintr. It loops continuously until you press the (DEL) key, at which time it displays a message and returns control to the Shell.

```
# demonstration of onintr
onintr close
while (1 == 1)
        echo 'Program is running.'
        sleep 2
end
close:
echo 'End of program.'
```

If Then Else

The three forms of the If Then Else control structure are shown below.

Form 1

```
if (expression) then
        commands
endif
```

Form 2

```
if (expression) then
        commands
else
        commands
endif
```

Form 3

```
if (expression) then
        commands
else if (expression) then
        commands
        .
        .
        .
else
        commands
endif
```

The first form is an extension of the simple If structure, executing more complex **commands** or a series of **commands** if the **expression** is true. This form is still a one-way branch.

The second form is a two-way branch. If the **expression** is true, the first set of **commands** is executed. If it is false, the set of **commands** following Else is executed.

The third form is similar to the If Then Elif structure of the Bourne Shell. It performs tests until it finds an **expression** that is true and then executes the corresponding **commands**.

```
# routine to categorize the first
# command line argument
#
set class
set number = $argv[1]
#
if ($number < 0) then
     @ class = 0
else if (0 <= $number && $number < 100) then
     @ class = 1
else if (100 <= $number && $number < 200) then
     @ class = 2
else
     @ class = 3
endif
#
echo 'The number' $number 'is in class' ${class}'.'
```

The example program above assigns a value of 0-3 to the variable **class**, based on the value of the first command line argument. The variable **class** is declared at the beginning of the program for clarity; it does not need to be declared before its first use. Again, for clarity, **number** is assigned the value of the first command line argument. The first If statement tests to see whether **number** is less than zero. If it is, the script assigns zero to **class**. If it is not, the second If tests to see whether the number is between 0 and 100. The && is a logical And, yielding a value of true if the expression on each side is true. If the number is between 0 and 100, 1 is assigned to **class**. A similar test determines whether the number is between 100 and 200. If it is not, the final Else assigns 3 to **class**. Endif closes the If control structure.

The final statement uses braces to isolate the variable **class** from the following period. Again, this is done for clarity; the Shell does not consider a punctuation mark as part of a variable name. The braces would be required if you wanted other characters to follow immediately after the variable.

Foreach

The Foreach structure parallels the For In structure of the Bourne Shell. Its format follows.

```
foreach loop-index (argument-list)
       commands
end
```

This structure loops through the **commands**. The first time through the loop, the structure assigns the value of the first argument in the **argument-list** to the **loop-index**. When control reaches the End statement, the value of the next argument from the **argument-list** is assigned to the **loop-index** and the commands are executed again. This procedure is repeated until the **argument-list** is exhausted.

```
# routine to zero-fill argv to 20 arguments
#
set buffer = (0 0 0 0 0 0 0 0 0 0 0 0 0 0 0 0 0 0 0 0)
set count = 1
#
if ($#argv > 20) goto toomany
#
       foreach argument ($argv[*])
       set buffer[$count] = $argument
       @ count++
       end
#
# REPLACE argtest ON THE NEXT LINE WITH
# THE PROGRAM YOU WANT TO CALL.
exec argtest $buffer[*]
exit
#
toomany:
echo 'There are more than 20 arguments.'
```

The program above calls another program named **argtest** with a command line guaranteed to contain twenty arguments. If this program is called with fewer than twenty arguments, it fills the command line with zeros to complete the twenty arguments for **argtest**. More than 20 arguments cause it to display an error message.

The Foreach structure loops through the commands one time for each of the command line arguments. Each time through the loop, it assigns the value of the next argument from the command line to the variable **argu-**

ment. Each of these values is assigned to an element of the array **buffer**. The variable **count** maintains the index for the **buffer** array. **count** is incremented by a postfix operator, using the @ command (@ **count**++). An Exec command (refer to Chapter 8) calls **argtest** so that a new process is not initiated. (Once **argtest** is called, the process running this routine will no longer be needed, so there is no need for a new process.)

Break and Continue

A Foreach loop can be interrupted by a Break or Continue statement. These statements cause the remaining commands on the line to be executed before they transfer control. Break transfers control to the statement after the End statement, terminating execution of the loop. Continue transfers control to the End statement, which continues execution of the loop.

While

The format of the While structure is shown below.

```
while (expression)
     commands
end
```

This structure continues to loop through the **commands** *while* the **expression** is true. If the **expression** is false the first time it is evaluated, the **commands** are never executed. Break and Continue statements can be used in a While structure; refer to the previous discussion.

```
# Demonstration of a While control structure.
# This routine sums the numbers between 1 and
# n, n being the first argument on the command
# line.
#
set limit = $argv[1]
set index = 1
set sum = 0
#
     while ($index <= $limit)
     @ sum += $index
     @ index++
     end
#
echo 'The sum is' $sum
```

This program computes the sum of all the integers up to and including n, where n is the first argument on the command line. The += operator assigns the value of **sum + index** to **sum**.

Switch

This structure is analogous to the Case structure of the Bourne Shell.

```
switch (test-string)

        case pattern:
                commands
        breaksw

        case pattern:
                commands
        breaksw
                .
                .
                .
        default:
                commands
        breaksw

endsw
```

Refer to the discussion of the Case statement in Chapter 8 for a discussion of special characters that can be used within the patterns.

```
# Demonstration of a Switch control structure.
# This routine tests the first command line argument
# for yes or no, any combination of upper and lower
# case characters.
#
# test that argv[1] exists
if ($#argv == 0) then
        echo 'Argument one does not exist.'
else
        # argv[1] exists, set up switch based on its value
        switch ($argv[1])
        #
        # case of YES
            case [yY][eE][sS]:
            echo 'Argument one is yes.'
            breaksw
        #
        # case of NO
            case [nN][oO]:
            echo 'Argument one is no.'
            breaksw
        #
        # default case
            default:
            echo 'Argument one is neither yes nor no.'
            breaksw
        endsw
endif
```

Reading User Input

Some implementations of the C Shell have no provision for getting a line of input from the terminal (refer to the Bourne Shell Read command, Chapter 8). Appendix B contains a simple C language program that performs this function. Some implementations use a Set command to read a line from the terminal and assign it to a variable. The following portion of a Shell script prompts the user and reads a line of input into the variable **input_line**.

```
echo 'Input the next condition: '
set input_line = $<
```

BUILT-IN COMMANDS

Built-in commands are part of (built into) the C Shell.

When you give a command, the Shell searches the directory structure for the program you want, using the **path** variable as a guide. When it finds the program, the Shell forks a new process to execute it.

The Shell executes a built-in command as part of the calling process. It does not spawn a new process to execute the command. It does not need to search the directory structure for the command program because the program is immediately available to the Shell. The following list describes the built-in commands.

@ This command is similar to the Set command, but is used to evaluate expressions. See "Variables," page 225.

Alias This command creates and displays Aliases. See "Aliases," page 222.

Cd (or Chdir) This command changes working directories. Refer to the **cd** utility in Part II for more information.

Echo This command is similar to the **echo** utility that is used from the Bourne Shell, but is built in to the C Shell. Refer to the **echo** utility in Part II for more information.

Exec This command is similar to the Exec command of the Bourne Shell. Exec replaces the program that is currently being executed with another program in the same Shell. The original program is lost. Refer to the "Exec" command in Chapter 8 for more information; also refer to "Source" on the following page.

Exit This command is used to exit from a C Shell. When it is followed by an argument that is a number, the number is the exit status that the Shell return to its parent process. Refer to the **status** variable, page 234.

Foreach This is the first keyword in a Foreach control structure. See "Control Structures," page 241.

Goto This command transfers control to a labeled line. See "Control Structures," page 238.

History   This command is used to display the History list of commands. See "History," page 217.

If   This is the first keyword for a If control structure. See "Control Structures," page 238.

Login   This command, which can be followed by a user name, logs in a user. It automatically logs the current user off.

Logout   This command ends a session if you are using your original (login) Shell. See "Shell Scrips," page 237.

Onintr   This command controls the behavior of a Shell script when it is interrupted. See "Control Structures," page 238.

Repeat   This command is followed by two arguments, a count and simple command (no pipes or lists of commands). It repeats the command the specified number of times.

Set   This command is used to declare, initialize, and display the value of local variables. See page 226.

Setenv   This command is used to declare and initialize the value of global variables. See page 225. Many systems include a Printenv command that displays the values of global variables.

Shift   This command is analogous to the Bourne Shell Shift command (page 179). When used without an argument, Shift promotes the indices of the **argv[*]** array. You can use it with an argument to perform the same operation on another array.

Source   Source causes the current C Shell to execute a Shell script given as its argument. It is similar to the . command, except that you do not require execute access permission to the Script. Source expects a C Shell script, so no leading sharp sign is required. The current Shell executes Source so that the Script can contain commands such as Set, that affect the current Shell. Source can be used to execute **.cshrc** or **.login** files from within a Shell.

Switch   This is the first keyword of a Switch control structure. See "Control Structures," page 243.

Time   Time executes the command that you give it as an argument. It displays the elapsed time, the system time, and the execution time for the command. When given without an argument, time displays the times for the current Shell and its children.

Unalias   This command removes an Alias. See "Alias," page 222.

Unset   This command removes a variable declaration. See "Variables," page 226.

Wait   This command causes the Shell to wait for all child processes. When you give a **wait** command in response to a C Shell prompt, the C Shell will not display a prompt and will not accept a command until all background processes have finished execution. If you interrupt it (using (DEL)), Wait displays a list of outstanding processes before returning control to the Shell.

While   This is the first keyword of the While control structure. See "Control structures," page 242.

SUMMARY

The C Shell, like the Bourne Shell, is both a command interpreter and a programming language. It was developed at the University of California at Berkeley and has most of the facilities of the Bourne Shell, plus some others.
   Among its most important features, the C Shell can:

- evaluate logical and numerical expressions
- process arrays of variables representing numbers and strings
- protect against overwriting files and accidentally logging off
- maintain a history of recent commands
- provide an alias mechanism for altering commands
- execute specific files when you log on, log off, and fork a new Shell
- use control structures to control execution within a Shell script

   Although the C Shell is not part of the standard UNIX system, many of its features are available on many systems.

Part II
THE UNIX
UTILITY
PROGRAMS

Part II of this book is a reference section that covers some of the most useful standard UNIX utility programs. It is compact and presents the utilities in a consistent format so that you can quickly find what you are looking for. A tutorial example is given at the end of each utility to show how to use it. Part II lists the utilities alphabetically. Below is a list of the utilities grouped by function.

Utilities That Display and Manipulate Files

awk—search for and process a pattern in a file (page 255)
cat—display a text file (page 263)
comm—compare files (page 271)
cp—copy file (page 273)
diff—display the differences between two files (page 275)
find—find files (page 291)
grep—search for a pattern in a file (page 297)
ln—make a link to a file (page 303)
lpr—print file (page 305)
ls—display information about a file (page 307)
mkdir—make a directory (page 325)
more—display a file (page 326)
mv—rename a file (page 327)
od—dump a file (page 329)
pr—paginate file (page 331)
rm—delete a file (page 336)
rmdir—delete a directory (page 338)
sed—editor (noninteractive) (page 339)
sort—sort and/or merge files (page 352)
spell—check a file for spelling errors (page 360)
tail—display the last part of a file (page 365)
uniq—display lines of a file that are unique (page 374)
wc—display a line, word, and character count (page 377)

Communication Utilities

mail—send or receive mail (page 314)
mesg—enable/disable reception of messages (page 324)
write—send a message to another user (page 379)

Documentation Utility

man—display pages from the system manual (page 38)

Utilities That Display and Alter Status

cd—change to another working directory (page 267)
chmod—change the access mode of a file (page 268)
file—display file classification (page 290)
kill—terminate a process (page 301)
ps—display process status (page 333)
sleep—put process to sleep (page 351)
stty—display or establish terminal parameters (page 361)
who—display names of users (page 378)

Utilities That Are Programming Tools

cc—C compiler (page 265)
make—keep a set of programs current (page 317)
touch—update a file's modification time (page 372)

Miscellaneous Utilities

at—execute a Shell script at a specified time (page 253)
cal—display calendar (page 261)
echo—display a message (page 283)
expr—evaluate an expression (page 284)
tee—copy the standard input to the standard output and one or more files (page 367)
test—evaluate an expression (page 368)
tty—display the terminal pathname (page 373)

The sections below are in the format used throughout Part II. They explain what you can expect to find under each heading within each utility.

utility

This section gives the name of the utility followed by a very brief description.

Format
The way you call the utility, including options and arguments, is listed here. Arguments enclosed in square brackets — [ ] — are optional.

Hyphenated words identify single arguments (e.g., source-file) or groups of similar arguments (e.g., directory-list). As an example, "file-list" means a list of one or more files.

Summary
Unless stated otherwise, the output from a utility goes to the standard output. The "Standard Input and Standard Output" section on page 76 explains how to redirect output so that it goes to a file other than the terminal.

The statement that a utility "takes its input from files specified on the command line or from the standard input," indicates that the utility is a member of the class of UNIX utility programs that takes input from files specified on the command line, or if no filename is specified, from the standard input. It also means that the utility can receive redirected input. See page 80.

Options
The options section lists the common options that you can use with the utility. Unless specified otherwise, you must precede all options with a hyphen. Most utilities accept a single hyphen before multiple options. See page 73.

Arguments
This section describes the arguments that you use when you call the utility. The argument itself, as shown in the preceding "Format" section, is printed in **bold type**.

Notes
Miscellaneous notes, some important and others merely interesting, can be found here.

Examples
You will find examples of the use of the utility in this section. It is tutorial, and is more casual than the preceding sections of the utility description.

at

Execute a Shell script at a specified time.

Format   at time [day] [file]

Summary   at causes the contents of a file to be executed as a Shell script in the working directory at the time specified.

at takes its input from a file specified on the command line or from the standard input.

When at causes a file to be executed, the standard output of the resulting process is not directed to the terminal. Any output that you do not redirect will be lost.

Options   There are no options.

Arguments The **time** is the time of day you want at to execute the contents of the **file**. You can specify the **time** as a one, two, three, or four digit number. One and two digit numbers only specify an hour, while three and four digit numbers specify an hour and minute. at assumes a twenty-four hour clock, unless you place one of the letters **a** (or **am**), **p** (or **pm**), **m** (midnight), or **n** (noon) immediately after the number. If one of these letters is included in the time, at uses a 12-hour clock.

The **day** is the day or date you want at to execute the contents of the **file**. You can abbreviate a day of the week as long as the meaning is not ambiguous. The word **week** can follow the day, indicating that at should not execute the file until one week from the day you specify. If the **day** is specified as a date, it must contain a month name (abbreviations are allowed) followed by a number indicating the day of the month.

Notes   Although at is not available with more recent versions of the UNIX system, there is frequently a similar installation-dependent utility that you can use.

at does not require you to have execute access permission to the **file**. You must, however, be able to read the file.

When you execute at, it creates a file that the Shell executes at the specified time. This file contains the contents of **file**, preceded by two items that insure the proper environment at the time the Shell executes the file. The

253

first is a **cd** command that changes the working directory of the process to the one you were using when you executed **at**. The second is a group of assignment statements that insure that all Shell variables that were present when you executed **at** are present for the execution of the file. The Shell executes the file with the user and group ID of the user that executed **at**.

The exact time of execution of the **file** is installation-dependent. Some systems check to see if there is an **at** file they need to execute every five minutes, some less frequently.

Examples
To paginate and print **long_file** at two o'clock the next morning, create a file containing the necessary command (**file3** below) and execute the **at** utility.

```
$ cat file3
pr long_file | lpr

$ at 2am file3
$
```

The next example executes **cmdfile** at 3:30pm (1530 hours) a week from next Thursday.

```
$ at 1530 thurs week cmdfile
$
```

The final example executes **qtr** on October 1 at 6am.

```
$ at 6 oct 1 qtr
$
```

awk

Search for and process a pattern in a file.

Format

```
awk -f program-file [file-list]
```
or
```
awk program [file-list]
```

Summary

awk is a programming language that searches one or more files to see if they contain lines that match specified patterns. When awk finds a match, it performs an action such as writing the line to the standard output or incrementing a counter. awk can perform simple arithmetic needed to compile many reports and tables. It is similar to grep, but much more powerful.

awk takes its input from files specified on the command line, or from the standard input.

Options

If you do not use the **-f** option, awk uses the first command line argument as its program.

-f (file) This option causes awk to read its program from the **program-file** given as the first command line argument.

Arguments

The **program-file** is the pathname of a file containing an awk program. awk programs are described below.

The **program** is an awk program included on the command line. This format allows you to write simple, short awk programs without creating a separate **program-file**.

The **file-list** contains pathnames of the plain files that awk processes. These are the input files.

Description

An awk program consists of one or more program lines containing a *pattern* and/or *action* in the following format.

```
pattern { action }
```

awk uses the pattern to select lines from the input file. You must enclose the action within braces so that awk can differentiate it from the pattern. awk takes the action on all lines selected by the pattern. If a program line does not contain a pattern, awk selects all lines in the input file. If a program line does not contain an action, awk copies the selected lines to the standard output.

255

awk compares the first line in the input file (from the **file-list**) with each pattern in the **program-file**. If a pattern selects the line (if there is a match), awk takes the action associated with the pattern. If the line is not selected, awk takes no action. When awk has completed its comparisons for the first line of the input file, it repeats the process for the next. It continues this process, comparing subsequent lines in the input file, until it has read the entire **file-list**.

If several patterns select the same line, awk takes the actions associated with each of the patterns. It is therefore possible for awk to send a single line from the input file to the standard output more than once.

Patterns

You can use a regular expression (refer to Appendix A), enclosed within slashes, as a pattern. A field or variable can be tested to see if it matches a regular expression by using the ˜ operator, or if it does not match by using the !˜ operator. awk can process arithmetic and character-relational expressions using the following relational operators.

<	less than
<=	less than or equal to
==	equal to
!=	not equal to
>=	greater than or equal to
>	greater than

You can combine any of the patterns described above using the boolean operators || (Or) or && (And).

If you use two patterns separated by a comma on a single awk program line, awk selects a range of lines beginning with the first line that contains the first pattern. The last line awk selects is the next subsequent line that contains the second pattern.

awk provides two unique patterns so that you can execute instructions before awk starts its processing or after it finishes. awk executes the actions associated with the **BEGIN** pattern before, and with the **END** pattern after, it processes all of the files in the **file-list**.

Actions

The action portion of an **awk** command causes something to happen when a pattern is matched. If you do not specify an action, **awk** assumes { **print** }. This action copies the record (normally a line—see "Variables" below) from the input file to the standard output. You can follow a Print instruction with arguments, causing **awk** to print just the arguments. The arguments can be variables or string constants. **awk** allows you to send the output from a Print instruction to a file (>), to append it to a file (> >), or to pipe it to the input of another program (|).

awk catenates items that Print outputs unless they are separated by commas, in which case the items are separated by the output field separator (normally a SPACE—see "Variables" below).

Comments

awk disregards anything on a program line following a sharp sign (#). You can document an **awk** program by preceding comments with this symbol.

Variables

You declare and initialize user variables when you use them. In addition, **awk** maintains program variables for your use. You can use both user and program variables in the pattern *and* in the action portion of an **awk** program. Following is a list of program variables.

NR	record number of current record
$0	the current record (as a single variable)
NF	number of fields in the current record
$1–$n	fields in the current record
FS	input field separator (SPACE or TAB)
OFS	output field separator (SPACE)
RS	input record separator (NEWLINE)
ORS	output record separator (NEWLINE)
FILENAME	name of the current input file

The input and output record separators are, by default, NEWLINE characters. Thus, **awk** takes each line in the input file to be a separate record and appends a NEWLINE to the end of each record that it sends to the standard output. The input field separators are, by default, SPACEs and TABs. The output field separator is a

(SPACE). You can change the value of any of the separators at any time by assigning a new value to its associated variable.

Functions

The functions that **awk** provides for manipulating numbers and strings are listed below.

length   returns the number of characters in its argument—if no argument is given, it returns the number of characters in the current input record

int   returns the integer portion of its argument

substr(string,index,length)

         returns the substring of **string** that starts at string (**index**) and is **length** characters long.

Operators

The following are valid **awk** arithmetic operators.

```
+= * / %
++ --
+= -= *= /= %=
```

Examples

A simple **awk** program is shown below.

```
{ print }
```

This program consists of one program line that is an action. It uses no pattern. Because the pattern is missing, **awk** selects all lines in the input file. Without any arguments, the Print instruction prints each selected line in its entirety. This program copies the input file to the standard output.

The following program has a pattern part without an explicit action.

```
/jenny/
```

In this case, **awk** selects all lines from the input file that contain the string jenny. When you do not specify an action, **awk** assumes Print. This program copies all the lines in the input file that contain jenny to the standard output.

The next program prints the record number (the program variable **NR**) followed by the third field (the program variable $3) for each record that contains the string jenny.

```
/jenny/ { print NR $3 }
```

awk can produce reports, as shown in the following example.

```
{ total += $2 }
END { print "total is " total }
```

This program calculates the sum of the contents of the second field of each record, keeping a running total in the user variable **total**. **awk** ignores records containing text in this field. **awk** executes the action associated with the pattern **END** after it has processed all the records in the input file. Here it prints the string total is followed by the value of the variable **total**.

The next example selects all records that begin with a (first field is less than b) and keeps running totals of the second and third fields. **awk** does not print anything until it has processed all the input records.

```
$1 < "b" { sum1 += $2; sum2 += $3 }
END     {
        print "total of column two is " sum1;
        print "total of column three is " sum2
        }
```

Next, two patterns separated by a comma select a range of lines. This program copies the 26th through 50th records from the input file to the standard output.

```
NR == 26, NR == 50
```

You can use the Length function to eliminate empty lines. This **awk** program selects lines that have a length greater than zero and copies them to the standard output. It also maintains a count of the number of selected lines and displays this count when it finishes processing the input file.

```
length > 0 { print; count++ }
END { print count " lines" }
```

The example below prints and counts all the lines that have only a single digit in their second field. The ~ operator tests for equality between a pattern and a field.

```
$2 ~ /[0-9]/ { print; count++ }
END { print count " lines" }
```

The final example displays all lines in a file in which field number four differs from the previous line. The first line is always displayed because the variable **remember** is not initialized before **awk** performs the test on the first line.

```
$4 != remember { remember = $4; print }
```

The != operator tests for inequality between a field and a variable. When **awk** reads the first line in the example above, the variable **remember** has a null value so that unless **$4** is null, **$4** and **remember** are not equal. **awk** takes the action within the braces: it assigns the value of the fourth field to **remember** and displays the line. The next line that **awk** selects is the next line that has a value of **$4** different from the value stored in **remember**. **awk** repeats the process, displaying only the lines it selects on the basis of the fourth field.

cal

Display calendar.

Format cal [month] year

Summary cal displays a calendar for a month or year.

Options There are no options.

Arguments The arguments specify the month and year cal displays a calendar for. The **month** is a decimal integer from 1 to 12 and the **year** is a decimal integer.

Notes Do not abbreviate the year. The year 82 does not represent the same year as 1982.

Examples The following command displays a calendar for November 1982.

```
$ cal 11 1982


        November  1982
    S   M Tu  W Th   F   S
        1   2   3   4   5   6
    7   8   9  10  11  12  13
   14  15  16  17  18  19  20
   21  22  23  24  25  26  27
   28  29  30
```

The next command displays a calendar for all of 1949.

```
$ cal 1949

                        1949

        Jan                   Feb                   Mar
 S  M Tu  W Th  F  S    S  M Tu  W Th  F  S    S  M Tu  W Th  F  S
                   1          1  2  3  4  5             1  2  3  4  5
 2  3  4  5  6  7  8    6  7  8  9 10 11 12    6  7  8  9 10 11 12
 9 10 11 12 13 14 15   13 14 15 16 17 18 19   13 14 15 16 17 18 19
16 17 18 19 20 21 22   20 21 22 23 24 25 26   20 21 22 23 24 25 26
23 24 25 26 27 28 29   27 28                  27 28 29 30 31
30 31
        Apr                   May                   Jun
 S  M Tu  W Th  F  S    S  M Tu  W Th  F  S    S  M Tu  W Th  F  S
                1  2    1  2  3  4  5  6  7             1  2  3  4
 3  4  5  6  7  8  9    8  9 10 11 12 13 14    5  6  7  8  9 10 11
 .
 .
 .
$
```

calendar

Reminder calendar.

Format   (not normally called by the user)

Summary   calendar is normally a service provided by the UNIX system. Once a day, this utility reviews the file named **calendar** in each user's home directory and sends any line containing that or the next day's date to that user via the mail utility.

Options   There are no options.

Arguments   There are no arguments.

Notes   During the weekend, the *next day* is considered to go through Monday.

The **calendar** file *must* be in your home directory. The dates can appear anywhere on the line in the file, in various formats, but must show the month preceding the day of the month.

When you execute calendar, or have your **.profile** or **.login** file execute it, calendar displays any lines in the **calendar** file that contain that or the next day's date.

calendar ignores any reference to a year as part of the date.

Examples   The following example of a **calendar** file shows some of the ways you can express the date. If you place this file in your home directory, each of the three lines will be sent to you by mail on the date specified, and one day previous to it.

```
$ cat calendar
This line will be displayed on 11/20/82
Nov 28: remember to call Frank
On november 30 five years ago. . .
$
```

262

cat

Display a text file.

Format

```
cat [file-list]
```

Summary

cat displays the contents of one or more plain text files. It takes its input from files specified on the command line or from the standard input.

Options

There are no options. (The Berkeley UNIX system uses **−v** to make nonprinting characters visible, **−e** to show the end of a line with a dollar sign, and **−t** to show (TAB) characters.)

Arguments

The **file-list** is composed of pathnames of one or more plain text files that cat displays. You can use a hyphen in place of a filename to cause cat to read the standard input (e.g., **cat a − b** gets its input from file **a**, the standard input (terminated by a (CONTROL-D)), and then file **b**).

Notes

Use the **od** utility (also covered in Part II) to display the contents of a file that does not contain text (e.g., an executable program file).

A command line such as the following destroys the input file (**letter**) before reading it.

```
$ cat memo letter > letter
$
```

The name cat is derived from one of the functions of this utility, *catenate,* which means to join together sequentially, or end to end.

Examples

The following command line displays the contents of the text file named **memo** on the terminal.

```
$ cat memo
.
.
.
$
```

The next example catenates three files and redirects the output to a file named **all**.

```
$ cat page1 letter memo > all
$
```

263

You can use cat to create short text files without using an editor. Enter the command line shown below, type the text that you want in the file, and then press (CONTROL-D) on a line by itself. cat takes its input from the standard input (the terminal) and the Shell redirects its standard output (a copy of the input) to the specified file. The (CONTROL-D) signals an end of file and causes cat to return control to the Shell. (Also see page 79).

```
$ cat > new_file
.
.
.
(text)
.
.
.
(CONTROL-D)
$
```

cc

C compiler.

Format

cc [options] file-list

Summary

Based on the command line options, **cc** compiles, assembles, and loads C language source programs. It can also assemble and load assembly language source programs, or merely load object programs.

cc uses the following file-naming conventions.

1. A filename extension of **.c** indicates a C language source program.
2. A filename extension of **.s** indicates an assembly language source program.
3. A filename extension of **.o** indicates an object program.

cc takes its input from files specified on the command line. Unless you use the **-o** option, **cc** stores the executable program it produces in **a.out**.

Options

Without any options, **cc** accepts C language source programs, assembly language source programs, and object programs that follow the file-naming conventions outlined above. It compiles, assembles, and loads these programs as appropriate, producing an executable file named **a.out**. **cc** puts the object programs in files with the same base filename as their source, but with a filename extension of **.o**. If a single C program is compiled, assembled, and loaded with one command, **cc** deletes the object program.

-c (compile) Do not load object files. This option causes **cc** to compile and/or assemble source programs and leave the corresponding object programs in files with filename extensions of **.o**.

-o **file**

(output) Place executable program in **file** instead of **a.out**. You can use any filename in place of **file**.

-O (optimize) Optimize C source program compilation.

-S (compile only) Only compile C source programs. This option causes **cc** to compile C programs and

265

leave the corresponding assembly language source programs in files with filename extensions of **.s**.

–l   **arg**

(search library) Search the **/lib/lib***arg*. **a** and **/usr /lib/lib***arg*. **a** libraries. Load any required functions. For example, the **–lm** option normally loads the standard math library.

The position of this option is significant; it is generally placed at the end of the command line. The loader only uses the library to resolve undefined symbols from modules that *precede* the library option on the command line.

Arguments   The **file-list** contains the pathnames of the programs that **CC** is to compile, assemble, and/or load.

Examples   The first example compiles, assembles, and loads a single C program, **compute.c**. The executable output is put in **a.out**. **CC** deletes the object file.

```
$ cc compute.c
$
```

Next, the same program is compiled using the C optimizer (**–O** option). The optimized code is assembled and then loaded. The executable output is put in **compute** as specified by the **–o** option.

```
$ cc –O compute.c –o compute
$
```

Next, a C program, an assembly language program, and an object program are compiled, assembled, and loaded. The executable output is saved in the **progo** file.

```
$ cc procom.c profast.s proout.o –o progo
$
```

The final example causes **CC** to search the standard math library stored in **/lib/libm.a** when it is loading the **himath** program. The executable output is placed in **a.out**.

```
$ cc himath.c –lm
$
```

cd or chdir

Change to another working directory.

Format   cd [directory]

Summary   When you specify a directory, that directory becomes the working directory. If you do not specify a directory on the command line, cd makes your home directory become the working directory.

Options   There are no options.

Argument The **directory** is the pathname of the directory that you want to become the working directory.

Notes   cd is not really a utility, but a built-in command in both the C and Bourne Shells. Refer to the discussion of the **HOME** Bourne Shell variable in Chapter 8 and the **home** C Shell variable in Chapter 9. Chapter 4 contains a discussion of cd.

Examples The following command makes your home directory become the working directory.

```
$ cd
$
```

The next command specifies a directory that the user wants to make the working directory.

```
$ cd /usr/alex/literature
$
```

chmod

Change the access mode of a file.

Format `chmod who[operation][permission] file-list`

Summary **chmod** changes the ways in which a file can be accessed by the owner of the file, the group to which the owner belongs, and/or all other users. Only the owner of a file or the super user can change the access mode of a file.

Options There are no options.

Arguments Arguments give **chmod** information about what files are to have their modes changed in what way.

chmod changes the access permission for the class of user specified by **who**. The class of user is designated by one or more of the following letters.

u   (user) owner of the file
g   (group) group to which the owner belongs
o   (other) all other users
a   (all) can be used in place of u, g, and o above

The **operation** to be performed is defined by the following list.

+   add permission for the specified user
−   remove permission for the specified user
=   set permission for the specified user—all other permissions for that user are reset

The access **permission** is defined by the following list.

r   read permission
w   write permission
x   execute permission
s   set user ID or set group ID (depending on the **who** argument) to that of the owner of the file while the file is being executed

Notes The only time the **permission** can be omitted from the command line is when the **operation** is = . This omission takes away all permissions. You can use the **ls** utility (with the −1 option) to display file access privileges (page 307).

Chapter 4 contains a description of file access privileges.

Examples   The following examples show how to use the **chmod** utility. A file named **temp** is used in the examples. The initial
access mode of **temp** is shown by ls.

```
$ ls -l temp
-rw-rw-r--  1 alex    57 Dec  5 16:47 temp
$
```

The command line below removes all access permissions for the group and all other users so that only the
owner has access to the file. When you do not follow an
equal sign with a permission, chmod removes all permissions for the specified user class. The ls utility verifies the
change.

```
$ chmod go= temp

$ ls -l temp
-rw-------  1 alex    57 Dec  5 16:47 temp
$
```

The next command changes the access modes for all
users (user, group, and all others) to read and write. Now
anyone can read from or write to the file. Again, ls verifies the change.

```
$ chmod a=rw temp

$ ls -l temp
-rw-rw-rw-  1 alex    57 Dec  5 16:47 temp
$
```

The following command removes the write access
privilege for all other users. This change means that
members of the owner's group can still read from and
write to the file, but other users can only read from the
file.

```
$ chmod o-w temp

$ ls -l temp
-rw-rw-r--  1 alex    57 Dec  5 16:47 temp
$
```

The final command adds execute access privilege for all other users. If **temp** is a Shell script or other executable file, all other users can now execute it.

```
$ chmod o+x temp

$ ls -l temp
-rw-rw-r-x  1 alex   57 Dec 5 16:47 temp
$
```

comm
Compare files.

Format

comm [options] file1 file2

Summary

comm displays a line-by-line comparison of two sorted files. (If the files have not been sorted, **comm** will not work properly.) The display is in three columns. The first column lists all lines found only in **file1**, the second column lists lines found only in **file2**, and the third lists those common to both files.

Input comes from the files specified on the command line. (Refer to "Arguments" below for an exception.)

Options

You can use the options, **−1**, **−2**, and **−3**, individually or in combination.

−1 **comm** does not display column one.

−2 **comm** does not display column two.

−3 **comm** does not display column three.

Arguments

The **file1** and **file2** are pathnames of the files that **comm** compares. You can use a hyphen in place of **file1** or **file2** to cause **comm** to use the standard input.

Examples

The following examples use two files, **c** and **d**, that are in the working directory. The contents of these files are shown below. As with all input to **comm**, the files are in sorted order. Refer to the **sort** utility for information on sorting files.

File c	File d
bbbbb	aaaaa
ccccc	ddddd
ddddd	eeeee
eeeee	ggggg
fffff	hhhhh

The first command (below) calls **comm** without any options. **comm** displays three columns. The first column lists those lines found only in file **c**, the second column lists those found in **d**, and the third lists the lines found in both **c** and **d**.

```
$ comm c d
        aaaaa
bbbbb
ccccc
                    ddddd
                    eeeee
fffff
        ggggg
        hhhhh
$
```

The next example shows the use of options to prevent **comm** from displaying columns one and two. The result is column three, a list of the lines common to files **c** and **d**.

```
$ comm −12 c d
ddddd
eeeee
$
```

cp
Copy file.

Format

```
cp source-file destination-file
```
or
```
cp source-file-list destination-directory
```

Summary

cp copies one or more plain files, including text and executable program files. cp has two modes of operation. The first copies one file to another. The second copies one or more files to a directory.

Options

There are no options.

Arguments

The **source-file** is the pathname of the plain file that cp is going to copy. The **destination-file** is the pathname that cp will assign to the resulting copy of the file.

The **source-file-list** is one or more pathnames of plain files that cp is going to copy. The **destination-directory** is the pathname of the directory in which cp will place the resulting copied files. When you specify a **destination-directory**, cp gives each of the copied files the same simple filename as its **source-file**. If, for example, you copy **/usr/jenny/memo.416** to the **/usr/jenny/archives** directory, the copy will also have the simple filename **memo.416**, but its pathname will be **/usr/jenny/archives/memo.416**.

Notes

If the **destination-file** exists before you execute cp, cp overwrites the file, destroying the contents but leaving the access privileges and owner associated with the file as they were. If it does not exist, the access privileges for, and the owner of, the **destination-file** are the same as those of the **source-file**.

Examples

The first command makes a copy of the file **letter** in the working directory. The name of the copy is **letter.sav**.

```
$ cp letter letter.sav
$
```

The next command copies all the files with filenames ending in .c into the **archives** file, a subdirectory of the

273

working directory. The copied files each maintain their simple filenames but have new pathnames.

```
$ cp *.c archives
$
```

The final command copies two files named **memo** and **letter** into another directory. The copies have the same simple filenames as the source files (**memo** and **letter**), but they have different pathnames. The pathnames of the copied files are **/usr/jenny/memo** and **/usr/jenny/letter**.

```
$ cp memo letter /usr/jenny
$
```

diff

Display the differences between two files.

Format   `diff [options] file1 file2`

Summary   **diff** displays the differences between two files on a line-by-line basis. It displays the differences as instructions that you can use to edit one of the files to make it the same as the other.

Input comes from the files specified on the command line. (Refer to "Arguments" for an exception.)

Options   Without any options, **diff** produces a series of lines containing **a** (Add), **d** (Delete), and **c** (Change) instructions. Each of these lines is followed by the lines from the file that need to be added, deleted, or changed. Lines from **file1** are preceded by a less-than symbol (<). A greater-than symbol (>) precedes lines from **file2**. **diff** produces output in the formats shown below. A pair of line numbers separated by a comma represents a range of lines, and can be replaced by a single line number that represents a single line.

Instruction	Meaning (changing file1 to file2)
linc1 a linc2,line3 > lines from file2	Append lines from file2 after line1 in file1
line1,line2 d line3 < lines from file1	Delete line1 through line2 from file1
line1,line2 c line3, line4 < lines from file1 --- > lines from file2	Change line1 through line2 in file1 to lines from file2

diff assumes that you are going to convert **file1** to **file2**. The line numbers to the left of each of the **a**, **c**, or **d** instructions always pertain to **file1**; numbers to the right of the instructions apply to **file2**. To convert **file1** to **file2**, ignore the line numbers to the right of the instructions. (To convert **file2** to **file1**, use a **d** in place of each **a**, an **a** in place of each **d**, and use the line numbers to the right of the instructions.)

-e This option creates an **ed** script that will edit **file1** to make it the same as **file2**. You must add **w** (Write) and **q** (Quit) instructions to the end of the script if you are going to redirect it as input to **ed**.

Arguments The **file1** and **file2** are pathnames of the files that **diff** works on. You can use a hyphen in place of **file1** or **file2** to cause **diff** to use the standard input.

Examples The first example shows how **diff** displays the differences between two short, similar files.

```
$ cat m
aaaaa
bbbbb
ccccc

$ cat n
aaaaa
ccccc

$ diff m n
2d1
< bbbbb
$
```

The difference between files **m** and **n** is that the second line from file **m** (bbbbb) is missing from file **n**. The first line that **diff** displays (2d1) indicates that you need to delete the second line from file1 (**m**) to make it the same as file2 (**n**). Unless you are editing file2 to make it the same as file1, ignore the numbers following the letters on the instruction lines. The next line **diff** displays starts with a less-than symbol (<) indicating that this line of text is from file1. In this example you do not need this information—all you need to know is the line number so that you can delete the line.

The next example uses the same **m** file and a new file, **p**, to demonstrate **diff** issuing an **a** (Append) instruction.

```
$ cat p
aaaaa
bbbbb
rrrrr
ccccc
```

```
$ diff m p
2a3
> rrrrr
$
```

diff issues the instruction 2a3 to indicate that you must append a line to file **m**, after line two, to make it the same as file **p**. The second line that **diff** displays indicates that the line is from file **p** (the line begins with >, indicating file2). In this example you need the information on this line—the appended line must contain the text rrrrr.

The next example uses **m** again, this time with file **r**, to show how **diff** indicates a line that needs to be changed.

```
$ cat r
aaaaa
qqqqq
ccccc

$ diff m r
2c2
< bbbbb
---
> qqqqq
$
```

The difference between the two files is in line two: file **m** contains bbbbb while file **r** contains qqqqq. **diff** displays 2c2 to indicate that line two needs to be changed. After indicating that a change is needed, **diff** shows that line two in file **m** (bbbbb) must be changed to line two in file **r** (qqqqq) to make the files the same. The three hyphens indicate the end of the text in file **m** that needs to be changed, and the start of the text in file **r** that is to replace it.

Next, a *group* of lines in file **m** needs to be changed to make it the same as file **t**.

```
$ cat t
aaaaa
|||||
sssss
nnnnn

$ diff m t
2,3c2,4
< bbbbb
< ccccc
---
> |||||
> sssss
> nnnnn
$
```

diff indicates that lines two through three (2,3) in file **m** need to be changed from **bbbbb** and **ccccc** to ||||||, sssss, and nnnnn.

The next set of examples demonstrates how to use **diff** to keep track of versions of a file that is repeatedly updated, without maintaining a library of each version in its entirety. When used with the **–e** option, **diff** displays an **ed** script that can recreate the second file from the first. If you keep a copy of the original file and the **ed** script that **diff** creates, each time you update the file, you can recreate any version of the file. Because these scripts are usually shorter than the files they are relating, the scripts can help conserve disk space.

In these examples, **menu1** is the original file. When it needs to be updated, it is copied to **menu2** and the changes are made to the copy of the file. The resulting files are shown below.

```
$ cat menu1
BREAKFAST
        scrambled eggs
        toast
        orange juice

LUNCH
        hamburger on roll
        small salad
        milkshake

DINNER
        sirloin steak
        peas
        potato
        vanilla ice cream

$ cat menu2
BREAKFAST
        poached eggs
        toast
        orange juice

LUNCH
        hamburger on roll
        french fries
        milkshake

DINNER
        chef's salad
        fruit
        cheese
$
```

diff with the **−e** option produces an **ed** script that details the changes between the two versions of the file. The first command line below redirects the output from **diff** to **2changes**; **cat** displays the resulting file. The **ed** Change Mode is invoked by the **c** command. In this mode, the lines that you specify in the command are replaced by the text that you enter following the command. A period instructs **ed** to terminate the Change Mode and return to the Command Mode.

```
$ diff -e menu1 menu2 > 2changes

$ cat 2changes
12,15c
        chef's salad
        fruit
        cheese
.
8c
        french fries
.
2c
        poached eggs
.
$
```

The only commands missing from the **ed** script that **diff** creates are **w** (Write) and **q** (Quit). Below, these are appended to **2changes**. (You can also use an editor to add the commands to the file.)

```
$ cat >> 2changes
w
q
CONTROL-D
$
```

Next, the process is repeated when the file is updated for the second time. The file is copied (to **menu3**), the changes are made to the copy, and the original (**menu2** in this case) and the edited copy are processed by **diff**. The **ed** script is displayed after the necessary commands have been added to it.

```
$ cat menu3
BREAKFAST
        poached eggs
        toast
        grapefruit juice

LUNCH
        tuna sandwich
        french fries

DINNER
        potluck

$ diff -e menu2 menu3 > 3changes

$ cat >> 3changes
w
q
CONTROL-D

$ cat 3changes
12,,14c
        potluck
.
9d
7c
        tuna sandwich
.
4c
        grapefruit juice
.
w
q
$
```

The **menu2** and **menu3** files are no longer needed; they can be recreated from **menu1**, **2change**, and **3change**. The process of recreating a file is shown below. First, the original file is copied to a file that will become the updated file. (If you make changes to the original file, you may not be able to go back and recreate one of the intermediate files.)

```
$ copy menu1 recreate
$
```

Next, the copy of the original file (**recreate**) is edited by **ed** with input from **2changes**. **ed** displays the number of characters it reads and writes. After it has been edited with **2changes**, the file is the same as the original **menu2**.

```
$ ed recreate < 2changes
155
134

$ cat recreate
BREAKFAST
        poached eggs
        eggs
        orange juice

LUNCH
        hamburger on roll
        french fries
        milkshake

DINNER
        chef's salad
        fruit
        cheese
$
```

If you just want **menu2** you can stop at this point. By editing the recreated **menu2** (now **recreate**) with input from **3changes**, **menu3** is recreated below.

```
$ ed recreate < 3changes
134
104

$ cat recreate
BREAKFAST
        poached eggs
        toast
        grapefruit juice

LUNCH
        tuna sandwich
        french fries

DINNER
        potluck
$
```

echo

Display a message.

Format `echo [option] message`

Summary **echo** copies its arguments, followed by a (NEWLINE), to the standard output.

Option −n (no (NEWLINE)) This option causes **echo** not to display a (NEWLINE) at the end of the message.

Arguments The **message** is one or more arguments. These arguments can include quoted strings, ambiguous file references, and Shell variables. Each argument is separated from the others by a (SPACE). The Shell recognizes unquoted special characters in the arguments (e.g., the Shell expands an asterisk into a list of all of the filenames in the working directory).

Notes You can use **echo** to send messages to the terminal from a Shell script. For other uses of **echo**, refer to the discussion of **echo** at the end of Chapter 5.

   echo is called as a utility from the Bourne Shell. It is a built-in command in the C Shell. Some versions of the C Shell command do not have a **−n** option.

Examples The following examples demonstrate the use of the **echo** utility.

```
$ echo 'Today is Friday.'
Today is Friday.

$ echo -n 'There is no newline after this.'
There is no newline after this.$
```

expr

Evaluate an expression.

Format `expr expression`

Summary **expr** evaluates an expression and displays the result. It evaluates character strings that represent either numeric or non-numeric values. Operators separate the strings to form expressions.

Options There are no options.

Arguments The **expression** is composed of other expressions and strings with operators in between. Each string and operator is a separate argument and must be separated from other arguments by a (SPACE). The following list of **expr** operators is in order of decreasing precedence. You can change the order of evaluation by using parentheses.

: comparison operator
This operator compares two strings, starting with the first character in each string and ending with the last character in the second string. If there is a match, it displays the number of characters in the second string. If there is no match, it displays a zero.

* multiplication operator
/ division operator
% remainder operator
These operators only work on strings that contain the numerals 0 through 9. They convert the strings to integer numbers, perform the specified arithmetic operation on numbers, and convert the result back to a string before displaying it.

\+ addition operator
– subtraction operator
These operators function in the same manner as those described above.

<	less than
<=	less than or equal to
=	equal to
!=	not equal to
>=	greater than or equal to
>	greater than

These relational operators work on both numeric and non-numeric arguments. If one or both of the arguments is non-numeric, the comparison is non-numeric, using the machine collating sequence. If both arguments are numeric, the comparison is numeric. **expr** displays a one if the comparison is true and a zero if it is false.

& And operator
The And operator evaluates both of its arguments. If neither is zero or a null string, it displays the value of the first argument. Otherwise, it displays a zero. You must quote this operator.

| Or operator
This operator evaluates the first argument. If it is neither zero nor a null string, it displays the value of the first argument. Otherwise, it displays the value of the second argument. You must quote this operator.

Notes **expr** returns an exit status of zero if the expression is neither a null string nor the number zero, one if the expression is null or zero, and two if the expression is invalid.

expr is useful in Bourne Shell scripts. Because the C Shell has the equivalent of **expr** built into it, **expr** is not normally used from the C Shell.

Although **expr** and this discussion distinguish between numeric and non-numeric arguments, all arguments to **expr** are actually non-numeric (character strings). When applicable, **expr** converts an argument to a number (e.g., when using the + operator). If a string contains characters other than 0 through 9, expr cannot convert it. Specifically, if a string contains a plus sign, a minus sign, or a decimal point, expr considers it to be non-numeric.

Examples   The following examples show expr being used from the command line to evaluate constants. You can also use expr to evaluate variables in a Shell script.

Although expr can yield a negative number as the result of an operation, it cannot accept a negative number as an argument. The third command line causes expr to display an error message.

```
$ expr 17 + 40
57

$ expr 10 - 24
-14

$ expr -17 + 20
non-numeric argument
$
```

The multiplication (*), division (/), and remainder (%) operators provide additional arithmetic power as demonstrated below. You must quote the multiplication operator (precede it with a backslash) so that the Shell does not treat it as a special character (an ambiguous file reference).

```
$ expr 5 \* 4
20
$

$ expr 21 / 7
3
$

$ expr 23 % 7
2
$
```

Parentheses can be used to change the order of evaluation as shown in the next two examples. Each parenthesis needs to be quoted and the backslash/parenthesis combination must be surrounded by blanks.

```
$ expr 2 \* 3 + 4
10
$

$ expr 2 \* \( 3 + 4 \)
14
$
```

You can use relational operators to determine the relationship between numeric or non-numeric arguments. The command below uses **expr** to compare two strings to see if they are equal. **expr** displays a zero when the relationship is false and a one when it is true.

```
$ expr fred = mark
0
$

$ expr mark = mark
1
$
```

Relational operators, which must also be quoted, can establish order between numeric or non-numeric arguments. Again, if a relationship is true, **expr** displays a one.

```
$ expr fred \> mark
0
$

$ expr fred \< mark
1
$

$ expr 5 \< 7
1
$
```

The next command compares **5** with **m**. When one of the arguments being compared by a relational operator is non-numeric, **expr** considers the other to be non-numeric. In this case, because **m** is non-numeric, **expr** treats **5** as a non-numeric argument. The comparison is between the ASCII (or other code) values of **m** and **5**.

The ASCII value of **m** is 109 and **5** is 53 so that expr evaluates the relationship as true.

```
$ expr 5 \< m
1
$
```

In the next example, the matching operator is shown determining that the four characters in the second string match the first four characters in the first string. expr displays a four.

```
$ expr abcdefghijkl : abcd
4
$
```

The **&** operator displays a zero if one or both of its arguments are zero or the null string. Otherwise, it displays the first argument.

```
$ expr '' \& book
0
$

$ expr magazine \& book
magazine
$

$ expr 5 \& 0
0
$

$ expr 5 \& 6
5
$
```

The **|** operator displays the first argument if it is not zero or the null string. Otherwise, it displays the second argument.

```
$ expr '' \| book
book
$

$ expr magazine \| book
magazine
$

$ expr 5 \| 0
5
$

$ expr 0 \| 5
5
$

$ expr 5 \| 6
5
$
```

file

Display file classification.

Format	`file file-list`
Summary	**file** classifies files according to their contents.
Options	There are no options.
Arguments	The **file-list** contains the pathnames of one or more files that **file** classifies. You can specify any kind of file, including plain, directory, and special files, in the **file-list**.
Notes	**file** works by examining the first part of a file, looking for keywords and special numbers that the linker uses. It also examines the access permissions associated with the file. The results of **file** are not always correct.
Examples	Some examples of file identification follow.

```
$ file memo proc new
memo:    English text
proc:    commands text
new:     empty
$
```

A few of the classifications that **file** displays are listed below.

```
English text
ascii text
c program text
cannot stat
commands text
data
directory
empty
executable
```

find

Find files.

Format	`find directory-list expression`
Summary	**find** selects files that are located in specified directories and are described by an expression. **find** does not generate any output without explicit instructions to do so.
Options	There are no options.
Arguments	The **directory-list** contains the pathnames of one or more directories that **find** is to search. When **find** searches a directory, it searches all subdirectories, to all levels.

The **expression** contains one or more criteria, as described in "Criteria." **find** tests each of the files in each of the directories in the **directory-list** to see if it meets the criteria described by the **expression**.

If two criteria are separated by a (SPACE), the criteria are anded: the file must meet *both* criteria to be selected. If two criteria are separated by **–o**, the criteria are ored: the file must meet one or the other (or both) of the criteria to be selected.

You can negate any criterion by preceding it with an exclamation point. **find** evaluates criteria from left to right unless you group them using parentheses.

Within the **expression** you must quote special characters so that the Shell does not interpret them, but passes them to the **find** utility. Special characters that you may frequently use with **find** are parentheses, square brackets, question marks, and asterisks.

Each element within the **expression** is a separate argument. You must separate arguments from each other with (SPACE)s. There must be a (SPACE) on both sides of each parenthesis, exclamation point, criteria, or other element. When you use a backslash to quote a special character, the (SPACE)s go on each side of the pair of characters (e.g., " \[").

Criteria

Following is a list of criteria that you can use within the **expression**. As used in this list, **±n** is a decimal integer that can be expressed as **+n** (meaning more than **n**), **−n** (meaning less than **n**), or **n** (meaning exactly **n**).

−name **filename**
The file being evaluated meets this criterion if **filename** matches its name. You can use ambiguous file references, but they must be quoted.

−type **filetype**
The file being evaluated meets this criterion if **filetype** specifies its file type. You can select a file type from the following list.

File Type	Description
b	block special file
c	character special file
d	directory file
f	plain file

−links **±n**
The file being evaluated meets this criterion if it has the number of links specified by **±n**.

−user **name**
The file being evaluated meets this criterion if it belongs to the user with the login name, **name**. You can use the numeric user ID in place of **name**.

−group **name**
The file being evaluated meets this criterion if it belongs to the group with the group name, **name**. You can use the numeric group ID in place of **name**.

−size **±n**
The file being evaluated meets this criterion if it is the size specified by **±n**, measured in bytes.

−atime **±n**
The file being evaluated meets this criterion if it was last accessed the number of days ago specified by **±n**.

−mtime **±n**
The file being evaluated meets this criterion if it was last modified the number of days ago specified by **±n**.

−newer **filename**
The file being evaluated meets this criterion if it was modified more recently than **filename**.

−print
The file being evaluated always meets this action criterion. When evaluation of the **expression** reaches this criterion, find displays the pathname of the file it is evaluating. If this is the only criterion in the **expression**, find displays the names of all the files in the **directory-list**. If this criterion is anded with other criteria, find displays the name only if the preceding criteria are met. Refer to "Discussion" and "Notes," below.

−exec **command**
The file being evaluated meets this action criterion if the **command** returns a zero (true value) as an exit status. You must terminate the **command** with a quoted semicolon. A pair of braces ({ }) within the **command** represents the filename of the file being evaluated.

You can use the **−exec** action criterion at the end of a group of other criteria to execute the **command** if the preceding criteria are met. Refer to the following "Discussion."

−ok **command**
This action criterion is the same as **−exec**, except that it displays each of the **command**s to be executed, enclosed in angle brackets. find only executes the **command** if it receives a **y** from the standard input.

Discussion   Assume that **x** and **y** are criteria. The following command line never tests to see if the file meets criterion **y** if criterion **x** is not met. Because the criteria are anded, once find determines that criterion **x** is not met, the file cannot meet the criteria, so find does not continue testing. Assume the file is in the **dir** directory. You can read the expression as "(test to see) if criterion **x** *and* (SPACE) means and) criterion **y** are met."

```
find dir x y
```

The next command line *always* tests the file against criterion **y** if criterion **x** is not met. The file can still meet the criteria, so find continues the evaluation. It is read as "(test to see) if criterion **x** *or* criterion **y** is met." If the file meets criterion **x**, find does not evaluate criterion **y**, as there is no need.

```
find dir x -o y
```

Certain "criteria" do not select files, but cause find to take action. The action is triggered when find evaluates one of these *action criteria*. Therefore, the position of an action criterion on the command line, and not the result of its evaluation, determines whether find takes the action.

The **–print** action criterion causes find to display the pathname of the file it is testing. The following command line displays the names of all files in the **dir** directory (and all subdirectories) that meet criterion **x**.

```
find dir x -print
```

The following command line displays the names of *all* the files in the **dir** directory.

```
find dir -print x
```

Notes find must be explicitly instructed to display filenames if you want it to do so. Unless you include the **–print** criterion or its equivalent on the command line, find does its work silently. Refer to the first example below.

You can use the **–a** operator between criteria for clarity. This causes two criteria to be anded, just as a (SPACE) does.

Examples   The following command line finds all the files in the working directory, and all subdirectories, that have filenames that begin with **a**. The command uses a period to designate the working directory, and quotes the ambiguous file reference. The command does not instruct **find** to do anything with these files—not even display their names. This is not a useful example, but it demonstrates a common problem when using **find**.

```
$ find . —name 'a*'
$
```

The next command line finds *and displays the filenames of* all the files in the working directory, and all subdirectories, that have filenames that begin with **a**.

```
$ find . —name 'a*' —print
.
.
.
$
```

The command line below finds, displays the filenames of, and deletes all the files in the working directory, and all subdirectories, that belong to Alex or Jenny.

The parentheses and the semicolon following **—exec** are quoted so that the Shell does not treat them as special characters. (SPACE)s separate the quoted parentheses from other elements on the command line. You can read this **find** command as, "**find**, in the working directory and all subdirectories (.), all files that belong to Alex (**—user alex**) *or* (**—o**) belong to Jenny (**—user jenny**) [if a file meets these criteria, continue with] *and* ((SPACE)) print (**—print**) the name of the file *and* ((SPACE)) delete the file (**—exec rm** {})."

```
$ find . \( —user alex —o —user jenny \) —print —exec rm {} \;
.
.
.
$
```

The next command finds all files in two user directories that are larger than 10000 bytes (**–size +10000**)
and have only been accessed more than five days ago—
that is, have not been accessed within the past five days
(**–atime +5**). This **find** command then asks whether you
want to delete the file (**–ok rm** { }). You must respond to
each of these queries with a **y** (for yes) or **n** (for no). The
delete command does not work if you do not have execute
and write access permission to the directory.

```
$ find /usr/alex /usr/barbara -size +10000 -atime +5 -ok rm {} \;
< rm . . . /usr/alex/notes >?    y
< rm . . . /usr/alex/letter >?    n
  .
  .
  .
$
```

grep

Search for a pattern in a file.

Format `grep [options] pattern [file-list]`

Summary **grep** searches one or more files, line by line, for a **pattern**. The **pattern** can be a simple string, or another form of a regular expression. **grep** takes various actions, specified by options, each time it finds a line that contains a match for the **pattern**.

    grep takes its input from files specified on the command line or from the standard input.

Options If you do not specify any options, **grep** sends its lines to the standard output. If you specify more than one file on the command line, **grep** precedes each line that it displays with the name of the file that it came from.

-c (count) **grep** only indicates the number of lines in each file that contain a match.

-e (expression) This option allows you to use a **pattern** beginning with a hyphen. If you do not use this option and specify a **pattern** that begins with a hyphen, **grep** assumes that the hyphen introduces an option and the search will not work.

-h (no header) **grep** does not list filenames. Use this option when you specify more than one file and want only a list of lines without filenames. The **-h** option is useful when you use **grep** within a pipe.

-l (list) **grep** displays the name of each file that contains one or more matches. **grep** displays each filename only once, even if the file contains more than one match.

-n (number) **grep** precedes each line by its line number in the file. The file does not need to contain line numbers—this number represents the number of lines in the file up to and including the displayed line.

-s (status) **grep** returns an exit status value without any output. (See "Notes" below.)

-v (reverse sense of test) This option causes lines *not* containing a match to satisfy the search. When you use this option by itself, **grep** displays all lines that do not contain a match.

-y This option causes lowercase letters in the pattern to match uppercase letters in the file. Use this option when searching for a word that may be at the beginning of a sentence (i.e., may or may not start with an uppercase letter).

Arguments   The **pattern** is a regular expression as defined in Appendix A. You must quote regular expressions that contain special characters, (SPACE)s, or (TAB)s. An easy way to quote these characters is to enclose the entire expression within apostrophes.

The **file-list** contains pathnames of plain text files that **grep** searches.

Notes   **grep** returns an exit status of zero if a match is found, one if no match is found, and two if the file is not accessible or there is a syntax error.

There are two utilities that perform functions similar to that of **grep**. The **egrep** utility can be faster than **grep**, but may also use more space. **fgrep** is fast and compact, but can process only simple strings, not regular expressions.

Examples   The following examples assume that the working directory contains three files: **testa**, **testb**, and **testc**. The contents of each file is shown below.

File testa	File testb	File testc
aaabb	aaaaa	AAAAA
bbbcc	bbbbb	BBBBB
ff–ff	ccccc	CCCCC
cccdd	ddddd	DDDDD
dddaa		

grep can search for a pattern that is a simple string of characters. The following command line searches **testa** for the string bb. **grep** displays each line containing bb.

```
$ grep bb testa
aaabb
bbbcc
$
```

The **−v** option reverses the sense of the test. The example below displays all the lines *without* bb.

```
$ grep −v bb testa
ff−ff
cccdd
dddaa
$
```

The **−n** flag displays the line number of each displayed line.

```
$ grep −n bb testa
1:aaabb
2:bbbcc
$
```

grep can search through more than one file. Below, **grep** searches through each file in the working directory. (The ambiguous file reference * matches all filenames.) The name of the file containing the string precedes each line of output.

```
$ grep bb *
testa:aaabb
testa:bbbcc
testa:bbbbb
$
```

The search that **grep** performs is case-sensitive. Because the previous examples specified lowercase bb, **grep** did not find the uppercase string, BBBBB, in **testc**. The **−y** option causes both uppercase *and* lowercase letters to match a pattern containing lowercase letters. Only uppercase letters ever match uppercase letters.

```
$ grep −y bb *
testa:aaabb
testa:bbbcc
testb:bbbbb
testc:BBBBB

$ grep −y BB *
testc:BBBBB
$
```

The **–c** option displays the name of each file, followed by the number of lines in the file that contain a match.

```
$ grep -c bb *
testa:2
testb:1
testc:0
$
```

The **–e** option searches for a string that begins with a hyphen. This option causes grep to accept the hyphen as part of the pattern and not as an indicator that an option follows.

```
$ grep -e -ff *
testa:ff-ff
$
```

The following command line displays lines from the file **text2** that contain a string of characters starting with st, followed by zero or more characters (. * represents zero or more characters in a regular expression — see Appendix A), and ending in ing.

```
$ grep 'st.*ing' text2
.
.
.
$
```

kill

Terminate a process.

Format   `kill [option] PID-list`

Summary   kill terminates one or more processes by sending them software termination signals (signal number 15). An option allows you to send another signal. The process must belong to the user executing the kill utility, except that the super user can terminate any process. kill displays a message when it terminates a process.

Options   You can specify a signal number (0-15) as an option before the **PID-list**. kill sends the signal you specify to the process.

Arguments   The **PID-list** contains process identification (PID) numbers of processes kill is to terminate.

Notes   The PID number of a background process is displayed when the process is initiated. You can also use the **ps** utility to determine PID numbers.

  If the termination signal does not terminate the process, try using a kill signal (signal number 9). A process can choose to ignore any signal except signal number 9.

  If you terminate process number zero, all processes that the current login process initiated are terminated and you are logged off.

Examples   The first example shows a command line executing the file **compute** as a background process and the kill utility terminating it.

```
$ compute &
17542

$ kill 17542
17542 Terminated
$
```

  The next example shows the **ps** utility determining the PID number of the background process running a

program named **xprog** and the **kill** utility terminating
xprog with a signal number 9.

```
$ ps
   PID TTY  TIME CMD
 22921  5m  0:10 -sh
 23714  5m  0:00 xprog
 23715  5m  0:03 ps

$ kill -9 23714
23714 Killed
$
```

ln

Make a link to a file.

Format

ln existing-file [new-link]

or

ln existing-file directory

Summary

ln makes a link to a plain file, and has two modes of operation. The first makes a link between an existing file and a new (optionally specified) filename. The second makes a link between an existing file and a new filename in a specified directory.

Options

There are no options.

Arguments

The **existing-file** is the pathname of the plain file you want to make a link to. If you do not specify **new-link**, the link appears as an entry in the working directory. The name of the entry is the same as the simple filename of the **existing-file**. If you specify a **new-link**, it is the pathname of the new link.

If the second argument is a **directory**, ln establishes the new link so that it appears in the specified directory. The name of the entry is the same as the simple filename of the **existing-file**.

Notes

A link is an entry in a directory that points to a file. The first link to a file is made when you create the file using an editor, a program, or redirected output. You can make additional links using ln, and remove links with rm. The ls utility, with the –l option, shows you how many links a file has. Refer to the end of Chapter 4 for a discussion of links.

ln displays an error message if you attempt to make a link across physical devices. Use cp to generate another copy of a file if you want it to appear on another physical device. (The Berkeley UNIX system allows *symbolic links* across physical devices, and even to unmounted devices.)

If you attempt to make a link to a directory, ln displays an error message.

Examples

The first command makes a link between the **memo2** file in the **/usr/alex/literature** directory and the working di-

303

rectory. The file appears as **memo2** (the simple filename of the existing-file) in the working directory.

```
$ ln /usr/alex/literature/memo2
$
```

The next command makes a link to the same file. This time, the file appears as **new_memo** in the working directory.

```
$ ln /usr/alex/literature/memo2 new_memo
$
```

The final command makes a link so that the file appears in another user's directory. You must have write access permission to the other user's directory for this command to work. You can use chmod to give the other user write access permission to the file.

```
$ ln /usr/alex/literature/memo2 /usr/jenny/new_memo
$
```

lpr
Print a file.

Format   lpr [options] [file-list]

Summary   **lpr** places one or more files in the line printer queue. It provides orderly access to the printer for several users or processes.

      lpr takes its input from files specified on the command line or from the standard input. The output from **lpr** is placed in the printer queue.

Options   Check with the system administrator about installation-dependent options.

     -c (copy file) **lpr** copies a file before placing it in the printer queue so that it cannot be changed. If you do not use this option, any changes you make to the file before its turn to be printed will be reflected in the printed copy.

     -m (mail report) **lpr** uses the **mail** utility to report when the file has finished printing.

     -r (remove file) **lpr** deletes the file after it has placed it in the printer queue.

Arguments   The **file-list** is a list of one or more pathnames of plain text files that **lpr** prints.

Examples   The following command line prints the file named **memo2**.

```
$ lpr memo2
$
```

     Below, a pipe sends the output of the **ls** utility to the printer.

```
$ ls | lpr
$
```

     Next, **nroff** (with the **-ms** macro package) formats **report7** and sends it to the printer via a pipe and **lpr**. The job runs in the background.

```
$ nroff -ms report | lpr&
$
```

305

The final examples send the **memo** file to the printer. The first does not paginate the output, while the second uses the **pr** utility as a filter to paginate the output. The third example shows another way of using **pr** to paginate and print **memo**. Refer to the **pr** utility for more information.

```
$ cat memo | lpr
$

$ cat memo | pr | lpr
$

$ pr memo | lpr
$
```

ls

Display information about a file.

Format   ls [options] [file-list]

Summary   **ls** displays information about one or more files. It lists the information alphabetically by filename unless you use an option to change the order.

Options   The options determine the type of information, and the order in which the information is displayed.

When you do not use an option, **ls** displays a short listing, containing only the names of files.

−a (all entries) Without a **file-list** (no arguments on the command line), this option causes **ls** to display information about all the files in the working directory, including invisible files. When you do not use this option, **ls** does not list information about invisible files unless you specifically request it.

In a similar manner, when you use this option with a **file-list** that includes an appropriate ambiguous file reference, **ls** displays information about invisible files.

−d (directory) This option causes **ls** to display the names of directories without displaying their contents. When you give this option without an argument, **ls** displays information about the working directory (**.**). This option displays plain files normally.

−g (group) This option causes **ls** to display group identification. When you use this option with the **−l** option, **ls** replaces the owner name in the display with the group name.

−l (long) This option causes **ls** to display eight columns of information about each file. These columns, displayed in Figure II-1, are described below.

The first column, which contains 11 characters, is divided as follows.

The first character describes the type of file.

− indicates a plain file
b indicates a block device file
c indicates a character device file
d indicates a directory file

307

Figure II-1: ls –l

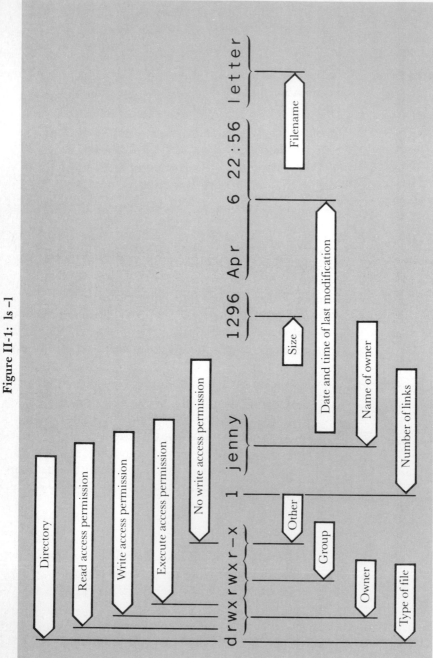

Refer to Chapter 4 for more information on types of files.

The next nine characters represent all the access permissions associated with the file. These nine characters are divided into three sets of three characters each.

The first three characters represent the owner's access permissions. If the owner has read access permission to the file, an **r** appears in the first character position. If the owner is not permitted to read the file, a hyphen appears in this position. The next two positions represent the owner's write and execute access permissions. A **w** appears in the second position if the owner is permitted to write to the file and an **x** appears in the third position if the owner is permitted to execute the file. An **s** in the third position indicates that the file has set user ID permission. A hyphen appears if the owner does not have the access permission associated with the character position.

In a similar manner, the second and third sets of three characters represent the access permissions of the user's group and other users. An **s** in the third position of the second set of characters indicates that the file has set group ID permission.

Refer to the **chmod** utility for information on changing access permissions.

The next column indicates the number of links to the file. Refer to Chapter 4 for more information on links.

The third column displays the name of the owner of the file.

The fourth column indicates the size of the file in bytes, or, if information about a device file is being displayed, the major and minor device numbers. In the case of a directory, this is the size of the actual directory file, not the size of the files that are entries within the directory.

The last two columns display the date and time the file was last modified.

-r (reverse) This option causes **ls** to display the list of filenames in reverse alphabetical order or, when used in conjunction with the **–t** or **–u** options, in reverse time order (least recently modified/accessed first).

-s (size) This option causes **ls** to display the size of each file in 512-byte blocks. The size precedes the filename.

When used with the **–l** option, the **–s** option causes **ls** to display the size in column one and to shift each of the other items over one column to the right.

-t (time modified) This option causes **ls** to display the list of filenames in order by the time of last modification. It displays the files that were modified most recently first.

-u (time accessed) This option causes **ls** to display the list of filenames together with the last time that each file was accessed. The list is in alphabetical order if you do not use an option that specifies another order.

Arguments When you do not use an argument, **ls** displays the names of all the files in the working directory.

The **file-list** contains one or more pathnames of files that **ls** displays information for. You can use the pathname of any plain, directory, or device file. These pathnames can include ambiguous file references.

When you give an ambiguous file reference, **ls** displays the names of all the files in any directories specified by the ambiguous file reference, in addition to files in the working directory.

When you specify a directory file, **ls** displays the contents of the directory. **ls** displays the name of the directory only when it is needed to avoid ambiguity (i.e., when **ls** is displaying the contents of more than one directory, it displays the names of the directories to indicate which files you can find in which directory). If you specify a plain file, **ls** displays information about just that file.

Examples All the following examples assume that the user does not change from the current working directory.

The first command line shows the ls utility without any options or arguments. ls displays an alphabetical list of the names of the files in the working directory.

```
$ ls
bin            calendar     letters
c              execute      shell
$
```

Next, the –l (long) option causes ls to display a long list. The files are still in alphabetical order.

```
$ ls -l
total 8
drwxrwxr-x  2 jenny    80 Nov 20 09:17 bin
drwxrwxr-x  2 jenny   144 Sep 26 11:59 c
-rw-rw-r--  1 jenny   104 Nov 28 11:44 calendar
-rwxrw-r--  1 jenny    85 Nov  6 08:27 execute
drwxrwxr-x  2 jenny    32 Apr  6 22:56 letters
drwxrwxr-x 16 jenny  1296 Dec  6 17:33 shell
$
```

The –a (all) option lists invisible files when you do not specify an argument.

```
$ ls -a
.          .profile   c            execute     shell
..         bin        calendar     letters
$
```

Combining the –a and –l options causes ls to display a long listing of all the files, including invisible files, in the working directory. This list is still in alphabetical order.

```
$ ls -al
total 12
drwxrwxr-x  6 jenny    480 Dec  6 17:42 .
drwxrwx--- 26 root     816 Dec  6 14:45 ..
-rw-rw-r--  1 jenny    161 Dec  6 17:15 .profile
drwxrwxr-x  2 jenny     80 Nov 20 09:17 bin
drwxrwxr-x  2 jenny    144 Sep 26 11:59 c
-rw-rw-r--  1 jenny    104 Nov 28 11:44 calendar
-rwxrw-r--  1 jenny     85 Nov  6 08:27 execute
drwxrwxr-x  2 jenny     32 Apr  6 22:56 letters
drwxrwxr-x 16 jenny   1296 Dec  6 17:33 shell
$
```

The −**r** (reverse order) option is added to the command line from the previous example. The list is now in reverse alphabetical order.

```
$ ls -ral
total 12
drwxrwxr-x 16 jenny    1296 Dec   6 17:33 shell
drwxrwxr-x  2 jenny      32 Apr   6 22:56 letters
-rwxrw-r--  1 jenny      85 Nov   6 08:27 execute
-rw-rw-r--  1 jenny     104 Nov  28 11:44 calendar
drwxrwxr-x  2 jenny     144 Sep  26 11:59 c
drwxrwxr-x  2 jenny      80 Nov  20 09:17 bin
-rw-rw-r--  1 jenny     161 Dec   6 17:15 .profile
drwxrwx---  26 root     816 Dec   6 14:45 ..
drwxrwxr-x  6 jenny     480 Dec   6 17:42 .
$
```

The −**t** (time) option causes **ls** to list files so that the most recently modified file appears at the top of the list.

```
$ ls -tl
total 8
drwxrwxr-x 16 jenny    1296 Dec   6 17:33 shell
-rw-rw-r--  1 jenny     104 Nov  28 11:44 calendar
drwxrwxr-x  2 jenny      80 Nov  20 09:17 bin
-rwxrw-r--  1 jenny      85 Nov   6 08:27 execute
drwxrwxr-x  2 jenny     144 Sep  26 11:59 c
drwxrwxr-x  2 jenny      32 Apr   6 22:56 letters
$
```

The −**r** option, when combined with the −**t** option, causes **ls** to list files so that the least recently modified file appears at the top of the list.

```
$ ls -trl
total 8
drwxrwxr-x  2 jenny      32 Apr   6 22:56 letters
drwxrwxr-x  2 jenny     144 Sep  26 11:59 c
-rwxrw-r--  1 jenny      85 Nov   6 08:27 execute
drwxrwxr-x  2 jenny      80 Nov  20 09:17 bin
-rw-rw-r--  1 jenny     104 Nov  28 11:44 calendar
drwxrwxr-x 16 jenny    1296 Dec   6 17:33 shell
$
```

The next example shows the ls utility with a directory filename as an argument. ls lists the contents of the directory in alphabetical order.

```
$ ls bin
c               e               lsdir
$
```

The –l option gives a long listing of the contents of the directory.

```
$ ls -l bin
total 3
-rwxrw-r-x  1 jenny     48 Oct  6 21:38 c
-rwxrw-r--  1 jenny    156 Oct  6 21:40 e
-rwxrw-r--  1 jenny    136 Nov  7 16:48 lsdir
$
```

To find out information about the directory file itself, use the –d (directory) option. This causes ls to only list information about the directory.

```
$ ls -dl bin
drwxrwxr-x  2 jenny     80 Nov 20 09:17 bin
$
```

mail

Send or receive mail.

Format

```
mail user-list
```
or
```
mail [options]
```

Summary

mail sends and receives mail between users. When you log on, the UNIX system informs you if another user has sent you mail.

Use the first format shown above to send mail to other users. When sending mail, **mail** accepts text from the standard input. The input can be redirected from a file or entered at the terminal. If you send mail from the terminal, it must be terminated by a (CONTROL-D) or a line with just a period on it. If you interrupt ((DEL)) **mail** when your are entering text at the terminal, the mail will not be sent.

Use the second format to display mail that you have received. When displaying mail, **mail** prompts you with a question mark following each piece of mail. The following are valid responses to this prompt.

?   A question mark causes **mail** to display a summary of valid responses.

!**command**   This response causes **mail** to exit to the Shell, execute **command**, and return to **mail** when the **command** has finished executing.

(CONTROL-D)   This response causes **mail** to stop and leave unexamined mail in the mailbox so that you can look at it the next time you run **mail**.

d   A **d** causes **mail** to delete the piece of mail it just displayed, and proceed to the next one.

m[**person**]   This response causes **mail** to remail the piece of mail to the specified **person** or people. If you do not specify a **person**, the mail is sent back to you again.

(RETURN)   Press the (RETURN) key to proceed to the next piece of mail.

p   A **p** causes **mail** to redisplay the previous piece of mail.

q   A **q** has the same effect as (CONTROL-D).

s[**file**]   This response causes **mail** to save the piece of mail in the file named **file** or **mbox** if you do not specify a filename.

w[**file**]   This response causes **mail** to save the piece of mail, without a header, in the file named **file** or **mbox** if you do not specify a filename.

x   This response causes **mail** to exit and not change the status of your mail.

Options   The following options affect mail that you have received and are displaying. They are not for use when you are sending mail.

–p (display mail, no questions) This option causes **mail** to display mail without prompting you after each piece of mail.

–q (quit on interrupt) Without this option, (DEL) stops **mail** from displaying the current piece of mail and allows it to proceed with the next. When you use this option, (DEL) stops execution of **mail** and returns you to the Shell without changing the status of your mail.

–r (reverse order) Without this option, **mail** displays mail in a last-piece-of-mail-received, first-piece-of-mail-displayed order. This option causes **mail** to display mail in chronological order.

Arguments   The **user-list** contains the user ID names of the users you want to send mail to.

Examples   Chapter 3 contains a tutorial session on using **mail**.
                     The first example below shows how to send a message to several users. In this case, **mail** sends the message to users with the login names of hls, alex, and jenny.

```
$ mail hls alex jenny
(message)

$
```

You can also compose a message in a file and then send it by redirecting the input to **mail**. The command line below sends the file **today** to barbara.

```
$ mail barbara < today
$
```

make

Keep a set of programs current.

Format

```
make [options] [target-files]
```

Summary

make is normally used to keep a set of executable programs current, based on differences in the modification times of the programs and the source programs that each is dependent on.

In its simplest use, **make** looks at *dependency lines* in a file named **makefile** in the working directory. The dependency lines indicate relationships between files, specifying a *target file* that is dependent on one or more *prerequisite* files. If any of the prerequisite files have been modified more recently than their target file, **make** updates the target file based on *construction commands* that follow the dependency line. **make** stops if it encounters an error.

Options

If the **–f** option is not used, **make** takes its input from **makefile** or **Makefile** in the working directory.

–f **file**
(input file) Use **file** as input in place of **makefile**. You can use any filename instead of **file**.

–n (no execution) This option causes **make** to display the commands it would execute to bring the **target-files** up to date, but not to actually execute the commands.

–t (touch) Update modification times of target files but do not execute any other commands. Refer to the **touch** utility.

Arguments

The **target-files** refer to targets on dependency lines in **makefile**. If you do not specify a **target-file**, **make** updates the target on the first dependency line in **makefile**.

Discussion

A simple **makefile** has the following format.

```
target: prerequisite-list
(TAB)    construction-commands
```

317

The dependency line is composed of the target and the prerequisite-list, separated by a colon. The construction-commands line must start with a (TAB) and must follow the dependency line.

The target is the name of the file that is dependent on the files in the prerequisite-list. The construction-commands are regular commands to the Shell that construct (usually compile and/or load) the target file. They are executed when the modification time of one or more of the files in the prerequisite-list is more recent than that of the target file.

In the following example, **payroll** is the target file. It is dependent on its prerequisites, **sales.c** and **salary.c**. An appropriate **CC** command is used to construct the target. (Refer to the **CC** utility.)

```
payroll: sales.c salary.c
        cc sales.c salary.c -o payroll
```

Each of the prerequisites on one dependency line can be targets on other dependency lines. The nesting of these dependency specifications can continue, creating a complex hierarchy that specifies dependencies for entire sets of programs.

Below, **form** is dependent on two object files, while the object files are each dependent on their respective source files and a header file (**form.h**). In turn, the header file is dependent on two other header files. The last line illustrates the fact that *any* command to the Shell can be put on a construction line. Here, **cat** creates the header file.

```
form:   size.o length.o
        cc size.o length.o -o form

size.o:   size.c form.h
        cc -c size.c

length.o: length.c form.h
        cc -c length.c

form.h: num.h table.h
        cat num.h table.h > form.h
```

Implied Dependencies

make can rely on implied dependencies and construction commands to make your job of writing a **makefile** easier. If you do not include a dependency line for a file, **make** assumes that object program files are dependent on compiler and assembler source code files. Thus, if a prerequisite for a target file is **xxx.o**, and **xxx.o** is not a target with its own prerequisite, **make** looks for one of the following files in the working directory.

File	Type of File
xxx.c	C source code
xxx.r	RATFOR source code
xxx.f	FORTRAN source code
xxx.y	YACC source code
xxx.l	Lex source code
xxx.s	Assembler source code

If you do not include a construction command for one of the types of files listed above, **make** provides a default construction command line that calls the proper compiler or the assembler to create the object file.

Macros

make has a macro facility that enables you to create and use macros within the **makefile**. The format of a macro definition is shown below.

```
ID = list
```

After this macro definition, $(ID) represents list in the **makefile**. Replace ID with an identifying name and list with a list of files. An example of the use of a macro appears on page 322.

By default, **make** invokes the C compiler without any options (except the −c option when it is appropriate to compile but not to load a file). You can use a macro definition, as shown below, to cause **make** to call the C compiler with any specified flags.

```
CFLAGS = flags
```

Replace flags with the flags you want to use. See page 322 for an example.

Comments   Because **make** ignores lines that begin with sharp signs (#), you can use sharp signs to set off comment lines.

Notes   You can use the **−t** option to touch all relevant files so that **make** considers everything to be up-to-date. This option is useful if you modify source files in a way that will not affect compilation (e.g., adding comments). If, on the other hand, you want to compile every program in the set that **make** maintains, you can use the **touch** utility to update the modification times of all the source files so that **make** considers that nothing is up-to-date. **make** will then recompile the entire set of programs.

Examples   The first example shows a **makefile** that keeps a file named **compute** up to date. The first three lines (each beginning with a sharp sign) are comment lines. The first dependency line shows that **compute** is dependent on two object files: **compute.o** and **calc.o**. The corresponding construction line gives the command needed to produce **compute**. The next dependency line shows that **compute.o** is not only dependent on its C source file, but on a header file, **compute.h**. The construction line for **compute.o** uses the C compiler optimizer (**−O** option). The final dependency and construction lines are not required. In their absence, **make** would infer that **calc.o** was dependent on **calc.c** and produce the command line needed for the compilation.

```
$ cat makefile
#
# makefile number one
#

compute: compute.o calc.o
        cc compute.o calc.o -o compute

compute.o: compute.c compute.h
        cc -c -O compute.c

# The next two lines are not required.
# Make assumes that calc.o is dependent on
# calc.c and that the C compiler is used to
# construct calc.o.
#
calc.o: calc.c
        cc -c calc.c
$
```

Following are some sample executions of **make**, based on the previous **makefile**. You can simulate this example by creating a directory with the files listed below, and using the **−n** option with **make**. When you use **−n**, **make** does not examine the contents of the program files, but only looks at the names and modification times. Because the contents are not examined, you can use null files. Because the **makefile** tells **make** what to do, it must contain the proper information as shown above.

```
$ ls
calc.c     compute.c     compute.h     makefile

$ make
cc −c −O compute.c
cc −c calc.c
cc compute.o calc.o −o compute
$
```

If you run **make** again without making any changes to the prerequisite files, you are told that the program is up-to-date. Below, **touch** is used to change the modification time of two of the prerequisite files. This simulates what would happen if you made a change to the file. **make** only executes the commands necessary to make the out-of-date files up-to-date and construct the target. In the first case, **compute.c** did not need to be compiled. In the second case, **compute.h** was modified. **compute.c** was recompiled because it is dependent on **compute.h**. In both cases the executable file was recreated.

```
$ make
'compute' is up to date.

$ touch calc.c

$ make
cc −c calc.c
cc compute.o calc.o −o compute

$ touch compute.h

$ make
cc −c −O compute.c
cc compute.o calc.o −o compute
$
```

The following **makefile** demonstrates some additional features and uses of **make**. It uses macros, implied dependencies, and constructions.

```
#
# makefile number two
#

CFLAGS  = -O
FILES = in.c out.c ratio.c process.c tally.c
OBJECTS = in.o out.o ratio.o process.o tally.o
HEADERS = names.h companies.h conventions.h

report:  $(OBJECTS)
        cc $(OBJECTS) -o report

ratio.o: $(HEADERS)

process.o: $(HEADERS)

tally.o: $(HEADERS)

print:
        pr $(FILES) $(HEADERS) | lpr

printf:
        pr $(FILES) | lpr

printh:
        pr $(HEADERS) | lpr
```

Following the comment lines, the **makefile** above uses CFLAGS to make sure that the C optimizer (**-O** option) is always selected when **make** invokes the C compiler because of an implied construction. (Whenever you put a construction line in a **makefile**, your construction line overrides CFLAGS and any other implied construction lines.)

Following CFLAGS, the FILES, OBJECTS, and HEADERS macros are defined. Each of these macros defines a list of files.

The first dependency line shows that **report** is dependent on the list of files that OBJECTS defines. The corresponding construction line loads the OBJECTS and creates an executable file named **report**.

The next three dependency lines show that three object files are dependent on the list of files that HEADERS defines. There are no construction lines, so when it is necessary **make** looks for a source code file corresponding to each of the object files and compiles it. The purpose of these three dependency lines is to insure that the object files are recompiled if any of the header files is changed.

You can combine several targets on one dependency line, so these three dependency lines could have been combined into one line, as follows.

```
ratio.o process.o tally.o:  $(HEADERS)
```

The final three dependency lines are used to send source and header files to the printer. They have nothing to do with compiling the **report** file. Each of these targets (print, printf, and printh) is not dependent on anything. When you call one of these targets from the command line, **make** executes the construction line following it. As an example, the next command prints all the source files that are defined by FILES.

```
$ make printf
$
```

mesg

Enable/disable reception of messages.

Format   `mesg [y/n]`

Summary   **mesg** enables or disables reception of messages sent by another user via the **write** utility. When you call **mesg** without an option, it tells you whether messages are enabled or disabled.

Options   There are no options.

Arguments   The **n** (no) disables reception of messages and the **y** (yes) enables reception.

Notes   When you first log on, messages are enabled. Messages are automatically disabled by **nroff** and **pr** while they are producing output.

Examples   The following example demonstrates how to disable messages.

```
$ mesg n
$
```

The next example calls **mesg** without an option and verifies that you disabled messages.

```
$ mesg
is n
$
```

mkdir

Make a directory.

Format   mkdir directory-list

Summary   mkdir creates one or more directories.

Options   There are no options.

Arguments   The **directory-list** contains one or more pathnames of directories that mkdir creates.

Notes   You must have write and execute access permission to the parent directory of the directory you are creating. The directories that mkdir creates contain the standard invisible entries . (representing the directory itself) and .. (representing the parent directory).

Examples   The following command creates a directory named **accounts** as a subdirectory of the working directory.

```
$ mkdir accounts
$
```

Below, without changing working directories, the same user creates two subdirectories within the accounts directory.

```
$ mkdir accounts/prospective accounts/existing
$
```

more

Display a file, one screenful at a time.

Format   `more file-list`

Summary   **more** allows you to view a text file at a terminal without missing any of the file. It is similar to **cat**, but pauses each time it fills the screen. In response to the **more** prompt, you can press the (SPACE) bar to view another screenful, (RETURN) to view another line, and (DEL) to terminate the program. (CONTROL-D) causes **more** to display one-half of another screenful of the file; a slash followed by a regular expression causes **more** to display the next match of the expression near the top of the screen. The percent that **more** displays as part of its prompt represents the portion of the file remaining to be seen.

This utility takes its input from files specified on the command line or from the standard input.

Options   There are no options.

Arguments   The **file-list** is the list of files that you want to view.

Notes   This utility was developed at Berkeley and is not available at all installations.

Examples   The following command line presents the file **letter** for viewing. To view more of **letter**, the user pressed the (SPACE) bar in response to the **more** prompt.

```
$ more letter
.
.
.
--More--(71%) (SPACE)
.
.
$
```

mv

Move (rename) a file.

Format

mv existing-file new-file-name

or

mv existing-file-list directory

Summary

mv moves, or renames, one or more files. It has two formats. The first renames a single file with a new, specified name. The second renames one or more files so that they appear in a specified directory. The file is physically moved if it is not possible to rename it (i.e., if you move it from one physical device to another).

Options

There are no options.

Arguments

In the first form of mv, the **existing-file** is a pathname that specifies the plain file that you want to rename. The **new-file-name** is the new pathname of the file.

In the second form, the **existing-file-list** contains the pathnames of the files that you want to rename, while the **directory** specifies the new parent directory of the files. The files that you rename will have the same names as the simple filenames of each of the files in the **existing-file-list**.

Notes

The UNIX system implements mv as ln and rm. When you execute the mv utility, it first makes a link (ln) to the **new-file** and then deletes (rm) the **existing-file**. If the **new-file** already exists, mv deletes it before creating the link.

As with rm, you must have write and execute access permission to the parent directory of the **existing-file**, but do not require read or write access permission to the file itself. If you are running mv from a terminal (i.e., if mv's standard input comes from a terminal) and you do not have write access permission to the file, mv displays your access permission and waits for a response. If you enter **y** or **yes**, mv renames the file; otherwise it does not. If the standard input is not coming from the terminal, mv renames the file without question.

327

If the **existing-file** and the **new-file** or **directory** are on different physical devices, the UNIX system implements mv as cp and rm. In this case, mv actually moves the file instead of just renaming it. After a file is moved, the user who moved the file becomes the owner of the file. mv will not move a file onto itself.

Examples
The first command line renames **letter**, a file in the working directory, as **letter.1201**.

```
$ mv letter letter.1201
$
```

The next command line renames the file so that it appears, with the same simple filename, in the **/usr/archives** directory.

```
$ mv letter.1201 /usr/archives
$
```

The next example renames all the files in the working directory with filenames that begin with memo so that they appear in the **/usr/backup** directory.

```
$ mv memo* /usr/backup
$
```

od

Dump the contents of a file.

Format   `od [options] file`

Summary   The **od** utility dumps the contents of a file. It is useful for viewing executable (object) files and text files with embedded nonprinting characters. This utility takes its input from the file specified on the command line or from the standard input.

Options   If you do not specify an option, the dump is in octal.

-c (character) This option produces a character dump. **od** displays certain nonprinting characters as printing characters preceded by a backslash. Any nonprinting characters that are not in the following list are displayed as 3-digit octal numbers.

Symbol	Character
\0	null
\b	backspace
\f	formfeed
\n	NEWLINE
\r	RETURN
\t	TAB

-d (decimal) This option produces a decimal dump.
-x (hexadecimal) This option produces a hexadecimal dump.

Arguments   The **file** is the pathname of the file that **od** dumps.

Notes   The name **od** is short for *octal dump*.

Examples   The example below shows the **sample** file displayed by **cat** and **od** with a **−c** option. The numbers to the left of the characters in the dump are the hexadecimal byte numbers of the first character on each line.

```
$ cat sample
This is a sample file.

It includes TABs:   , and NEWLINEs.
Here's what a dumped number looks like: 755.

$ od −c sample
0000000   T   h   i   s       i   s       a       s   a   m   p   l   e
0000020       f   i   l   e   .  \n  \n   I   t       i   n   c   l   u
0000040   d   e   s       T   A   B   s   :  \t   ,           a   n   d
0000060   N   E   W   L   I   N   E   s   .  \n   H   e   r   e   '   s
0000100       w   h   a   t       a       d   u   m   p   e   d       n
0000120   u   m   b   e   r       l   o   o   k   s       l   i   k   e
0000140   :       7   5   5   .  \n  \0
0000147
```

pr

Paginate file for printing.

Format   pr [options] file-list

Summary   **pr** breaks files into pages, usually in preparation for printing. Each page has a header with the name of the file, date, time, and page number.

    pr takes its input from files specified on the command line or from the standard input. The output from **pr** goes to the standard output, and is frequently redirected by a pipe to the **lpr** utility for printing.

Options   You can embed options within the **file-list**. An embedded option only affects files following the option on the command line.

-h   (header) The argument following this option is the page header. **pr** displays this header at the top of each page in place of the filename. If the header contains (SPACE)s, you must enclose it within apostrophes.

-ln (length) This option changes the page length from the standard 66 lines to **n** lines.

-m (multiple columns) This option causes **pr** to display *all* specified files simultaneously in multiple columns.

+n (page) This option causes **pr** to begin its output with page **n**. You must precede this option with a *plus sign,* not a hyphen.

-n (columns) This option causes **pr** to display its output in **n** columns. Precede this option with a hyphen.

-sx (separate) This option causes **pr** to separate columns with the single character **x** instead of (SPACE)s. If you do not specify **x**, **pr** uses (TAB)s as separation characters.

-t (no header or trailer) This option causes **pr** to refrain from displaying the 5-line page header and trailer. The header that **pr** normally displays includes the name of the file, the date, time, and page number. The trailer is five blank lines.

-wn (width) This option changes the page width from its standard 72 columns to **n** columns.

Arguments   The **file-list** contains the pathnames of plain text files that **pr** paginates.

Notes   The **write** utility can't send messages to your terminal while you are running **pr**. This prevents another user from sending you a message and disrupting **pr**'s output to your screen.

Examples   The first command line shows **pr** paginating a file named **memo** and sending its output, via a pipe, to **lpr** for printing.

```
$ pr memo | lpr
$
```

Next, **memo** is again sent to the printer, this time with a special heading at the top of each page. The job is run in the background.

```
$ pr -h 'MEMO FROM AC TO HS REGARDING BOOK' memo | lpr &
$
```

The final command displays the **memo** file on the terminal, without any header, starting with page 3.

```
$ pr -t +3 memo
.
.
.
$
```

ps

Display process status.

Format   ps [options]

Summary   **ps** displays status information about active processes.

Options   Without any options, **ps** displays the status of all active processes that your terminal controls. **ps** displays four columns, each with one of the following headings.

PID   This column lists the process ID number of the process.

TTY   This column lists the number of the terminal that controls the process.

TIME   This column lists the number of seconds the process has been executing for.

CMD   This column lists the command line the process was called with.

–a (all) This option causes **ps** to display status information for all active processes that any terminal controls. Some systems use a **–e** option in place of **–a**.

–l (long) This option causes **ps** to display a complete status report. **ps** displays 14 columns, each with one of the following headings.

F (flags) This column lists the flags associated with the process.

S (state) This column lists the state of the process.

UID (user ID) This is the user ID number of the owner of the process.

PID (as above)

PPID (parent PID) This is the process ID number of the parent process.

CPU (central processor utilization)

PRI (priority) This is the priority of the process. The higher the number, the lower the priority of the process.

NICE This number is established by the **nice** utility. It is used in computing the priority of the process.

ADDR (address)

SZ (size in blocks)

WCHAN This column is blank for running processes. If the process is waiting or sleeping, this is the event it is waiting for.
TTY (as above)
TIME (as above)
CMD (as above)

-x This option causes **ps** to display status information about all active processes, even those a terminal does not control.

Arguments There are no arguments.

Notes Because of the way **ps** obtains the command line, the CMD column may not be accurate.

Examples The first example shows the **ps** utility, without any options, displaying the user's active processes. The first process is the Shell (−sh) while the second is the process executing the **ps** utility.

```
$ ps
    PID TTY     TIME CMD
  24059 5m      0:05 −sh
  24259 5m      0:02 ps
$
```

When used with the **−1** (long) option, **ps** displays more information about each of the processes.

```
$ ps −l
 F S UID    PID  PPID CPU PRI NICE  ADDR  SZ  WCHAN TTY    TIME CMD
 1 S 108 24059     1   0  30   20   146  16  11502 5m     0:05 −sh
 1 R 108 24260 24059  78  54   20   371  24        5m     0:03 ps −l
$
```

The next sequence of commands shows how to use **ps** to determine the process number of a process running in the background and how to terminate that process using the **kill** utility. In this case, it is not necessary to use **ps** because the Shell displays the process number of the background processes. **ps** verifies the PID number.

First, **program** is executed in the background. The Shell displays the PID number of the process and gives the user a prompt.

```
$ program &
24264
$
```

Next, **ps** confirms the PID number of the background task. If you did not already know this number, **ps** would be the only way to find it out.

```
$ ps
    PID TTY   TIME CMD
  24059 5m    0:05 -sh
  24264 5m    0:05 program
  24267 5m    0:03 ps
$
```

Finally, the **kill** utility terminates the process. Refer to the **kill** utility for more information.

```
$ kill 24264
24264 Terminated
$
```

rm

Delete a file (remove a link).

Format

rm [options] file-list

Summary

rm removes links to one or more files. When you remove the last link, you can no longer access the file and the system releases the space the file occupied on the disk for use by another file (i.e., the file is deleted).

To delete a file, you must have execute and write access permission to the parent directory of the file, but you do not need read or write access permission to the file itself. If you are running rm from a terminal (i.e., rm's standard input is coming from a terminal) and you do not have write access permission to the file, rm displays your access permission and waits for you to respond. If you enter **y** or **yes**, rm deletes the file; otherwise it does not. If the standard input is not coming from the terminal, rm deletes the file without question.

Options

–f   (force) This option causes rm to remove files for which you do not have write access permission, without asking for your consent.

–i   (interactive) This option causes rm to ask you before removing each file. If you use the **–r** option with this option, rm also asks you before examining each directory. When you use the **–i** option with the * ambiguous file reference, rm can delete files with characters in their filenames that prevent you from deleting the files by other means. If you are using the C Shell, you can put the following command in your **.login** file to reduce the chances of accidentally deleting a file.

    alias rm rm -i

–r   (recursive) This option causes rm to delete the contents of the specified directory and the directory itself. Use this option cautiously.

Arguments   The **file-list** contains the list of files that rm deletes. The list can include ambiguous file references. Because you can remove a large number of files with a single command, use rm with an ambiguous file reference cautiously. If you are in doubt as to the effect of an rm command with an ambiguous file reference, use the echo utility with the same file reference first. echo displays the list of files that rm will delete.

Notes   The ln utility and Chapter 4 both contain discussions about removing links.

Refer to the rmdir utility in this chapter if you need to remove an empty directory.

Examples   The following command lines delete files, both in the working directory and in another directory.

```
$ rm memo
$ rm letter memo1 memo2
$ rm /usr/jenny/temp
$
```

rmdir

Delete a directory.

Format   `rmdir directory-list`

Summary   **rmdir** deletes empty directories from the file system by removing links to those directories.

Options   There are no options.

Arguments   The **directory-list** contains pathnames of empty directories that **rmdir** removes.

Notes   Refer to the **rm** utility with the **−r** option if you need to remove directories that are not empty, together with their contents.

Examples   The following command line deletes the empty **literature** directory from the working directory.

```
$ rmdir literature
$
```

The next command line removes the **letters** directory using an absolute pathname.

```
$ rmdir /usr/jenny/letters
$
```

sed

Editor (noninteractive).

Format
```
sed [-n] -f program-file [file-list]
```
or
```
sed [-n] program [file-list]
```

Summary
sed is a batch (noninteractive) editor. **sed** commands are usually stored in a **program-file**, although simple **sed** commands can be given on the command line. By default, **sed** copies lines from the **file-list** to the standard output, editing the lines in the process. **sed** selects lines to be edited by position within the file (line number) or context (pattern matching).

   sed takes its input from files specified on the command line or from the standard input. Unless a **sed** program directs its output elsewhere, it goes to the standard output.

Options
If you do not use the **-f** option, **sed** uses the first command line argument as its program.

-f (file) This option causes **sed** to read its program from the **program** file given as the first command line argument.

-n (no print) **sed** does not copy lines to the standard output except as specified by the Print (**p**) instruction or flag.

Arguments
The **program-file** is the pathname of a file containing a **sed** program. **sed** programs are described below.

   The **program** is a **sed** program, included on the command line. This format allows you to write simple, short **sed** programs without creating a separate program file.

   The **file-list** contains pathnames of the plain files that **sed** processes. These are the input files.

Description
A **sed** program consists of one or more lines in the following format.

```
[address[,address]] instruction [argument-list]
```

The addresses are optional. They select the line(s) the instruction part of the command operates on. The instruction is the editing instruction that modifies the text. The number and kinds of arguments depend on the instruction.

sed processes an input file as follows.

1. sed reads one line from the input file (**file-list**).
2. sed reads the first command from the **program-file** (or command line) and, if the address part of the command selects the input line, sed performs the instruction part of the command.
3. sed reads the next command from the **program-file**. If the address part of the command selects the input line, sed performs the instruction part of the command.
4. sed repeats Step 3 until it has executed all of the commands in the **program-file**.
5. If there is another line in the input file, sed starts over again with Step 1; otherwise it is finished.

Addresses   A line number is an address that selects a line. As a special case, the line number **$** represents the last line of the last file in the **file-list**.

A regular expression (refer to Appendix A) is an address that selects the lines that contain a string that the expression matches. Slashes must delimit a regular expression used as an address.

Except as noted, zero, one, or two addresses can precede an instruction. If you do not use an address, sed selects all lines, causing the instruction to act on every input line. One address causes the instruction to act on each input line that the address selects. Two addresses cause the instruction to act on groups of lines. The first address selects the first line in the first group. The second address selects the next subsequent line that it matches; this is the last line in the first group. After sed selects the last line in a group, it starts the selection process over again, looking for the next subsequent line that the first address matches. This line is the first line in the next group. sed continues this process until it has finished going through the file.

Instructions

d (delete) The Delete instruction causes **sed** not to write the selected line(s) to the standard output. **sed** also does not finish processing the line. It reads another line from the input and begins over again with the first command in the **program-file**.

n (next) The Next instruction reads the next input line from the **file-list**. It writes out the currently selected line, if appropriate, and starts processing the new line with the next command in the **program-file**.

a (append) The Append instruction appends one or more lines to the currently selected line. If you do not precede the Append command with an address, it appends to each line in the input. **sed** does not accept an Append instruction preceded by two addresses. An Append command has the following format.

```
[address] a\
text \
text \
  .
  .
  .
text
```

You must end each line of appended text except the last with a backslash. (The backslash quotes the following (NEWLINE).) The appended text concludes with a line that does not end with a backslash. **sed** *always* writes out appended text, regardless of how you set the **-n** flag on the command line. It even writes out the text if you delete the line that you appended the text to.

i (insert) The Insert instruction is identical to the Append instruction except that it places the new text *before* the selected line.

c (change) The Change instruction is similar to Append and Insert except that it changes the selected lines so that they contain the new text. This command can be used with two addresses. If an address range is specified, Change replaces the entire range of lines with a single occurrence of the new text.

s   (substitute) The Substitute instruction is akin to that of **ed** and **vi**. It has the following format.

```
[address[,address]] s/pattern/replacement-string/[g][p][w]
```

The pattern is a regular expression that is delimited by any character (other than a (SPACE) or (NEWLINE)). The replacement string starts immediately following the second delimiter and must be terminated by the same delimiter. The final (third) delimiter is required. The replacement string can contain an ampersand (**&**), which **sed** replaces with the matched pattern. Unless you use the **g** flag, the Substitute instruction replaces only the first occurrence of the pattern on each selected line.

g   (global flag) This flag causes the Substitute instruction to replace all non-overlapping occurrences of the pattern on the selected lines.

p   (print flag) This flag causes **sed** to send all lines on which it makes substitutions to the standard output. If it makes more than one substitution on a line, the line is sent to the standard output once for each substitution. This flag overrides the **-n** option on the command line.

w   (write flag) This flag is similar to the **p** flag, except that it sends the output to a specified file. A single (SPACE) and the name of a file must follow the Write flag.

p   (print) The Print instruction writes the selected lines to the standard output. It writes the lines immediately, and does not reflect subsequent changes to the line. This instruction overrides the **-n** option on the command line.

w   (write) This instruction is similar to the **p** instruction, except that it sends the output to a specified file. A single (SPACE) and the name of a file must follow the Write instruction.

r   (read) The Read instruction reads the contents of the specified file and appends it to the selected line. **sed** does not accept two addresses preceding a Read instruction. A single (SPACE) and the name of a file must follow a Read instruction.

Control Structures

! (not) The not structure causes **sed** to apply the following instruction, located on the same line, to each of the lines *not* selected by the address portion of the command.

{} (group instructions) When a group of instructions is enclosed within a pair of braces, a single address (or address pair) selects the lines that the group of instructions operates on.

Examples

Unless you specifically instruct it not to, **sed** copies all lines, selected or not, to the standard output. **sed** only copies specified lines when you use the **−n** option on the command line.

The input file **new**, used in the following examples, is shown below.

```
$ cat new
Line one.
The second line.
The third.
This is line four.
Five.
This is the sixth sentence.
This is line seven.
Eighth and last.
$
```

The following command line displays all the lines in the **new** file that contain the word line (all lowercase). The command uses the address /line/, a regular expression. **sed** selects each of the lines that contain a match for that pattern. The Print (**p**) instruction displays each of the selected lines.

```
$ sed "/line/ p" new
Line one.
The second line.
The second line.
The third.
This is line four.
This is line four.
Five.
This is the sixth sentence.
This is line seven.
This is line seven.
Eighth and last.
$
```

The preceding command does not use the **−n** option, so it displays all the lines in the input file at least once. It displays the selected lines an additional time because of the Print instruction.

The following command uses the **−n** option so that **sed** only displays the selected lines.

```
$ sed −n "/line/ p" new
The second line.
This is line four.
This is line seven.
$
```

Below, **sed** copies part of a file based on line numbers. The Print instruction selects and displays lines three through six.

```
$ sed −n "3,6 p" new
The third.
This is line four.
Five.
This is the sixth sentence.
$
```

When you need to give **sed** more complex or lengthy commands, you can use a program file. The following program file (**pgm**) and command line perform the same function as the command line in the previous example.

```
$ cat pgm
3,6 p

$ sed −n −f pgm new
The third.
This is line four.
Five.
This is the sixth sentence.
$
```

The **sed** program **prg1** on the following page demonstrates the Append instruction. The command in the program file selects line two and appends a (NEWLINE) and the text AFTER. to the selected line. Because the command line does not include the **−n** option, **sed** copies all the lines from the input file **new**.

```
$ cat prg1
2 a\
AFTER.

$ sed -f prg1 new
Line one.
The second line.
AFTER.
The third.
This is line four.
Five.
This is the sixth sentence.
This is line seven.
Eighth and last.
$
```

prg2 selects all the lines containing the string This and inserts a ⟨NEWLINE⟩ and the text BEFORE. before the selected lines.

```
$ cat prg2
/This/ i\
BEFORE.

$ sed -f prg2 new
Line one.
The second line.
The third.
BEFORE.
This is line four.
Five.
BEFORE.
This is the sixth sentence.
BEFORE.
This is line seven.
Eighth and last.
$
```

The next example demonstrates a Change instruction preceded by an address range. When you give a Change instruction a range of lines, it does not change each line within the range, but rather changes the block of text to a single occurrence of the new text.

```
$ cat prg3
2,4 c\
SED WILL INSERT THESE\
THREE LINES IN PLACE\
OF THE SELECTED LINES.

$ sed -f prg3 new
Line one.
SED WILL INSERT THESE
THREE LINES IN PLACE
OF THE SELECTED LINES.
Five.
This is the sixth sentence.
This is line seven.
Eighth and last.
$
```

The next example demonstrates a Substitute command. **sed** selects all lines because the command has no address portion. Each occurrence of the string line is replaced by sentence, and the resulting line displayed. The **p** flag displays each line in which a substitution is made. The command line calls **sed** with the **-n** option so that only the lines that the program explicitly requests **sed** to display are displayed.

```
$ cat prg4
s/line/sentence/p

$ sed -n -f prg4 new
The second sentence.
This is sentence four.
This is sentence seven.
$
```

The next example is very similar to the preceding one, except the **w** flag is used at the end of the Substitute command, causing **sed** to create the file **temp**, as specified following the **w**. The command line does not include a **-n** option, so all lines, including those that **sed** changes, are displayed. The contents of the file **temp** is displayed by **cat**. The word Line (starting with an uppercase letter) is not changed.

```
$ cat prg5
s/line/sentence/gw temp

$ sed -f prg5 new
Line one.
The second sentence.
The third.
This is sentence four.
Five.
This is the sixth sentence.
This is sentence seven.
Eighth and last.

$ cat temp
The second sentence.
This is sentence four.
This is sentence seven.
$
```

Below, the Write command writes the selected lines to a file named **temp2**. The range of lines two through four is selected by the line numbers 2 and 4, separated by a comma.

```
$ cat prg6
2,4 w temp2

$ sed -n -f prg6 new

$ cat temp2
The second line.
The third.
This is line four.
$
```

The program **prg7** is very similar to **prg6** except that it precedes the **write** command with the not operator (!), causing **sed** to write the lines *not* selected by the address to the specified file.

```
$ cat prg7
2,4 !w temp2

$ sed -n -f prg7 new

$ cat temp2
Line one.
Five.
This is the sixth sentence.
This is line seven.
Eighth and last.
$
```

prg9 demonstrates the Next instruction. When **sed** processes the selected line (line three) it immediately starts processing the next line, without printing line three. Thus, line three is not displayed.

```
$ cat prg9
3 n
p
```

```
$ sed -n -f prg9 new
Line one.
The second line.
This is line four.
Five.
This is the sixth sentence.
This is line seven.
Eighth and last.
$
```

The next example uses a textual address. The sixth line contains the string the, so the Next command causes **sed** not to display it.

```
$ cat prg10
/the/ n
p
```

```
$ sed -n -f prg10 new
Line one.
The second line.
The third.
This is line four.
Five.
This is line seven.
Eighth and last.
$
```

The next set of examples uses the file **compound.in** to demonstrate how **sed** instructions work in conjunction with each other.

```
$ cat compound.in
1. The words on this page. . .
2. The words on this page. . .
3. The words on this page. . .
4. The words on this page. . .
$
```

The following example substitutes the string words with text on lines one, two, and three, and the string text with TEXT on lines two, three, and four. It also selects and deletes line three. The result is text on line one, TEXT on line two, no line three, and words on line four. sed made two substitutions on line two: text was substituted for words and TEXT was substituted for text.

```
$ cat compound
1,3 s/words/text/
2,4 s/text/TEXT/
3 d

$ sed -f compound compound.in
1. The text on this page. . .
2. The TEXT on this page. . .
4. The words on this page. . .
$
```

The next example shows that the ordering of instructions within a sed program file is critical. After line two substitutes the string TEXT in place of text, the third line displays all of the lines that contain TEXT. No lines, or different lines, would have been displayed by the Print instruction if it had been moved one line before or after its present location.

```
$ cat compound2
1,3 s/words/text/g
2,4 s/text/TEXT/g
/TEXT/ p
3 d

$ sed -f compound2 compound.in
1. The text on this page. . .
2. The TEXT on this page. . .
2. The TEXT on this page. . .
3. The TEXT on this page. . .
4. The words on this page. . .
$
```

compound3 appends two lines to line two. All of the lines from the file are displayed once, because no -n option was given on the command line. Line three is displayed an additional time because of the Print instruction at the end of the program file.

```
$ cat compound3
2 a\
This is line 2a.\
This is line 2b.
3 p

$ sed -f compound3 compound.in
1. The words on this page. . .
2. .The words on this page. . .
This is line 2a.
This is line 2b.
3. The words on this page. . .
3. The words on this page. . .
4. The words on this page. . .
$
```

The final example shows that appended text is always displayed. Here line two is deleted, but the Append instruction has already displayed the two lines that were appended to it. Appended lines are displayed even if you use the **-n** option on the command line.

```
$ cat compound4
2 a\
This is line 2a.\
This is line 2b.
2 d

$ sed -f compound4 compound.in
1. The words on this page. . .
This is line 2a.
This is line 2b.
3. The words on this page. . .
4. The words on this page. . .
$
```

sleep
Put the current process to sleep.

Format sleep time

Summary **sleep** causes the process executing it to go to sleep for the specified time.

Options There are no options.

Arguments The **time** is the length of time, in seconds, that the process will sleep.

Notes The time must be less than 65,536 seconds.

Examples Sleep can be used from the command line to execute a command after a period of time. The example below executes a process in the background that will remind you to make a phone call in 20 minutes (1200 seconds).

```
$ (sleep 1200; echo 'Remember to make phone call.') &
PID = xxxx
$
```

Sleep can also be used within a Shell script to execute a command at specified regular intervals. The **per** Shell script below executes a program named **update** every 90 seconds.

```
$ cat per
while (true)
    do
    update
    sleep 90
    done
$
```

If you execute a Shell script such as **per** in the background, you can only terminate it by using the **kill** utility.

sort

Sort and/or merge files.

Format

```
sort [options] [field-specifier-list]
     [file-list]
```

Summary

The **sort** utility sorts and/or merges one or more text files in sequence. When you use the **−n** option, **sort** performs a numeric sort.

sort takes its input from files specified on the command line or from the standard input. Unless you use the **−o** option, output from **sort** goes to the standard output.

Options

If you do not specify an option, **sort** orders the file in the machine collating (ASCII) sequence. You can embed options within the **field-specifier-list**.

−b (ignore leading blanks) Blanks ((TAB) and (SPACE) characters) are normally field delimiters in the input file. Unless you use this option, **sort** *also* considers leading blanks to be part of the field they precede. This option causes sort to consider multiple blanks as field delimiters, with no intrinsic value, so that **sort** does not consider these characters in sort comparisons.

−c (check only) This option causes the **sort** to check to see that the file is properly sorted. **sort** does not display anything if everything is in order. **sort** displays a message if the file is not in sorted order.

−d (sort in dictionary order) This option causes **sort** to ignore all characters that are not alphanumeric characters or blanks. Specifically, **sort** does not consider punctuation and (CONTROL) characters.

−f (fold uppercase into lowercase) This option causes **sort** to consider all uppercase letters to be lowercase letters. Use this option when you are sorting a file that contains both uppercase and lowercase text.

−m (merge) This option causes the **sort** to assume that multiple input files are in sorted order. **sort** merges these files without verifying that they are sorted.

−n (numeric sort) When you use this option, minus signs and decimal points take on their arithmetic meaning and the **−b** option is implied. **sort** does not order lines or sort-fields in the machine collating sequence, but rather in arithmetic order.

-o (specify output file) You must place a filename after this option on the command line. **sort** sends its output to this file instead of to the standard output.

-r (reverse sense) This option reverses the sense of the sort (e.g., z precedes a).

-tx (set tab character) When you use this option, replace the **x** with the character that is the field delimiter in the input file. This new character replaces blanks, which become regular (nondelimiting) characters.

-u (unique lines) This option causes **sort** to output repeated lines only once. **sort** outputs lines that are not repeated as it would without this option.

Arguments   The **field-specifier-list** selects one or more sort-fields within each line to be sorted. The **sort** utility uses the sort-fields to sort the lines. The **file-list** contains pathnames of one or more plain files that contain the text to be sorted. **sort** sorts and merges the files unless you use the **−m** option, in which case, **sort** only merges the files.

Description   In the following description, a *line-field* is a sequence of characters on a line in the input file. These sequences are bounded by blanks and the beginning and end of the line. Line-fields are used to define a sort-field.

A *sort-field* is a sequence of characters that **sort** uses to put lines in order. The description of a sort-field is based on line-fields. A sort-field can contain part or all of one or more line-fields. Refer to Figure II-2.

The **field-specifier-list** contains pairs of pointers that define subsections of each line (sort-fields) for comparison. If you omit the second pointer from a pair, **sort** assumes the end of the line. A pointer is in the form $\pm\mathbf{f.c}$. The first of each pair of pointers begins with a plus sign, while the second begins with a hyphen.

You can make a pointer ($\mathbf{f.c}$) point to any character on a line. The $\mathbf{f}$ is the number of line-fields you want to skip, counting from the beginning of the line. The $\mathbf{c}$ is the number of characters you want to skip, counting from the end of the last line-field you skipped with the $\mathbf{f}$.

The **–b** option causes **sort** to count multiple leading blanks as a *single* line-field delimiter character. If you do not use this option, **sort** considers each leading blank to be a character in the sort-field, and includes it in the sort comparison.

You can specify options that pertain only to a given sort-field by immediately following the field specifier by one of the options **b**; **d**, **f**, **i**, **n**, or **r**. In this case, you must *not* precede the options with a hyphen.

If you specify more than one sort-field, **sort** examines them in the order that you specify them on the command line. If the first sort-field of two lines is the same, **sort** examines the second sort-field. If these are again the same, **sort** looks at the third field. This process continues for all the sort-fields you specify. If all the sort-fields are the same, **sort** examines the entire line.

If you do not use any options or arguments, the sort is based on entire lines.

Examples
The following examples assume that a file named **list** is in the working directory. All the blanks are ⟨SPACE⟩s, not ⟨TAB⟩s.

```
$ cat list
Tom Winstrom          94201
Janet Dempsey         94111
Alice MacLeod         94114
David Mack            94114
Toni Barnett          95020
Jack Cooper           94072
Richard MacDonald     95510
$
```

The first example demonstrates **sort** without any options or arguments, other than a filename. **sort** sorts the file on a line-by-line basis. If the first characters on two lines are the same, **sort** looks at the second characters to determine the proper sorted order. If the second characters are the same, **sort** looks at the third characters. This process continues until **sort** finds a character that differs between the lines. If the lines are identical, it doesn't matter which one **sort** puts first. The **sort** command in this example only needs to examine the first three letters

Figure II-2: Line-Fields and Sort-Fields

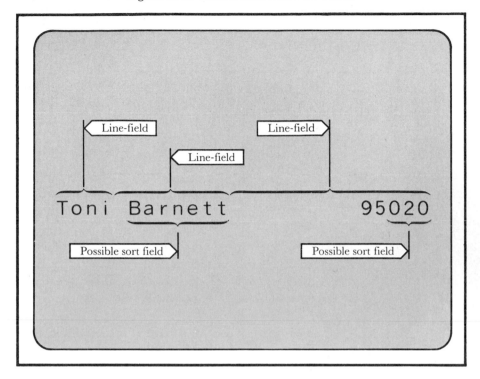

(at most) of each line. **sort** displays a list that is in alphabetical order by first name.

```
$ sort list
Alice MacLeod        94114
David Mack           94114
Jack Cooper          94072
Janet Dempsey        94111
Richard MacDonald    95510
Tom Winstrom         94201
Toni Barnett         95020
$
```

sort can skip any number of line-fields and characters on a line before beginning its comparison. Blanks normally separate one line-field from another. The next example sorts the same list by last name, the second line-field. The **+1** argument indicates that **sort** is to *skip one line-field* before beginning its comparison. It skips the first-name field. Because there is no second pointer, the sort-field extends to the end of the line. Now the list is almost in last name order, but there is a problem with `Mac`.

```
$ sort +1 list
Toni Barnett          95020
Jack Cooper           94072
Janet Dempsey         94111
Richard MacDonald     95510
Alice MacLeod         94114
David Mack            94114
Tom Winstrom          94201
$
```

In the example above, `MacLeod` comes before `Mack`. `sort` found the sort-fields of these two lines the same through the third letter (Mac). Then it put L before k because it arranges lines in the order of ASCII (or other) character codes. In this ordering, uppercase letters come before lowercase ones and therefore L comes before k.

The −f option makes `sort` treat uppercase and lowercase letters as equals, and thus fixes the problem with `MacLeod` and `Mack`.

```
$ sort −f +1 list
Toni Barnett          95020
Jack Cooper           94072
Janet Dempsey         94111
Richard MacDonald     95510
David Mack            94114
Alice MacLeod         94114
Tom Winstrom          94201
$
```

The next example attempts to sort **list** on the third line-field, the zip code. `sort` does not put the numbers in order, but puts the shortest name first in the sorted list and the longest name last. With the argument of **+2**, `sort` *skips* two line-fields and counts the (SPACE)s after the second line-field (last name) as part of the sort-field. The ASCII value of a (SPACE) character is less than that of any other printable character, so `sort` puts the zip code that is preceded by the greatest number of (SPACE)s first, and the zip code that is preceded by the fewest (SPACE)s last.

```
$ sort +2 list
David Mack             94114
Jack Cooper            94072
Tom Winstrom           94201
Toni Barnett           95020
Janet Dempsey          94111
Alice MacLeod          94114
Richard MacDonald      95510
$
```

The **−b** option causes **sort** to ignore leading (SPACE)s. With the **−b** option, the zip codes come out in the proper order (see following example).

When **sort** determines that MacLeod and Mack have the same zip codes, it compares the entire lines. The Mack/MacLeod problem crops up again because the **−f** option is not used.

```
$ sort −b +2 list
Jack Cooper            94072
Janet Dempsey          94111
Alice MacLeod          94114
David Mack             94114
Tom Winstrom           94201
Toni Barnett           95020
Richard MacDonald      95510
$
```

The next example shows a **sort** command that not only skips line-fields, but skips characters as well. The **+2.3** causes **sort** to skip two line-fields and then skip three characters before starting its comparisons. The sort-field is, and the list below is sorted in order of, the last two digits in the zip code. (The **−f** option is included to take care of **MacLeod** and **Mack**.)

```
$ sort −f −b +2.3 list
Tom Winstrom           94201
Richard MacDonald      95510
Janet Dempsey          94111
David Mack             94114
Alice MacLeod          94114
Toni Barnett           95020
Jack Cooper            94072
$
```

The next example uses a different file, **list2**, to demonstrate the **–n** option. This file contains text that represents numbers and includes minus signs and decimal
points.

```
$ cat list2
.7
1.1
-11
10.0
0.5
-1.1
$
```

When **sort** processes this list of numbers, it sorts
them according to the machine collating sequence. They
are not put in arithmetic order.

```
$ sort list2
-1.1
-11
.7
0.5
1.1
10.0
$
```

The **–n** option causes **sort** to put the list of numbers—including symbols—in its proper, arithmetic
sequence.

```
$ sort -n list2
-11
-1.1
0.5
.7
1.1
10.1
$
```

The final **sort** example demonstrates a more complex use of options and arguments. **cat** displays the
words file used in this example.

```
$ cat words
apple
pear
peach
apple
Apple
Pear
prune
Plum
peach
orange
pear
plum
pumpkin
$
```

The following **sort** command sorts **words** and displays only one copy of each line (**−u** option). The arguments cause **sort** to evaluate each line twice.

```
$ sort −u +0f +0 words
Apple
apple
orange
peach
Pear
pear
Plum
plum
prune
pumpkin
$
```

Just as the argument **+1** causes **sort** to skip one line-field, **+0** causes **sort** to skip zero fields; **sort** examines the first line-field.

The **+0f** argument causes **sort** to evaluate the first line-field through the end of the line (the entire word) as though it were lowercase. The **−f** option is used to fold uppercase into lowercase and is not preceded by a hyphen because it follows a field specifier. The second argument, **+0**, evaluates each word, differentiating between uppercase and lowercase letters. The result is a list of all the words, in alphabetical order, differentiating between upper- and lowercase letters, displaying only one copy of each word.

spell

Check a file for spelling errors.

Format `spell [options] file-list`

Summary The **spell** utility checks the words in a file against a dictionary file. It displays a list of words that it cannot either find in the dictionary or derive from one of the words in the dictionary. This utility takes its input from files listed on the command line or from the standard input.

Options −v This option displays all words that are not literally in the dictionary. As in the example below, it gives a proposed derivation for words that it would normally accept.

−b This option allows British spellings to be accepted.

Arguments The **file-list** is a list of files that **spell** checks. If you specify more than one file, **spell** generates one list of words for all the files.

Notes **spell** is not a foolproof way of finding spelling errors. It also does not check for misused, but properly spelled words (e.g., read instead of red).

Examples The examples below use **spell** to check the spelling in the **check** file. When used with the **−v** option, **spell** displays all words that are not actually in its dictionary.

```
$ cat check
Here's a sampel document that is tobe
used with th Spell utilitey.
It obviously needs proofing quite badly.

$ spell check
sampel
th
tobe
utilitey

$ spell -v check
sampel
th
tobe
utilitey
+ly     badly
+'s     Here's
+s      needs
+ly     obviously
+ing    proofing
+d      used
$
```

stty

Display or establish terminal parameters.

Format   stty [arguments]

Summary   When used without any arguments, stty displays certain parameters affecting the operation of the terminal. For a complete list of these parameters and an explanation of each, see the following arguments section. When used with arguments, stty establishes or changes the specified parameter(s).

Options   There are no options.

Arguments   The arguments specify which terminal parameters stty is to alter. Each of the parameters that is preceded by an optional hyphen (indicated in the following list as [-]) is turned on by specifying the parameter without the hyphen and turned off by specifying it with the hyphen. The descriptions describe the parameters in their *on* states.

Modes of Data Transmission
[-]even   even parity
[-]odd   odd parity
even odd   When even and odd parity are both specified as on, no parity bit is used.
[-]raw   The normal state is –raw. When input is read in its raw form, the following special characters are not interpreted by the Shell: delete character (erase-#), delete line (kill-@), interrupt execution ($\boxed{\text{DEL}}$), and EOF ($\boxed{\text{CONTROL-D}}$). In addition, parity bits are not used.
[-]cbreak   The normal state is –cbreak. When cbreak is in effect, each character is available to the read routine as it is entered at the terminal. The erase and kill characters are nonfunctional.

Treatment of Characters
[-]nl   Only a $\boxed{\text{NEWLINE}}$ character is accepted as a line terminator. With –nl in effect, a $\boxed{\text{RETURN}}$ character from the terminal is accepted as a $\boxed{\text{NEWLINE}}$ while a $\boxed{\text{RETURN}}$ $\boxed{\text{LINE-FEED}}$ sequence is sent to the terminal in place of a $\boxed{\text{NEWLINE}}$.

361

[–]echo	Echo characters as they are typed; this is full duplex operation. If a terminal displays two characters for each one it should display, turn the echo parameter off (–echo).
[–]lcase	For uppercase only terminals, translate all uppercase characters into lowercase as they are entered.
[–]tabs	Transmit each (TAB) character to the terminal as a (TAB) character. When tabs is turned off (–tabs), each (TAB) character is translated into the appropriate number of (SPACE)s and these (SPACE)s are transmitted to the terminal.

Data Line Specifications

[–]hup	Disconnect telephone line when user logs off.
0	Disconnect telephone line immediately.
50 75 110 134 150 200 300 600 1200 1800 2400 4800 9600	Set the terminal baud rate as specified by one of these numbers.

Special Keys

ek	Set the delete character and delete line keys to their default values: # and @.
erase **x**	Set the delete character key to **x**. To indicate a (CONTROL) character, precede the **x** with a caret and enclose both characters within apostrophes (e.g., '∧H' for (CONTROL-H)).
kill **x**	Set the delete line key to **x**. To indicate a (CONTROL) character, precede the **x** with a caret and enclose both characters within apostrophes (e.g., '∧U' for (CONTROL-U)).

Transmission Delays

You can specify any one of each of these sets of parameters. Except for zero, the numbers following the letters do not have special significance but represent a different amount of delay following the transmission of the character. Zero always means no delay.

cr0 cr1 cr2 cr3	delay following a RETURN
nl0 nl1 nl2 nl3	delay following a NEWLINE
tab0 tab1 tab2 tab3	delay following a TAB
ff0 ff1	delay following a formfeed
bs0 bs1	delay following a backspace

Notes

stty normally affects the terminal attached to its standard output. You can view or change the characteristics of a terminal other than the one you are using, by redirecting the output from stty. Refer to the following command.

```
$ stty [arguments] >/dev/ttyxx
$
```

The **ttyxx** is the terminal device number of the target terminal. You can only change the characteristics of a terminal if you own its device file. (Some systems require you to redirect the **input** instead of the **output** for this form of the command to work properly—use < in place of > in the above example).

Examples

The first example shows stty without any arguments, displaying several terminal operation parameters.

```
$ stty
speed 1200 baud
erase = '^H'; kill = '^U'
even odd -nl echo
$
```

Next the **ek** argument is used to return the delete character and delete line keys to their default values.

```
$ stty ek
$
```

The next example sets the erase special character to
(CONTROL-H). An ∧ followed by an h represents the
(CONTROL) character. Even though a lowercase h was en-
tered, the following display shows that **stty** stores it as
(CONTROL-H).

```
$ stty erase '∧h'
$ stty
speed 1200 baud
erase = '∧H'; kill = '@'
even odd −nl echo
$
```

Below, **stty** turns off (TAB)s so that the appropriate
number of (SPACE)s are sent to the terminal in place of a
(TAB). Use this command if a terminal cannot automatically expand (TAB)s.

```
$ stty −tabs
$
```

If you log on and everything that appears on the terminal is in uppercase letters, give the following command.

```
$ STTY −LCASE
$
```

Turn on **lcase** if a terminal cannot display lowercase
characters.

tail

Display the last part (tail) of a file.

Format   `tail ±number[options] [file]`

Summary   **tail** displays the last part of a file. It takes its input from the file specified on the command line or from the standard input.

Options   When used without any options, **tail** counts by lines. If options are used, they must follow immediately after the **number** and not be preceded by a hyphen or a (SPACE).

b   (blocks) Count by blocks.
c   (characters) Count by characters.
l   (lines) Count by lines (default).

Arguments   If the **number** is preceded by a plus sign, **tail** counts the number of units specified by the **number** and any option, from the beginning of the file. If the **number** is preceded by a hyphen, **tail** counts from the end of the file.

Examples   The following examples are based on the **lines** file shown below.

```
$ cat lines
line one
line two
line three
line four
line five
line six
line seven
line eight
line nine
line ten
$
```

The first example displays the last three lines (-3, no option) of the file.

```
$ tail -3 lines
line eight
line nine
line ten
$
```

The next example displays the file, starting at line eight (+8, no option).

```
$ tail +8 lines
line eight
line nine
line ten
$
```

The final example displays the last six characters in the file (–6c). Only five characters are evident (e ten); the sixth is a (NEWLINE).

```
$ tail –6c lines
e ten
$
```

tee

Copy the standard input to the standard output and one or more files.

Format

```
tee [options] file-list
```

Summary

tee copies its standard input to its standard output *and* to one or more files as specified on the command line.

Options

Without any options, **tee** overwrites the output files if they exist and responds to interrupts.

−i (no interrupts) When this option is used, **tee** does not respond to interrupts.

−a (append) Append output to files (do not overwrite them).

Arguments

The **file-list** contains the pathnames of files that receive output from **tee**.

Examples

In the following example, output from the **date** utility is sent via a pipe, to **tee**, which copies it to the standard output and the file **hold.date**. The copy that goes to the standard output appears on the screen. **cat** displays the copy that was sent to the file.

```
$ date | tee hold.date
Sat Jun 25 16:46:18 PDT 1983

$ cat hold.date
Sat Jun 25 16:46:18 PDT 1983
$
```

test

Evaluate an expression.

Format

```
test expression
```

Summary

test evaluates an expression and returns a condition code indicating that the expression is either true or false. A condition code of zero means that the expression is true. A nonzero code means that it is false.

Options

There are no options.

Arguments

The **expression** contains one or more criteria (see the following list) that **test** evaluates. If –**a** separates two criteria, the criteria are anded: both criteria must be true for **test** to return a condition code of true. If –**o** separates two criteria, the criteria are ored: one or the other (or both) of the criteria must be true for **test** to return a condition code of true.

You can negate any criterion by preceding it with an exclamation point (!). You can group criteria with parentheses. If there are no parentheses, –**a** takes precedence over –**o** and operators of equal precedence are evaluated from left to right.

Within the **expression**, you must quote special characters, such as parentheses, so that the Shell does not interpret them, but passes them on to **test**.

Each element (such as a criterion, string, or variable) within the **expression** is a separate argument and must be separated from other elements by a (SPACE).

Following is a list of criteria that you can use within the **expression**.

string
This criterion is true if the **string** is not a null string.

–n **string**
This criterion is true if the **string** has a length greater than zero.

–z **string**
This criterion is true if the **string** has a length of zero.

string1 = **string2**
This criterion is true if **string1** is equal to **string2**.

string1 ! = string2
This criterion is true if **string1** is not equal to **string2**.

int1 relop **int2**
This criterion is true if integer **int1** has the specified algebraic relationship to integer **int2**. The **relop** is a relational operator from the following list.

Relop	Description
−gt	greater than
−ge	greater than or equal to
−eq	equal to
−ne	not equal to
−le	less than or equal to
−lt	less than

−r **filename**
This criterion is true if the file named **filename** exists and you have read access permission to it.

−w **filename**
This criterion is true if the file named **filename** exists and you have write access permission to it.

−f **filename**
This criterion is true if the file named **filename** exists and is not a directory.

−d **filename**
This criterion is true if the file named **filename** exists and is a directory.

−s **filename**
This criterion is true if the file named **filename** exists and contains information (has a size greater than zero bytes).

−t **file-descriptor**
This criterion is true if the open file with the file descriptor number **file-descriptor** is associated with a terminal. If you do not specify a **file-descriptor**, number one (standard output) is assumed.

Notes   test is useful in Bourne Shell scripts. Because the C Shell has the equivalent of test built into it, test is not normally used from the C Shell.

Examples   The following examples show how to use the test utility in Shell scripts. Although test will work from a command line, it is more commonly used in Shell scripts to test input or verify access to a file.

The first two examples show incomplete Shell scripts. They are not complete because they do not test for upper as well as lowercase input or inappropriate responses and do not acknowledge more than one response.

The first example prompts the user, reads a line of input into the user variable **user_input**, and uses test to see if the user variable **user_input** matches the quoted string **yes**. Refer to Chapter 8 for more information on variables, Read, and If.

```
$ cat user_in
echo -n 'Input yes or no: '
read user_input
if (test $user_input = 'yes')
        then echo 'You input yes.'
fi
$
```

The next example prompts the user for a filename and then uses test to see if the user has read access permission (**-r**) for the file *and* (**-a**) if the file contains more than zero bytes (**-s**).

```
$ cat validate
echo -n 'Enter filename: '
read filename
if (test -r $filename -a -s $filename)
      then echo 'File' $filename 'exists and contains information.'
      echo 'You have read access permission to the file.'
fi
$
```

When used without a number, the **−t** criterion assumes a value of one for the file descriptor and causes the **test** utility to determine whether the process running **test** is sending output to the user's terminal. **test** returns a value of true (**0**) if the process is sending its output to a terminal. Following is a listing of the Shell script **term** that runs **test**.

```
$ cat term
test -t
echo 'This program is (=0) or is not (=1)
sending its output to a terminal:' $?
$
```

First, **term** is run with the output going to the terminal, i.e., the output is not redirected to a file. **test** returns a zero. The Shell stores this value in the Shell variable that records the condition code of the last process, **$?**. **echo** displays this value.

```
$ term
This program is (=0) or is not (=1)
sending its output to a terminal: 0
$
```

The next example runs **term** and redirects the output to a file. Following this is a listing of the file **temp** that received the output of **term**. **test** returned a one, indicating that its output was not going to a terminal.

```
$ term > temp
$ cat temp
This program is (=0) or is not (=1)
sending its output to a terminal: 1
$
```

touch

Update a file's modification time.

Format   `touch [option] file-list`

Summary   **touch** reads a byte from a file and writes it back to make the time (date) last modified associated with the file current. This utility is used in conjunction with the **make** utility.

Options   When you do not specify the **–c** option, **touch** creates the file if it does not exist.

–c (no create) Do not create the file if it does not already exist.

Arguments   The **file-list** contains the pathnames of the files to be updated.

Examples   The following examples demonstrate how **touch** functions. The first examples show **touch** updating an existing file. **ls** with the **–l** option displays the modification time of the file. The last three command lines show **touch** creating a file.

```
$ ls -l program.c
-rw-rw-r--  1 jenny     136 Nov  7 16:48 program.c

$ touch program.c

$ ls -l program.c
-rw-rw-r--  1 jenny     136 Jun 25 16:33 program.c

$ ls -l read.c
read.c not found

$ touch read.c

$ ls -l read.c
-rw-rw-r--  1 jenny       0 Jun 25 16:35 read.c
$
```

tty

Display the terminal pathname.

Format   `tty`

Summary   tty displays the pathname of the standard input file if it is a terminal.

Options   There are no options.

Arguments There are no arguments.

Notes   If the standard input is not a terminal, tty displays not a tty.

Examples   The following example illustrates the use of tty.

```
$ tty
/dev/tty5m
$
```

uniq
Display lines of a file that are unique.

Format

uniq [options] [-fields] [+characters]
       [input-file] [output-file]

Summary

uniq displays a file, removing all but one copy of successive repeated lines. If the file has been sorted (refer to the sort utility), uniq insures that no two lines that it displays are the same.

uniq takes its input from a file specified on the command line or from the standard input. Unless the output file is specified on the command line, output from uniq goes to the standard output.

Options

-c (count) This option causes uniq to precede each line with the number of occurrences of the line in the input file.

-d (repeated lines) This option causes uniq to display only lines that are repeated.

-u (unique lines) This option causes uniq to display only lines that are *not* repeated.

Arguments

In the following description, a **field** is any sequence of characters not containing a blank. Fields are bounded by one or more blanks or the beginning or end of the line.

The **-fields** causes uniq to ignore the first **n** fields of each line. uniq bases its comparison on the remainder of the line.

The **+characters** causes uniq to ignore the first **n** characters of each line. If you also use **-fields**, uniq ignores **+n** characters after the end of the last field that it ignores. The **+characters** does *not* ignore blanks following the last ignored field. You must take these blanks into account when you specify the number of characters to ignore.

You can specify the **input-file** on the command line. If you do not specify it, uniq uses its standard input.

You can specify the **output-file** on the command line. If you do not specify it, uniq uses its standard output.

Examples These examples assume that the file named **test** in the working directory contains the following text.

```
$ cat test
boy took bat home
boy took bat home
girl took bat home
dog brought hat home
dog brought hat home
dog brought hat home
$
```

When used without any options, uniq removes all but one copy of successive repeated lines.

```
$ uniq test
boy took bat home
girl took bat home
dog brought hat home
$
```

The –c option displays the number of consecutive occurrences of each line in the file.

```
$ uniq –c test
      2 boy took bat home
      1 girl took bat home
      3 dog brought hat home
$
```

The –d option displays only lines that are consecutively repeated in the file.

```
$ uniq –d test
boy took bat home
dog brought hat home
$
```

The –u option displays only lines that are *not* consecutively repeated in the file.

```
$ uniq –u test
girl took bat home
$
```

Below, the **–fields** argument (**–1**) skips the first field in each line. This causes the lines that begin with boy and the one that begins with g i r l to appear to be consecutive repeated lines. uniq only displays one occurrence of these lines.

```
$ uniq -1 test
boy took bat home
dog brought hat home
$
```

The final example uses both the **–fields** and **+characters** arguments (**–2** and **+2**) to first skip two fields and then skip two characters. The two characters that this command skips include the ⟨SPACE⟩ that separates the second and third fields and the first character of the third field. Ignoring these characters, all the lines appear to be consecutive repeated lines containing the string, at home. uniq only displays the first of these lines.

```
$ uniq -2 +2 test
boy took bat home
$
```

WC

Display the number of lines, words, and characters in a file.

Format   wc [options] file-list

Summary   WC displays the number of lines, words, and characters contained in one or more files. If you specify more than one file on the command line, WC displays totals for each file and totals for the group of files.

WC takes its input from files specified on the command line or from the standard input.

Options   −c (characters) This option causes WC to display only the number of characters in the file.

−l (lines) This option causes WC to display only the number of lines in the file.

−w (words) This option causes WC to display only the number of words in the file.

Arguments   The **file-list** contains the pathnames of one or more text files that WC analyzes.

Notes   A word is a sequence of characters bounded by (SPACE)s, (TAB)s, (NEWLINE)s, or a combination of these.

Examples   The following command line displays an analysis of the file named **memo**. The numbers represent the number of lines, words, and characters in the file.

```
$ wc memo
      5    31     146 memo
$
```

The next command line shows an analysis of three files. The line at the bottom, with the word total in the right-hand column, contains the sum of each of the columns.

```
$ wc memo1 memo2 memo3
      10    62     292    memo1
      12    74     341    memo2
      12    68     320    memo3
      34    204    953    total
$
```

who

Display names of users.

Format

who [am i]

Summary

who displays the names of users currently logged on, together with their terminal device numbers and times they logged on.

Options

There are no options.

Arguments

When given any two arguments, such as **am i**, **who** displays the login name the user giving the command, the terminal device number, and the time the user logged on.

Examples

The following examples demonstrate the use of the **who** utility.

```
$ who
jenny       tty1        Nov 29 11:01
alex        tty5m       Nov 29 18:11

$ who am i
alex        tty5m       Nov 29 18:11
$
```

write

Send a message to another user.

Format

```
write destination-user [tty-name]
```

Summary

You and another user can use **write** to establish two-way communication. Both of you must execute the **write** utility, each specifying the other user's name as the **destination-user**. **write** then copies text, on a line-by-line basis, from each terminal to the other.

When you execute the **write** utility, a message appears on the **destination-user**'s terminal indicating that you are about to transmit a message.

When you want to stop communicating with the other user, press (CONTROL-D) once (at the start of a line) or twice (elsewhere on a line) to return to the Shell. The other user must do the same.

Options

There are no options.

Arguments

The **destination-user** is the name of the user you are sending a message to. The **tty-name** can be used as a second argument, after the user name, to resolve ambiguities if a user is logged in on more than one terminal.

Notes

It may be helpful to set up a protocol for carrying on communication when using **write**. Try ending each message with **o** for over and ending the transmission with **oo** for over and out. This gives each user time to think and enter a complete message without the other user wondering whether the first user is finished.

While you are using **write**, any line beginning with an exclamation point causes **write** to pass the line, without the exclamation point, to the Shell for execution.

Each user controls permission to write to that user's terminal. Refer to the **mesg** utility.

Examples

Refer to Chapter 3 for an example of **write**.

APPENDICES

APPENDIX A

REGULAR EXPRESSIONS

A regular expression defines a set of one or more strings of characters. Several of the UNIX utility programs, including **ed**, **vi**, **grep**, and **sed**, use regular expressions to search for and replace strings.

A simple string of characters is a regular expression that defines one string of characters: itself. A more complex regular expression uses letters, numbers, and special characters to define many different strings of characters. A regular expression is said to *match* any string it defines.

CHARACTERS

As used in this appendix, a *character* is any character *except* a (NEWLINE). Most characters represent themselves within a regular expression. A *special character* is one that does not represent itself. If you need to use a special character to represent itself, see the section of this appendix on "Quoting Special Characters."

DELIMITERS

A character, called a *delimiter,* usually marks the beginning and end of a regular expression. The delimiter is always a special character for the regular expression it delimits (i.e., it does not represent itself, but marks the beginning and end of the expression). You can use any character as a delimiter, as long as you use the same character at both ends of the regular expression. For simplicity, all the regular expressions in this appendix use a forward slash as a delimiter. In some unambiguous cases, the second delimiter is not required. You can usually omit the second delimiter when it would be followed immediately by a (RETURN).

SIMPLE STRINGS

The most basic regular expression is a simple string that contains no special characters except the delimiters. A simple string matches only itself.

Regular expression	Meaning	Examples
/ring/	matches ring	ring, spring, ringing, stringing
/Thursday/	matches Thursday	Thursday, Thursday's
/or not/	matches or not	or not, poor nothing

SPECIAL CHARACTERS

You can use special characters within a regular expression to cause it to match more than one string. A regular expression that includes a special character always matches the longest possible string starting as far toward the beginning of the line as possible.

Period

A period matches any character.

Regular expression	Meaning	Examples
/.alk/	matches all strings that contain a (SPACE) followed by any character followed by alk	will talk, may balk
/.ing/	matches all strings with any character preceding ing	singing, ping, before inglenook

Square Brackets

Square brackets ([ ]) define a *character class* that matches any single character within the brackets. If the first character following the left square bracket is a caret (∧), the square brackets define a character class that matches any single character not within the brackets. You can use a hyphen to indicate a range of characters. Within a character class definition, backslashes, asterisks, and dollar signs (all described below) lose their special meanings. A right square bracket (appearing as a member of the character class) can only appear as the first character following the left square bracket, and a caret is only special if it is the first character following the left bracket.

Regular expression	Meaning	Examples
/[bB]ill/	defines the character class containing b and B— matches a member of the character class followed by ill	bill, Bill, billed

Regular expression	Meaning	Examples
/t[aeiou].k/	matches t followed by a lowercase vowel, any character, and a k.	talkative, took, teak, tanker
/number[6–9]/	matches number followed by a (SPACE) and a member of the character class.	number 6 number 8 number 9
/[∧a–ZA–Z]/	matches any character that is not a letter	1, 7, @, ., }

Asterisk

An asterisk can follow a regular expression to represent *zero* or more occurrences of a match of the regular expression preceding it. The regular expression can include any of the previously defined special characters (. [∧ –]). An asterisk following a period matches any string of characters. (A period matches any character and an asterisk matches zero or more occurrences of the preceding regular expression.) A character class definition followed by an asterisk matches any string of characters that are members of the character class.

Regular expression	Meaning	Examples
/ab*c/	matches a followed by zero or more bs followed by a c	ac, abc, abbc, abbbc
/ab.*c/	matches ab followed by a zero or more other characters followed by c	abc, abxc, ab45c, ab 756.345 x cat
/t.*ing/	matches t followed by zero or more characters followed by ing	thing, ting, thought of going
/[a–zA–Z]*	matches a string composed only of letters and (SPACE)s	any string without numbers or punctuation
/(.*)/	matches as long a string as possible between (and)	(this) and (that)
/([∧)]*)/	matches the shortest string possible that starts with (and ends with)	(this), (this and that)

Caret and Dollar Sign

A regular expression that begins with a caret (∧) can only match a string at the beginning of a line. In a similar manner, a dollar sign at the end of a regular expression matches the end of a line.

Regular expression	Meaning	Examples
/∧T/	matches a T at the beginning of a line	This line . . . That time . . .
/∧+[0-9]/	matches a plus sign followed by a number at the beginning of a line	+5 45.72 +759 Keep this . . .
/:$/	matches a colon that ends a line	. . . below:

Quoting Special Characters

You can quote any special character (but not a digit or a parenthesis) by preceding it with a backslash. Quoting a special character makes it represent itself.

Regular expression	Meaning	Examples
/end\./	matches all strings that contain end followed by a period.	The end., send. pretend.mail
/\\/	matches a single backslash	\
/*/	matches an asterisk	*.c, an asterisk (*)
/\[5\]/	matches the string [5]	it was five [5]
/and\/or/	matches and/or	and/or

RULES

The following rules govern the application of regular expressions.

Longest Match Possible

As stated previously, a regular expression always matches the longest possible string starting as far toward the beginning of the line as possible. For example, given the following string:

```
This (rug) is not what it once was (a long time ago), is it?
```

The expression: `/Th.*is/`
matches: `This (rug) is not what it once was (a long time ago), is`

and: `/(.*)/`
matches: `(rug) is not what it once was (a long time ago)`

however: `/([∧)]*)/`
matches: `(rug)`

One Regular Expression Does Not Exclude Another

If a regular expression is composed of two regular expressions, the first will match as long a string as possible, but will not exclude a match of the second. Given the following string:

```
singing songs, singing more and more
```

The expression: `/s.*ing/`
matches: `singing songs, singing`

and: `/s.*ing song/`
matches: `singing song`

Empty Regular Expressions

An empty regular expression always represents the last regular expression that you used. For example, if you give **vi** the following substitute command:

```
s/mike/robert/
```

and then you want to make the same substitution again, you can use the command:

```
s//robert/
```

The empty regular expression (//) represents the last regular expression you used (/mikc/).

BRACKETING EXPRESSIONS

Quoted parcntheses, \(and \), can be used to bracket a regular expression. The string that the bracketed regular expression matched can subsequently be used, as explained below in "Quotcd Digits." A regular expression does not attempt to match quoted parentheses. Thus, a regular expression enclosed within quoted parentheses matches what the same regular expression without the parentheses would match.

The expression: `/\(rexp\)/` matches what `/rexp/` would match
and: `/a\(b*\)c/` matches what `/ab*c/` would match

You can nest quoted parentheses. The following expression consists of two bracketed expressions, one within the other.

```
/\([a-z]\([A-Z]*\)\)/
```

The bracketed expressions are identified only by the opening \(s, so there is no ambiguity in identifying them.

THE REPLACEMENT STRING

Regular expressions are used as Search Strings within substitute commands in **vi** and **sed**. You can use two special characters, ampersands (**&**) and quoted digits (**\n**) to represent the matched strings within the corresponding Replacement String.

Ampersands

Within a Replacement String, an ampersand (**&**) takes on the value of the string that the Search String (regular expression) matched.

For example, the following substitute command surrounds a string of one or more numbers with **NN**. The ampersand in the Replacement String matches whatever string of numbers the regular expression (Search String) matched. Two character class definitions are required because the regular expression [0–9]* matches *zero* or more occurrences of a digit, and *any* character string is zero or more occurrences of a digit.

```
s/[0-9][0-9]*/NN&NN/
```

Quoted Digits

Within the regular expression itself, a quoted digit takes on the value of the string that the bracketed regular expression beginning with the nth \(matched.

Within a Replacement String, a quoted digit (\n) represents the string that the bracketed regular expression (portion of the Search String) beginning with the nth \(matched.

For example, you can take a list of people in the form

last-name, first-name initial

and put it in the following format

first-name initial last-name

with the following **vi** command.

```
1,$s/\([^,]*\), \(.*\)/\2 \1/
```

This command addresses all the lines in the file (1,$). The Substitute command (s) uses a Search String and a Replacement String delimited by forward slashes. The first bracketed regular expression within the Search String, \([^,]*\), matches what the same unbracketed regular expression, [^,]*, would match. This regular expression matches a string of zero or more characters not containing a comma (the **last-name**). Following the first bracketed regular expression is a comma and a (SPACE) that match themselves. The second bracketed expression \(.*\) matches any string of characters (the **first-name** and **initial**).

The Replacement String consists of what the second bracketed regular expression matched (\2) followed by a (SPACE) and what the first bracketed regular expression matched (\1).

SUMMARY

A regular expression defines a set of one or more strings of characters. A regular expression is said to match any string it defines.

The following characters are special within a regular expression.

Special character	Function
.	matches any single character
[xyz]	defines a character class that matches **x, y,** or **z**
[^xyz]	defines a character class that matches any character except **x, y,** or **z**
[x-z]	defines a character class that matches any character **x** through **z** inclusive
*	matches zero or more occurrences of a match of the preceding character
^	forces a match to the beginning of a line
$	forces a match to the end of a line
\	used to quote special characters
\(xyz\)	matches what **xyz** matches (a bracketed regular expression)

The following characters are special within a Replacement String.

Character	Function
&	represents what the regular expression (Search String) matched
\n	a quoted number, **n,** represents the nth bracketed regular expression in the Search String

APPENDIX B

A READ ROUTINE FOR THE C SHELL

Some versions of the C Shell implement a Read command as shown on page 244. Other versions have no provision for reading user input from a Shell script. The following C program performs this function.

```
% cat read.c
/*
C routine to read a line
from the standard input
*/
include stdio.h
main ()
{
char character;
while ((character = getchar ()) != '\n')
        {
        putchar (character);
        }
}
%
```

The program must be compiled, usually be giving a command such as **cc filename** (see **cc**, Part II) where filename is the name of the file containing the C program. Most compilers require that the program have a filename extension of **.c**. The compiler generates an executable file, usually named **a.out**. You can rename this file (using **mv**) anything you want; **read** is appropriate.

Have the system administrator put the **read** file in the program directory (usually **/bin** or **/usr/bin**) and you're set to write interactive C Shell scripts.

A sample C Shell script, **read_test**, that uses the **read** program follows. The **noglob** variable does not have to be set if you are not going to input any characters that the Shell interprets as ambiguous file references.

```
% cat read_test
#
set noglob
echo 'Please input a line:'
set input_line = `read`
echo 'You entered:' $input_line
%
```

APPENDIX C

GLOSSARY

Absolute Pathname A pathname that starts with the root directory (/). An absolute pathname locates a file without regard to the working directory.

Access In computer jargon, this word is frequently used as a verb to mean use, read from, or write to. Accessing a file means reading from or writing to the file.

Access Permission Permission to read from, write to, or execute a file. If you have "write access permission to a file," it means that you can write to the file.

Alphanumeric Character One of the characters, either uppercase or lowercase, from A to Z and 0 to 9, inclusive.

Ambiguous File Reference A reference to a file that does not necessarily specify any one file, but can be used to specify a group of files. The Shell expands an ambiguous file reference into a list of filenames. Special characters are used to represent single characters (?), strings of zero or more characters (*), and character classes ([ ]) within an ambiguous file reference.

Angle Bracket There is a left angle bracket (<) and a right angle bracket (>).

Append To add something to the end of something else. To append text to a file means to add the text to the end of the file.

Argument A number, letter, or word that gives some information to a program and is passed to the program at the time it is called. A command line argument is anything on a command line following the command itself.

Arithmetic Expression A group of numbers, operators, and parentheses that can be evaluated. When you evaluate an arithmetic expression, you end up with a number.

Array An arrangement of elements (numbers or strings of characters) in one or more dimensions. The C Shell can store and process arrays.

ASCII This acronym stands for the American National Standard Code for Information Interchange. It is a code that uses seven bits to represent both graphic (letters, numbers, and punctuation) and (CONTROL) characters. You can represent any textual information, including program source code and English text, in ASCII code. Because it is a standard, it is frequently used when exchanging information between computers.

There are extensions of the ASCII character set that make use of eight bits. The seven bit set is common; the eight bit extensions are still coming into popular use.

Asynchronous Event An event that does not occur regularly or synchronously with another event. UNIX system signals are asynchronous; they can occur at any time because they can be initiated by any number of irregular events.

Background Process A process that is not run in the foreground. Also called a detached process, a background process is initiated by a command line that ends with an ampersand (**&**). You do not have to wait for a background process to run to completion before giving the Shell additional commands.

Bit The smallest piece of information a computer can handle. A bit is either a one or zero (on or off).

Blank Character Either a (SPACE) or a (TAB) character, also called white space.

Block Device A disk or tape drive. A block device stores information in blocks of characters. As contrasted with a character device. A block device is represented by a block device (block special) file.

Block Number A disk or tape is divided into sections (usually 512 bytes long, but longer on some systems) that are numbered so that the UNIX system can keep track of the data on the device. These numbers are block numbers.

Braces There is a left brace ({) and a right brace (})

Bracket Either a square or angle bracket.

Branch In a tree structure, a branch connects nodes, leaves, and the root.

Buffer An area of memory that stores data until it can be used. When you write information to a file on a disk, the UNIX system stores the information in a disk buffer until there is enough to write to the disk or until the disk is ready to receive the information.

Byte Eight bits of information. A byte can store one character.

Calling Environment A list of variables and their values that is made available to a called program. See "Environment and Exporting Variables" in Chapter 8 and "Variable Substitution" in Chapter 9.

Case-sensitive Able to distinguish between uppercase and lowercase characters. Unless you set the **ignorecase** parameter, **vi** performs case-sensitive searches.

Catenate To join sequentially, or end to end. Also concatenate. The Unix **cat** utility catenates files—it displays them one after the other.

Character Class A group of characters that defines which characters can occupy a single character position. A character class definition is usually surrounded by square brackets. The character class defined by [abcr] represents a character position that can be occupied by a, b, c, or r.

Character Device A terminal, printer, or modem. A character device stores or displays characters one at a time. As contrasted with a block device. A character device is represented by a character device (character special) file.

Command Line A line of instructions and arguments that executes a command. This term usually refers to a line that you enter in response to a Shell prompt.

Concatenate See catenate.

Condition Code See exit status.

⸤CONTROL⸣ **Character** A character that is not a graphic character such as a letter, number, or punctuation mark. They are called ⸤CONTROL⸣ characters because they frequently act to control a peripheral device. ⸤RETURN⸣ and **LINE-FEED** are ⸤CONTROL⸣ characters that control a terminal or printer.

The word ⸤CONTROL⸣ is printed in uppercase letters in this book because it is a key that appears on most terminal keyboards. It may be labeled **CNTRL** or **CTRL** on your terminal. ⸤CONTROL⸣ characters, frequently called nonprinting characters, are represented by ASCII codes less than 32 (decimal).

Current (Process, Line, Character, Directory, Event, etc.) The item that is immediately available, working, or being used. The current process is the process that is controlling the program you are running; the current line or character is the one the cursor is on; the current directory is the working directory.

Cursor A small lighted rectangle or underscore that appears on the terminal screen and indicates where the next character is going to appear.

Debug To correct a program.

Default Something that is selected without being explicitly specified. When used without an argument, **ls** displays a short list of the files in the working directory by default.

Detached Process See background process.

Device See peripheral device.

Device Driver The program that controls a device such as a terminal, disk drive, or printer.

Device File A file that represents a device. There are three kinds of UNIX system files: plain, directory, and device (special) files.

Device Number A number assigned to a device at the time the system is generated. Device numbers are listed when you use **ls** to list the /**dev** directory.

Directory Short for directory file. A file that contains a list of other files.

Element One thing, usually a basic part of a group of things. An element of a numeric array is one of the numbers that is stored in the array.

Environment See calling environment.

EOF An acronym for End Of File.

Exit Status The status returned by a process; either successful (usually zero) or unsuccessful (one).

Expression See logical expression and arithmetic expression.

File A collection of related information, referred to by a filename. The UNIX system views peripheral devices as files, allowing a program to read from or write to a device, just as it would to a file.

Filename The name of a file. You use a filename to refer to a file.

Filename Extension The part of a filename following a period.

Footer The part of a format that goes at the bottom (or foot) of a page.

Foreground Process When a program is run in the foreground, it is attached to the terminal. You must wait for a foreground process to run to completion before you can give the Shell another command. As contrasted with background.

Header The part of a format that goes at the top (or head) or a page.

Hexadecimal Number A base 16 number. Hexadecimal numbers are composed of the hexadecimal digits 0-9 and A-F. Refer to the following table.

Decimal	Hexadecimal	Decimal	Hexadecimal
1	1	14	E
2	2	15	F
3	3	16	10
4	4	17	11
5	5	20	14
6	6	31	1F
7	7	32	20
8	8	33	21
9	9	64	40
10	A	96	60
11	B	100	64
12	C	128	80
13	D	256	100

Home Directory The directory that is the working directory that you will be using when you first log on. The pathname of this directory is stored in the **PATH** (Bourne Shell) or **path** (C Shell) variable.

Indention When speaking of text, the blank space between the margin and the beginning of a line that is set in from the margin.

Inode   A part of the directory structure that contains information about a file.

Input   Information that is fed to a program from a terminal or other file.

Installation   A computer at a specific location. Some aspects of the UNIX system are installation-dependent.

Invisible File   A file whose filename starts with a period. These files are called invisible because the ls utility does not normally list them. Use the –a option of ls to list all files, including invisible ones.

Justify   To expand a line of type all the way to the right margin. A line is justified by increasing the space between words and sometimes between letters on the line.

Kernel   The heart of the UNIX operating system. The kernel is the part of the operating system that allocates resources and controls processes. The design strategy has been to keep the kernel as small as possible and to put the rest of the UNIX operating system into separately compiled and executed programs.

Leaf   In a tree structure, the end of a branch that cannot support other branches. As contrasted with a node.

Logical Expression   A collection of strings separated by logical operators (> , > = , = , < = , and <) that can be evaluated as true or false.

Login Name   The name you enter in response to the login: prompt. Other users use your login name when they send you mail or write to you.

Login Shell   The Shell that you are using when you first log on. The login Shell can fork other processes that can run other Shells.

Log Off   To stop using a terminal on a UNIX system so that another user can log on.

Log On   To gain access to a UNIX system by responding correctly to the login: and password: prompts.

Machine Collating Sequence   The sequence that the computer orders characters in. The machine collating sequence affects the outcome of sorts and other procedures that put lists in alphabetic order. Most computers use ASCII.

Macro   A single instruction that a program replaces by several (usually more complex) instructions. A C Shell Alias is a macro.

Major Device Number   A number assigned to a class of devices such as terminals, printers, or disk drives. Using the ls utility with the –l option to list the contents of the /dev directory displays the major and minor device numbers for all devices (as major:minor).

Merge   To combine two ordered lists so that the resulting list is still in order.

Minor Device Number   A number assigned to a specific device within a class of devices. See major device number.

Node   In a tree structure, the end of a branch that can support other branches. As contrasted with a leaf.

Nonprintable Character   See (CONTROL) character. Also, nonprinting character.

Null String   A string that could contain characters, but doesn't.

Octal Number   A base eight number. Octal numbers are composed of the digits 0-7 inclusive.

Output   Information that a program sends to the terminal or other file.

Pathname   A list of directories, separated by slashes (/). A pathname is used to trace a path through the file structure to locate or identify a file.

Pathname Element   One of the filenames that comprise a pathname.

Pathname, Last Element of a   The part of a pathname following the final /, or the whole filename if there is no /. A simple filename.

Peripheral Device   A disk drive, printer, terminal, plotter, or other input/output unit that can be attached to the computer.

Physical Device   A device such as a disk drive that is physically—as well as logically—separate from other similar devices.

PID   This acronym stands for *Process ID*entification and is usually followed by the word number. The UNIX system assigns a unique PID number to each process when it is initiated.

Pipe   A connection between two programs such that the standard output of one is connected to the standard input of the other. Also, pipeline.

Plain File   A file that is used to store a program, text, or other user data. As contrasted with a directory file or a device file.

Printable Character   One of the graphics characters: a letter, number, or punctuation mark. As contrasted with a nonprintable or (CONTROL) character. Also, printing character.

Process   The means by which UNIX executes a program.

Prompt   A cue from a program, usually displayed on the terminal, indicating that it is waiting for input.

Quote   When you quote a character, you take away any special meaning that it has. You can quote a character by preceding it with a backslash or surrounding it with single quotation marks. For example, the Shell expands * into a list of the files in the working directory. The command **echo** * displays a list of these files. The command **echo** * or **echo** ' * ' displays *.

Recursive Routine   A program or subroutine that calls itself, either directly or indirectly.

Redirection   The process of directing the standard input for a program to come from a file other than the terminal or directing the standard output to go to a file other than the terminal.

Regular Character   A character that always represents itself. As contrasted with a special character.

Regular Expression   A string—composed of letters, numbers, and special symbols—that defines one or more strings. See Appendix A.

Relative Pathname   A pathname that starts from the working directory. As contrasted with an absolute pathname.

Return Code   See exit status.

Root Directory   The ancestor of all directories and the start of all absolute pathnames.

Scroll   To move lines on a terminal up or down one line at a time.

Session   As used in this book, the sequence of events between when you start using a program such as an editor and when you finish, or between when you log on and the next time you log off.

Shell   The UNIX system command processor.

Shell Script   A program composed of Shell commands. Also, Shell program.

Signal   A very brief message that the UNIX system can send to a process, apart from the process' standard input.

Simple Filename   A single filename, containing no slashes (/). A simple filename is the simplest form of a pathname. Also, the last element of a pathname.

Sort   To put in a specified order, usually alphabetic or numeric.

(SPACE) **Character**   A character that appears as the absence of a visible character. Even though you cannot see it, a (SPACE) is a printable character. It is represented by the ASCII code 32 (decimal).

Special Character   A character that does not represent itself unless it is quoted. Special characters for the Shell include the * and ? ambiguous file references.

Special File   See device file.

Spool   To place items in a queue, each waiting its turn for some action. Often used when speaking about the **lpr** utility and the printer: **lpr** spools files for the printer.

Square Bracket   There is a left square bracket ([) and a right square bracket (]).

Standard Error Output   A file that a program can send output to. Usually, this file is reserved for error messages. Unless you instruct the Shell otherwise, it directs this output to the terminal.

Standard Input   A file that a program can receive input from. Unless you instruct the Shell otherwise, it directs this input so that it comes from the terminal. See Chapter 4.

Standard Output   A file to which a program can send output. Unless you instruct the Shell otherwise, it directs this output to the terminal. See Chapter 4.

Status Line   The bottom (usually the 24th) line of the terminal.

String   A sequence of characters.

Subdirectory   A directory that is located within another directory.

Super User   A privileged user who has access to anything any other system user has access to, and more. The system administrator must be able to become a super user in order to establish new accounts, change passwords, and perform other administrative tasks.

Swap   To move a process from memory to a disk or vice versa. Swapping a process to the disk allows another process to begin or continue execution.

System Administrator   The person who is responsible for the upkeep of the system.

Termcap   An abbreviation of *term*inal *cap*ability. The **termcap** file contains a list of various types of terminals and their characteristics. Visually oriented programs, such as **vi**, make use of this file.

tty   A terminal: tty is an abbreviation of *telety*pewriter.

User ID   A number that the **/etc/passwd** file associates with a login name.

Variable   A name and an associated value used in a program such as a Shell script.

White Space   A collective name for (SPACE)s and/or (TAB)s.

Work Buffer   A location in memory where **ed** and **vi** store text while it is being edited.

Working Directory   The directory that you are associated with at any given time. The relative pathnames that you use are built upon the working directory.

APPENDIX D

THE XENIX OPERATING SYSTEM

Microsoft, a company that specializes in manufacturing software for microprocessor-based computers, has adapted Bell Lab's UNIX software for microprocessors. The XENIX operating system is the UNIX system with Microsoft's improvements and enhancements.

USING THE XENIX SYSTEM

Because XENIX is the UNIX system redesigned for microprocessors, almost all the techniques, programs, and examples in this book apply to the XENIX system.

IMPROVEMENTS

The UNIX system, as supplied by AT&T, is designed to run on minicomputers such as a PDP-11 or VAX and is designed to be maintained by a technical system administrator with programming experience. Microsoft has redesigned certain aspects of the UNIX system so that it is better suited for use on microprocessor-based computers.

Runs on Microprocessors

The UNIX system is largely written in C, although it is not totally machine-independent. In adapting XENIX to a number of different microprocessor chips, Microsoft has made the operating system more machine-independent and has isolated those aspects that *must* be machine-dependent. Improving machine independence allows XENIX to further the goals of the UNIX system, by making it easier to move both the operating system and application programs from one machine to another.

Easier Crash Recovery

When a power failure causes a computer system to crash, the system can write incorrect data on the disk. If the bad data is part of the file system index, the index must be repaired before the computer can be used again.

Using the UNIX system, system recovery procedures can be cumbersome, requiring an experienced system administrator to perform the recovery task. The XENIX system is designed to recover automatically after a system crash; each time the system is turned on, XENIX verifies the integrity of the disk. If XENIX detects a problem with the file system, it automatically makes the necessary repairs before allowing the user to log on.

More Tolerant of Faulty Disks

Hard disks, housing millions of pieces of information, are prone to having bad spots that cannot reliably record data. Some disks for minicomputers are certified free of defects. The UNIX system is designed to use these error-free disks.

Hard microcomputer disks, using Winchester technology, do not generally provide the option of error-free disks. The XENIX hard disk driver (the program that reads from and writes to the disk) is designed to accommodate flaws in a hard disk. The driver can keep track of where the bad spots are and not use them.

Runs Faster on Microcomputers

Because the UNIX system was designed to run on minicomputers, it takes advantage of the features of those machines. Minicomputers are characterized by having faster hard disks and smaller memories than microcomputers. Microsoft has redesigned portions of the UNIX system so that XENIX takes advantage of more available memory and uses the disk less.

Logs Errors

The XENIX software keeps a log of hardware errors for each device. By referring to these logs, the system administrator can avoid total equipment failure by catching problems early.

Easier to Configure

You can tailor a version of XENIX to your computer and to your needs by using an interactive program that allows you to specify various system parameters. The **configure** utility automatically generates and installs a XENIX system based on your specifications.

ENHANCEMENTS

The UNIX system was developed in a research environment, so it lacks some features that are required in a commercial environment. Microsoft has added some of these features.

Locks

When more than one person is updating a database at the same time, it is important that the software maintain the integrity of the data. A problem could arise when, for example, two salespeople taking orders for cars query the database at the same time and find one car left to be sold. If the software does not arbitrate this situation, both salespeople could sell the same car. With arbitration, one transaction will be forced to occur before the other. The computer will tell the second salesperson that there are no cars left to be sold.

The mechanism that insures the integrity of the data in this case is a *lock*. A lock ensures that, when one person is reading and/or writing data, no other request for the data is allowed until the first person is finished. XENIX can lock a record, a group of records, or an entire file at once.

Nonblocking Reads

Using the UNIX system, there is no way to determine whether someone has entered data at the terminal. If a program tries to read from the terminal and the user has not typed anything, the program will wait until a key is pressed before continuing. XENIX incorporates a feature that allows a program to poll an input file such as the terminal to see whether any data is available. A program that uses this feature can continue execution, if the user has not entered anything, and periodically check back for new data.

Other Features

Microsoft has incorporated other features into the XENIX operating system, such as synchronous writes to ensure that data is written out in a timely manner, scatter-loading of programs to take advantage of modern memory-management techniques, and semaphores to improve multitask synchronization.

APPENDIX E

UTILITY SUMMARY

This appendix summarizes the use of the UNIX utility programs covered in Part II of this book. An asterisk appearing after the first use of a utility name indicates that the utility can accept input from a file listed on the command line *or* from its standard input (i.e., you can redirect the standard input to these utilities so that it comes from another program).

at*

Execute a Shell script at a specified time.

Format `at time [day] [file]`

Arguments **time** 24 hour clock (HHMM)
     day day of week or date

awk*

Search for and process a pattern in a file.

Format-1 `awk -f program-file [file-list]`

Format-2 `awk program [file-list]`

Option   `-f`   read program from **program-file**

**Program
format**   `pattern { action }`

Pattern   composed of the following (two patterns separated by a
      comma indicate a range of lines)

      `<`
      `<=`   form relational expressions with
      `==`   numbers, fields, and variables
      `!=`   using these relational operators
      `>=`
      `>`
      `||`   Or (boolean operator)
      `&&`   And (boolean operator)
      BEGIN   pattern matches start of file
      END   pattern matches end of file
      regular expression (delimited by slashes)
       ~ expression is equal to field or variable
       !~ expression is not equal to field or variable

Action   print   display record
      `+ = */`
      `% ++ --` } perform arithmetic operation

**User
variables** use as needed, declared when used

**Program
variables**

NR	record number
$0	current record
NF	number of fields
$n	value of field **n**
FS	input field separator
OFS	output field separator
RS	input record separator
ORS	output record separator
FILENAME	current filename

cal

Display calendar.

Format   `cal [month] year`

Arguments   month and year are decimal integers

cat*

Display a text file.

Format   `cat [file-list]`

cc

C compiler

Format   `cc [options] file-list`

Options

-c	compile, do not load
-o file	put executable program in **file**
-O	optimize
-S	compile only, produce assembly code
-larg	search library **arg**

cd

Change to another working directory.

Format   `cd [directory]`

chmod

Change the access mode of a file.

Format	`chmod who[operation][permission] file-list`
Arguments	**who**

      u   user

      g   group

      o   other

      a   all

operation

      +   add permission

      −   remove permission

      =   set permission

permission

      r   read

      w   write

      x   execute

      s   set user or group ID

comm

Compare files.

Format	`comm [options] file1 file2`
Options	`-1` do not list lines found only in **file1**
	`-2` do not list lines found only in **file2**
	`-3` do not list lines found in both files

cp

Copy file.

Format-1	`cp source-file destination-file`
Format-2	`cp source-file-list destination-directory`

diff

Display the differences between two files.

Format	`diff [option] file1 file2`
Option	`-e` create **ed** script

echo
Display a message.

Format `echo [option] message`

Option `-n` no (NEWLINE) (only from the Bourne Shell)

expr
Evaluate an expression.

Format `expr expression`

Arguments (operators used in the expression)

:	comparison
*	multiplication
/	division
%	remainder
+	addition
–	subtraction
< <= = != >= >	} relational operators
&	And
|	Or

file
Display file classification.

Format `file file-list`

find
Find files.

Format   `find directory-list expression`

Arguments criteria used in the expression, ±**n** means either
1. +n = more than n,
2. −n = less than n, or
3.   n = exactly n.

And is implied unless Or (−**o**) is specified.

−name filename	name of file
−type filetype	type of file (b c d f)
−links ±n	number of links to file
−user name	name of owner
−group name	name of group
−size ±n	size in bytes
−atime ±n	last accessed **n** days ago
−mtime ±n	last modified **n** days ago
−newer filename	modified more recently than **filename**
−print	display filename
−exec command	execute command
−ok command	query and execute command

grep*
Search for a pattern in a file.

Format   `grep [options] pattern [file-list]`

Options

−c	(count) display number of lines only
−e	(expression) pattern can begin with hyphen
−h	(header) do not list filenames
−l	(list) display filenames only
−n	(number) display line numbers
−s	(status) return exit status only
−v	(reverse) reverse sense of test
−y	lowercase letters in the pattern match uppercase letters in the file

Arguments **pattern**   a regular expression, can be a simple string

kill

Terminate a process.

Format `kill [option] PID-list`

Options signal number

    −15   software termination (default)

    −9   kill (cannot be ignored)

    −3   terminal interrupt (DEL)

ln

Make a link to a file.

Format-1 `ln existing-file [new-link]`

Format-2 `ln existing-file directory`

lpr*

Print a file.

Format `lpr [options] [file-list]`

Options −c   copy file before printing

    −m   mail report

    −r   delete (remove) file

ls

Display information about a file.

Format `ls [options] [file-list]`

Options −a   all entries

    −d   directory

    −g   group

    −l   long

    −r   reverse

    −s   size in blocks

    −t   modified time

    −u   accessed time

mail*

Send or receive mail.

Format-1 `mail user-list`

Format-2 `mail [options]`

The first format sends mail to the user-list. The second format displays mail that you have received and prompts you with a ? following each letter.

Responses to ?
?	help
d	delete mail
q	quit
w	write to mbox
w file	write to **file**
(RETURN)	proceed to next letter
p	redisplay previous letter

Options
-p	display mail, no questions
-q	quit on interrupt
-r	reverse order

make

Keep a set of programs current.

Format `make [options] [target-files]`

Options
-f file	read input from **file** in place of **makefile**
-n	no execution
-t	touch only

Makefile format
`target:  prerequisite-list`
(TAB) `construction-commands`

mesg

Enable/disable reception of messages.

Format `mesg [y/n]`

mkdir
Make a directory.

Format   mkdir directory-list

more*
Display a file.

Format   more [file-list]

mv
Rename a file.

Format-1   mv existing-file new-file

Format-2   mv existing-file-list directory

od*
Dump a file.

Format   od [options] file

Options   (default is octal)
-c	character
-d	decimal
-x	hexadecimal

pr*
Paginate file.

Format   pr [options] file-list

Options
-h	(header) option must be followed by page header
-ln	(length) **n** is page length (default is 66)
-m	(multiple) display files simultaneously in multiple columns
+n	begin with page **n** (no hyphen)
-n	display **n** columns
-sx	(separate) use **x** to separate columns (default is TAB)
-t	do not display header and trailer
-wn	(width) **n** is page width (default is 72)

ps

Display process status.

Format   `ps [options]`

Options   −a   most processes (−e on some systems)
                −l   long list
                −x   all processes

rm

Delete a file.

Format   `rm [options] file-list`

Options   −f   force
                −i   interactive
                −r   recursive

rmdir

Delete a directory.

Format   `rmdir directory-list`

sed

Editor (noninteractive)

Format-1   sed [-n] -f program-file [file-list]

Format-2   sed [-n] program [file-list]

Options   -f   read program from **program-file**
               -n   (no print) do not copy lines to the standard
                            output unless specified by the Print
                            instruction or flag

Instructions   d   delete
                   n   next
                   a   append
                   i   insert
                   c   change
                   s   substitute
                     g   global substitute flag
                     p   display substitutions flag
                     w   write substitutions to file flag
                   p   print
                   w   write to file
                   r   read from file

sleep

Put process to sleep.

Format   sleep time

Arguments **time**   in seconds

sort*

Sort and/or merge files.

Format	`sort [options] [field-specifier-list]` `[file-list]`

Options

–b	(blanks) ignore leading blanks
–c	(check) check for proper sorting only
–d	(dictionary) ignore nonalphanumeric and blank characters
–f	(fold) sort uppercase letters as though they were lowercase
–m	(merge) merge only, assume sorted order
–n	(numeric) minus signs and decimal points take on their arithmetic value (implies **–b**)
–o	(output) must be followed by output filename
–r	(reverse) reverse sense of sort
–tx	(tab) **x** is input field delimiter
–u	(unique) do not display a repeated line more than once

Arguments   **field-specifier-list** specifies input fields by pairs of pointers as **+f.c –f.c** where **f** is the number of fields to skip and **c** is the number of characters to skip

spell*

Check a file for spelling errors.

Format	`spell [options] file-list`

Options

–v	display all words not actually in dictionary
–b	allow British spellings

stty

Display or establish terminal parameters.

Format	`stty [arguments]`

Arguments

[-]even	even parity
[-]odd	odd parity
even odd	no parity
[-]raw	raw input (default –raw)
[-]cbreak	cbreak input (default –cbreak)
[-]nl	(NEWLINE) terminal
[-]echo	full duplex
[-]lcase	uppercase only terminal
[-]tabs	use (TAB)s
[-]hup	disconnect when user logs off
0	disconnect immediately
50 75 110 134 150 200 300 600 1200 1800 2400 4800 9600	specify terminal baud rate
ek	set erase and kill characters to # and @
erase x	set erase character to **x**
kill x	set kill character to **x**
cr0 cr1 cr2 cr3	set delay following (RETURN)
nl0 nl1 nl2 nl3	set delay following (NEWLINE)
tab0 tab1 tab2 tab3	set delay following (TAB)
ff0 ff1	set delay following formfeed
bs0 bs1	set delay following backspace

tail*

Display the last part of a file.

Format   `tail ±number[option] [file]`

Options   -b   count by blocks
                  -c   count by characters
                  -l   count by lines (default)

Arguments   **+number**   counts from start of file
                  −number   counts from end of file

tee*

Copy the standard input to the standard output and one
    or more files.

Format   `tee [options] file-list`

Options   -i   no interrupts
                  -a   append to files

test

Evaluate an expression.

Format `test expression`

Arguments composed of criteria separated by the following operators:

!	negates criterion
-a	And operator
-o	Or operator
( )	as needed

Criteria

string	true if **string** is not null
-n string	true if length of **string** > 0
-z string	true if length of **string** $= 0$
string1 = string2	true if strings are equal
string1 ! = string2	true if strings are not equal
int1 relop int2	true if the two integers have the relationship specified by **relop** (**-gt -ge -eq -ne -le -lt**)
-r filename	true if **filename** exists and you can read it
-w filename	true if **filename** exists and you can write it
-f filename	true if **filename** exists and is not a directory
-d filename	true if **filename** is a directory
-s filename	true if **filename** is larger than 0 bytes
-t file-descriptor	true if **file-descriptor** is associated with the terminal

touch

Update a file's modification time.

Format `touch [option] file-list`

Option **-c** do not create file

uniq*
Display lines of a file that are unique.

Format `uniq [options] [-fields] [+characters]`
`[input-file] [output-file]`

Options `-c` (count) precede each line with the
number of occurrences

`-d` display only repeated lines

`-u` (unique) display only unique lines

Arguments **-fields** replace **fields** with a number and
skip that many fields

+characters replace **characters** with a number
and skip that many characters
after skipping fields

wc*
Display a line, word, and character count.

Format `wc [options] file-list`

Options `-c` (characters) display a character count only

`-l` (lines) display a line count only

`-w` (words) display a word count only

who
Display names of users.

Format `who [am i]`

Arguments **am i** display information about you

write
Send a message to another user.

Format `write destination-user [tty-name]`

Arguments **destination-user** person you want to send a message to

tty-name use to resolve ambiguity if the
destination-user is logged on
more than once

INDEX